THE
SECRET
LIFE
of the
SEINE

Le Havre

Tancarville

Villequier

Caudebec

Quillebeuf

Honfleur

Rouen

Amfreville

Les Andelys

Giverny

Vernon

Vétheuil

Limay

Mantes

L'OISE

Conflans-Ste.-Honorine

Paris

Bougival

Le Port à l'Anglais

LA MARNE

DA CAPO PRESS

THE
SECRET
LIFE
of the
SEINE

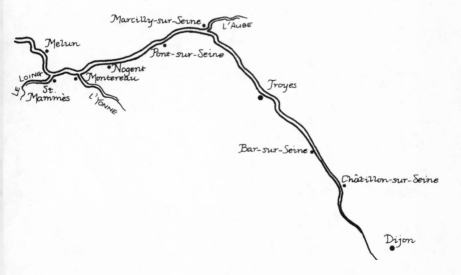

MORT ROSENBLUM

Copyright © 1994 by Mort Rosenblum

Designed by Dede Cummings
Set in 10 1/2-point Meridien by Pagesetters, Inc.

Cataloging-in-Publication data for this book is available from the Library of Congress.

First Da Capo Press edition 2001
ISBN 0–306–81074–3

Published by Da Capo Press
A Member of the Perseus Books Group
http://www.dacapopress.com

Da Capo Press books are available at special discounts for bulk purchases in the U.S. by corporations, institutions, and other organizations. For more information, please contact the Special Markets Department at the Perseus Books Group, 11 Cambridge Center, Cambridge, MA 02142, or call (617) 252-5298.

1 2 3 4 5 6 7 8 9 10—05 04 03 02 01

For Jeannette, who managed to cram a lifetime's stuff under a moldy bunk and never stopped smiling

Contents

AUTHOR'S NOTE   xiii

1. RIVER OF LIGHT   1

≋≋≋*Upstream*

2. THE SOURCE   29

3. ROLLING ON THE RIVER   49

4. RIDERS OF THE LONG DAYS   66

5. THE EDGE OF PARIS   80

≋≋≋*Paris*

6. PARIS-SUR-SEINE   91

7. WALKING ON WATER   121

8. LIFE ON THE *QUAIS*   137

9. GOOD NEIGHBORS   162

∾∾∾*Downstream*

10.   CONFLANS-SAINTE-HONORINE   173

11.   PLASTIC MAN'S MAGIC HAMMER   200

12.   MONET TO THE MONKS   219

13.   RONALD REAGAN ATE HERE   241

14.   BOVARY COUNTRY   252

15.   SURFING ON THE SEINE   269

16.   THE BIG ONE-HEARTED RIVER   277

∾∾∾*Glossary   289*

Author's
Note

SOME BOOKS WRITE THEMSELVES. The subject is so compelling that those connected with it are eager to talk and share experiences. I found this along the Seine, from Paul Lamarche at the source to Michel Lemoine at the mouth. To name them all would be to list the characters in the book, but I am grateful to each.

Specifically, my thanks to Jean-Pierre Ardouin, Jacques Donnez, Jillie Faraday, Annie Amirda, Charlie Godefroid, Olivier de Cornois, Françoise and Jean-Robert Villepigue, Hazel Young, Eric Tempe, Phil Cousineau, Christine Guyot, Jean Allardi and, at the top of the list, the mysterious Philippe. Also, of course, thanks to the boating party: Jeannette Hermann, Gretchen Hoff, Val Gardner, Dev Kernan, Jim Ravenscroft, Chuck McCutcheon, John Cooke, and Grabowski, wherever she is.

Amassing data and checking facts took a lot of help. For this, I thank Yota Milona, Alice Clark and Allison Penn.

Geri Thoma, pal and agent, persuaded me to put my

passion for the Seine between covers. She solicited the interest of Bill Patrick, pal and editor, who made it happen. The reader will join me in thanking Patrick for his loving little remarks on margins of the initial manuscript: "weak," "mundane," "yuk!" and so forth. In the nature of things, authors are to publishers as mongeese are to serpents. Not so here. I am grateful to the whole house of Addison-Wesley for embracing this project from its first moments.

                                                                M.R.

1 River
of Light

EVERY OTHER MORNING, my friend Paul slouched into the office with yet another hard-luck story about the boat he loved. The something-something had clogged and frozen his family overnight. A *bateau-mouche* had decked his poop, or pooped his deck. The river had risen, and he needed a dinghy to get home.

Paul slouched because he was six feet one inch high, and the saloon ceiling of *La Vieille* was not. Winter or summer, his clothes were ripe with mildew and diesel. One sleeting December night, his clothes smelled even worse. He had slipped on the gangway and belly flopped into the Seine.

Paul could talk your ear off about epoxy resin fatigue and wet carpets. He and his wife, Jill, had lived aboard *La Vieille* since the time they nursed her ancient teak timbers across the English Channel in 1967 and tied her up in the middle of Paris. That they had a son to rear on a fifty-four-foot boat didn't faze them, not even when young Ozzie grew so tall he could stand erect only with the hatch open.

During the decade that Paul and I worked together, I could never fathom his devotion to *La Vieille*. But I knew why he loved the Seine. There is not a river like it in the world, for beauty and passion along its banks. Its history is as old as the Jordan's, and it is no muddy stream across moonscape. If hardly a Mississippi, it still conceals treacherous sandbanks that keep boatmen anxiously marking their twain.

From the time I first gasped at the view from the Pont Marie, years ago, I was smitten by the Seine. And back then, I didn't know the half of it.

While Paul and Jill lived aboard *La Vieille*, I rented a country cottage four floors up in an old building in the heart of Paris, on the Ile Saint-Louis. Each time Paul lamented over his Webasto diesel heater, I thought of my cheery steam radiators and fireplaces on two floors. When winds and waves rocked the boat, I shut double doors to a terrace rose garden. I was a happy landlubber, and my clothes did not smell.

Late one night, I walked home across the Pont Sully. Golden light from the Quai d'Anjou glittered on the Seine. The narrow street curved by slate-roofed stone mansions that had sheltered the families, from the Voltaires to the Rothschilds, who had made France into France. Climbing the last steps to my door, I figured I had found the loveliest speck of real estate in the world. With any luck, I'd live there forever.

Inside, I exulted on the subject to my friend and roommate. "We have to leave," she said.

It was a typical low Parisian story. A local reptile who inherited some money had heard about the apartment and visited our landlord. The short version of the story is that we had a few months to clear out, with no idea where to go. I only knew that I had to be near the Seine.

Paul showed up for work, as usual, with another *La Vieille* hard-luck story. "You don't want to sell that old wreck, do you?" I asked. "I just might," he said. Not long after, I was the one telling the stories and reeking of old boat.

Paul and Jill had decided to move to England, and they were looking for friendly hands to take the helm. I was a reluctant candidate, a son of Arizona desert and a klutz with wrench or varnish brush. It took only one lunch on deck. The spring air was electric. Dutch barges lazed past, piloted by housewives in slippers and patrolled by stubby dogs trained to coil rope with their teeth. Tugs puffed by, their wakes sloshing the Burgundy in our glasses. On neighboring boats and along the quai, I watched characters Hugo had missed and Flaubert never imagined. Along with foul water, I saw waterfowl. It had to be Paris because the Eiffel Tower loomed over the golden cherubs on the Pont Alexandre III. But we were also somewhere else, in a place most Parisians seldom see.

Only a few nylon ropes, a power cable and a garden hose connected us to the real world. Suddenly, I understood why my friends loved *La Vieille* and had resolved to sell her with lumps in their throats. I had discovered the secret life of the Seine.

∞∞∞∞∞

A glance at the river in Paris tells you what is going on in France. If it is not slopping over its stone quais at the new year, farmers had a bad time with drought. When it runs fast, high, and cocoa brown in April, the skiing was terrific; keepers had to drop the sluice gates on the Marne to drain off melting snow. When France is happiest, for a bicentennial celebration of the revolution or only Bastille Day, barges and barks jam the Seine on their way to the fireworks.

You can gauge the crop of tourists by counting heads hanging over the rails of *bateaux-mouches*. When barges are so heavy with gravel that water splashes over their gunwales, construction is booming. Seine watchers knew France was hooked on American television when the police began blasting past in hot little patrol boats, driver erect at the wheel, bound for lunch à la *Miami Vice*.

And downstream past Rouen, that glance at the Seine can tell you the state of the world. Long before most people got their lips around a new household word, *perestroika*, Jacques Mevel knew the curtain was coming down. A river pilot, he travels the world each day without leaving the Seine. He noticed that Soviet sea captains suddenly started smiling and talking to strangers.

From the beginning, the French soul has bobbed in the waters of the Seine. On its bridges, love blooms; beneath them, lives end. Hardly anyone can tell you exactly where the river starts, or much else about it, but it flows through every romantic's spirit. It nourished Maupassant's pen and watered Monet's lily pond.

Paris was the City of Light long before there were switches to flip. The *rayonnement*, that radiance which the French have always beamed to the less enlightened, emanates from the pinks and oranges and sparkling flashes of the sun sinking into the Seine. When Baudelaire wrote that all around was nothing but *"ordre et beauté; luxe, calme et volupté,"* he was looking at the river off the Ile Saint-Louis.

A few generations ago, Guillaume Apollinaire mused:

> *Beneath the Pont Mirabeau flows the Seine*
> *And our love . . .*
> *While passes beneath the bridge of our arms*
> *The eternal gaze of the sultry waves.*

But the river is not always as the poets would have it, voluptuous and unchanging. In late winter, its mood shifts. When only slightly aroused, it floods the fast lanes along the Left Bank, gridlocking traffic from Saint-Michel to the Eiffel Tower. In 1910, hell-bent on mayhem, it went knee-deep into the fancy shops off the Champs-Elysées. A century ago, by the placid banks of a Normandy village, the current swallowed Victor Hugo's daughter Léopoldine, who toppled from a boat and sank in her Sunday best.

For two thousand years, the Seine was alimentary canal to a nation that took its nourishment seriously. Grain moved upriver, passing cargoes of wine headed downstream. Most food travels by road and rail these days, but a look at the Seine suggests that it is still at least France's digestive tract. By the time it reaches Paris, the river carries enough detritus of civilization to sicken your average sewer rat. This, of course, does not deter the swimmers who race periodically from Notre-Dame toward Neuilly, emerging undissolved. The Seine will confound you every time.

Visitors have never gotten enough of the river. Gertrude Stein ran her dogs by the Seine. Henry Miller walked off his excesses along it; in a houseboat, Anaïs Nin took hers to new levels. Fish was the first course of Hemingway's moveable feast; he loved to watch the anglers along the Pont des Arts footbridge: "It was easier to think . . . seeing people doing something they understood." The idea of Seine sushi is pretty revolting, but the old guys are still there in late spring when fishing is best.

Today's generation, if less lost than Hemingway's, still comes to the Seine in summer to shed inhibitions. Parisians strip down to nothing and sunbathe on its warm stone banks. They hide their wine in brown bags only when embarrassed by the label. On certain stretches of the quaiside,

Paris is gay. On others, kids and dogs frolic. Aging pigeon feeders occupy the benches by day, but lovers claim them at night.

Even its small mysteries intrigue. One evening a black wingtip shoe floated past my boat, dry inside, sole flat on the surface. Enough Parisians insist they can walk on water; would one of them shortly stride past? My upstream neighbor, Pierre Richard, did well as the lead in a film called *The Tall Blond Man with One Black Shoe*. Who knows?

People mark their history with memories of the Seine. One night in 1958, my friend Jo Menell stood on the Pont-Neuf and watched mysterious loglike shapes bobbing by the dozen in the swift current. France was at war to keep Algeria under her wing, and the shapes were Algerians murdered by French zealots who countered terror in Algiers with terror in Paris. Bodies, as tradition demanded, were dumped in the river.

Politics changed, but the eternal waves flowed on. A few years after Jo stood on the Pont-Neuf, Algeria and most other French colonies went free, and people of two dozen cultures crowded into the *métropole*. By 1993, France decided it was no longer a land of asylum. On that same bridge, police stopped an African and demanded his papers for a routine identity check. He flung himself over the stone parapet and drowned in the Seine.

"The Seine is the great receptacle which first receives the victims of assassination or despair," wrote Fanny Trollope in 1836. "But they are not long permitted to elude the vigilance of the Parisian police; a huge net, stretched across the river at Saint-Cloud, receives and retains whatever the stream brings down; and anything that retains a trace of human form which is found amidst the product of the fearful draught is daily conveyed to La Morgue;—DAILY; for rarely does it chance that for four-and-twenty hours its melancholy biers remain unoccupied; often do eight, ten, a dozen corpses at a time arrive by the frightful caravan from 'les filets de Saint-Cloud.' "

These days, the number is down. During 1992, Paris police recovered thirteen bodies from the Seine. They rescued another twenty-three people who had fallen in, accidentally or on purpose. And they extracted nine cars. It was an average year.

The net at Saint-Cloud is also down. Today, God knows what would shred it, or fill it, in minutes. When the current is fast, huge trees are hurled downstream, like battering rams. Other items, smaller than trees and sometimes unspeakable, also float down the Seine. Here, for example, is a brief sampling from the log of a young visitor to *La Vieille* who watched for half an hour: one mattress, countless Styrofoam containers, a bloated pig, several condoms, dead fish, live ducks, a television set, someone's jacket, someone else's trousers, many people's lunch—at one stage or another.

American scientists have found fifty-seven varieties of pollution in the Seine. Those racing swimmers notwithstanding, it carries a hundred times more bacteria than the European Community's safety level for swimming. In launching an ambitious campaign to clean up the river, Paris mayor Jacques Chirac announced that he would swim in it by 1994. The minister of health replied that he would be waiting on the bank with a towel and antibiotics. Chirac did not keep his promise.

Whatever Paris does, industries manage to elude measures to stop pollution. In 1991, Greenpeace blew the whistle. The group thrives in France under the slogan "You can't sink a Rainbow"—a reference to the incident a few years back, in New Zealand, when French agents blasted a hole in the Greenpeace flagship, *Rainbow Warrior*, and killed a crewman. Most Frenchmen laughed it off; that was about polluting the Pacific. When it comes to the Seine, officialdom is more sympathetic. Greenpeace eco-warriors welded shut the waste pipes of some major offenders, choking them in their own poisonous sludge, and authorities began enforcing the law. Sort of.

Beyond industrial waste, there is the aging and overtaxed Paris sewage system. Even a little rain channels filth to the river. At times during the year, the largest tributary of the Seine is a river of noxious effluent from the Achères treatment plant.

Today the river balances on an ecological edge. Its fish feel the slightest rattle of the food chain. Early in June 1992, I came home from a trip to find the river running thick with bloated bream and carp cadavers. And I was seeing only the first few. Over three weeks, firemen scooped out a thousand tons of rotting fish along a twenty-five-mile stretch of the Seine. It seems the river was low, the water was warm, and an oily film cut the level of oxygen. Heat triggered a rash of bacteria, which ate up even more oxygen. A biblical deluge backed up the Paris sewers, pouring filth into the river. Half the fish in the Paris area died that week. Then again, half lived. Judging from the size of those that didn't, the river is alive with fish the size of small sheep.

Within weeks, high-tech barges were pumping billions of bubbles of oxygen into the river, and Parisians shrugged off the expense. Fortunately, the incident coincided with the Earth Summit in Rio de Janeiro. And this was, after all, the Seine.

∞∞∞∞∞

Ichthyology aside, other species are endangered as modern times alter the course of the Seine. A whole class of freshwater salts, wharf rats, and river riders are also going. Like the fish, however, they are going slowly.

When I moved to the river, I found a cast of the old characters right off the end of my gangplank. Jean Privat looked after the quai at the Touring Club de France, where fifty converted barges and boats are settled in a floating community between the Pont de l'Alma and the footbridge just above the Pont de la Concorde. His job was to make sure nothing sank.

Winter and summer, he wore an increasingly off-white yachting cap and an American bomber jacket he picked up while working with U.S. forces in the war. A dashing figure, even when a liquid breakfast slurred his sentences, he always managed to have the last word. He spoke river, and urban mariners depended upon him for translation. When Jean died in 1990, he left in character. It was a busy day at the crematorium, and his family, having paid extra, refused to be shunted off to a chapel annex. The mortician was firm and so was the family, but Jean, of course, had the last word. The heavy caisson bearing his coffin suddenly rolled on its track—across the undertaker's toes.

After Jean's ashes were scattered on the water, his boat hook went to Jacques Donnez, who spells his name "Jack" (no one else does). Jacques looks like a cross between Jean-Paul Sartre and Popeye, with a raspy voice and a craggy squint behind opaque glasses. At first, for me, he was mainly prime character material. Then I asked him to teach me to navigate. By the third time he spared me from making chopsticks of a fine old boat, he was Captain, sir, and a friend.

Jacques was born afloat in 1939, an eighth-generation Seine boatman. He and wife, Lisette, married on a floating church barge, made a decent income ferrying coal, sand, grain, and wine while their laundry flapped in the wind on the aft deck. But trucks and trains cut deeply into the market. In 1976, they sold the barge for scrap and came ashore. He took a job on the quai, where he can fix anything made by man and wait out anything delivered by nature. He starts early, works hard, and does his level best to help Burgundy vineyards prosper.

"Ouuaais, je l'aime," says Jacques, a man of few words, when asked to rhapsodize on the Seine. The trick is to watch him look at the river; his eyes are as expressive as temperature gauges. When he furrows his brow at the rising current, it is time to get your car off the quai. He is like most hearty old marine equipment, utterly dependable as long as you check the meters. When his nose flashes red, for example, it is not the time to have him change your bilge pump.

※※※※

In no time at all, the river bewitched me. Most likely, it happened that July morning when I was wakened by a mother duck giving hell to eight fuzzy ducklings. With a fresh cup of coffee, I sat on deck to survey my new neighborhood. The Seine was calm but by 8 A.M. *La Vieille* was rocking gently, like a cradle. The air bore a pleasant nip and fresh river scent. The bridge statues gleamed gold. Suddenly, sweet notes of music wafted down to the deck. Up in the trees, masked by leaves, I saw a bandsman in blue and red with shiny brass buttons tuning a French horn.

On balmy summer nights, we sat on deck until the Eiffel Tower blinked off at 1 A.M. Then we drank wine and giggled, forgetting to go to bed, until it was time for sunrise and the duck serenade.

Soon, I started talking funny. When I remarked to a

normal person, "I've got dry rot in my head," he nodded in agreement, not aware that I was referring to the bathroom ceiling. At the time, the world was in turmoil, and my job as a reporter kept me nearer the Volga, the Vltava, and Victoria Falls. But every time I came home, the Seine had a new surprise. I decided I had to learn more about this magical river and the people who live on it.

The books lined up in *La Vieille*'s saloon were of some help. Mostly, they confirmed a single bit of nautical knowledge: deck leaks make pages stick together. Within a year I had hired storage space for a library that would have capsized the boat: old musings in heavy leather, mildewed maps and slim volumes of verse. I spent afternoons gazing at paintings to see what had captivated the impressionists. I studied the river's moods, attuned to rising currents and falling barometers. With the help of Captain Jacques, I got *La Vieille* ready to roll, and we snooped into the river's innermost secrets. The more I realized that the depths were unfathomable, the more I loved the mission.

Looking around, I found the river's rich history bubbled regularly to the surface, refusing to lie dead in books. One morning I returned to Paris to find a Viking longboat—gargoyles, oars and all—docked at the visitors' quai. This being the Seine, it would not have surprised me to find it full of hairy Norwegians in animal skins and pointy hélmets looking for loot after a thousand-year time warp. It was a replica, part of an exhibition at the Grand Palais.

Since Roman times, the Seine was an Old World thoroughfare. Norsemen routinely plundered riverside abbeys and towns until Charles the Simple bought off King Rollo in 911 with a spare daughter and Normandy. The Vikings turned their energies into taming the river; their channels and dikes lasted ten centuries. On the Seine, William the

Conqueror put together the flotilla that invaded England. He chased his cousins back to Scandinavia, and they have yet to return, except for Wimbledon.

Among the old stones of Paris are traces of walls built to repel the Vikings and remnants of later medieval forts that Napoléon III blasted away last century to let the river run free. By Notre-Dame, for instance, the Petit Pont has been around in one form or another since the birth of Christ. It was once flanked by wooden buildings, but they went in 1718, in a Parisian precursor to the Mrs. O'Leary cow incident. When things got lost in the Seine, back then, people went to a local convent for a hunk of bread blessed with a prayer to St. Nicolas. This, balanced on a plank along with a lighted candle, was placed in the river. Wherever the candle went out was the spot to look. A widow who lost her only son in the current launched a plank to find his body. The candle did not go out. It ignited a hay barge which struck the bridge, setting a three-day fire. Twenty-two houses burned to the pilings.

As the French went from monarchy to republic to empire to monarchy to empire to republic, the Seine remained their centerpiece. I had not only a river to explore but also a few thousand years of the soul of France.

〰〰〰

The Seine that is synonymous with Paris is actually 482 miles long. In a straight line, it travels only 250 miles, but the Seine is in no hurry. It wells up from three cracks at the foot of a limestone hill in a forest glade in the Côte d'Or province of Burgundy, thirty miles northwest of Dijon. The Gauls, knowing magic when they saw it, built a temple at the source to the river goddess, Sequana, whose name was later smoothed out into *Seine*. Until the fourth century A.D., when German invaders destroyed the temple, pagan Perrier cured ancient ailments. A few believers remain convinced.

For the first mile or so, you can pop a cork across the Seine while *déjeunering sur l'herbe*. By the time it reaches Le Havre, after twenty-five locks in all, the river has broadened to an estuary hardly distinguishable from the English Channel beyond. From source to mouth, the Seine drops only sixteen hundred feet. At its widest, it can be dead calm, translucent in deep green hues. Or it can look like café au lait on the boil.

"La Seine" is sanctified by signboard on an old stone bridge in the village of Billy-lès-Chanceaux, eight miles from the source. The water beneath is crystal clear and hardly deep enough to drown a dwarf. It twists and turns, picking up the odd stream, until it reaches the bottom of Champagne country. By then, its banks are dotted with the remains of wooden wheels that once ground flour or cranked up a few watts of electricity.

Châtillon-sur-Seine is a miniature Paris, Seine-wise; its oldest part nestles between two branches of the river. But neither branch is wider than ten yards or more than a yard deep. Navigation starts at Marcilly, 120 miles from the source. River traffic once reached the medieval port at Troyes via canal, but the grand waterway ordered by Napoléon was closed less than a century after it opened, one more casualty of a vanishing way of life.

At Montereau, the Seine gets significant. The Yonne joins in, doubling the flow and adding traffic from canals and rivers that reach the Mediterranean. Farther on, at the impressionists' paradise of Moret, there is the Loing. Soon after, the Essonne. Then the Marne empties in, bringing water from the mountains of the Vosges and barges from beyond the Rhine, as far away as the Black Sea. The Seine is swift and murky and ready for Paris.

From the City of Light, the Seine winds into the heart of darkness. Past the abandoned hulk of a Renault factory on the Ile Séguin outside Paris, the riverside homes peter out. Suddenly, it is as if you are on Conrad's steamer among mangrove swamps on the Congo. And then, just as abruptly, the river turns and you sense the luminosity that inspired so many painters.

The Oise comes in below Paris, and the Eure and others. Long past the wrought-iron terrace of La Fournaise, where Renoir painted the luncheon clientele and Maupassant scribbled on the walls, it passes near the village near Rouen where Flaubert's Emma Bovary learned home economics the hard way. Plaques along the way mark where battered Englishmen went home after their Hundred Years' War and where, a long time later, the English helped run off Germans. A little tower marks the spot where Napoléon's ashes came ashore, for a carriage ride to Paris, after sailing up the Seine in a frigate painted black.

On a map of Normandy, Sequana looks like an earthworm with stomach cramps. The river snakes among spectacular castles and abbeys, set against a backdrop of plunging white escarpments and thick woods. In spring, its lazy loops are flanked in the shocking pink of cherry orchards. It changes again and again, meandering through history and humdrum, on toward open waters.

No statesman has missed the significance of this varied thoroughfare. "Le Havre, Rouen, and Paris are a single town," Napoléon said, "and the Seine is Main Street." He planned to build canals so that boats from lesser states to the east could visit the capital of Europe by inland waterway.

The Rhône, wild and wide, was once a Roman freeway. The Loire, lovely and long, winds among sumptuous châteaux. Next to either, the Seine is a stream. Its normal flow, four hundred cubic meters a second, is a fifth of the Rhône's and a sixth of the Danube's. But the Seine and its tributaries water an area totaling 78,878 square kilometers, 15 percent of France. Seventeen million inhabitants, a third of the French population, live within its reach. More than half of France's heavy industry, 60 percent of the phosphoric acid plants, 37 percent of the petroleum works, and a pair of nuclear reactors flank the greater Seine. The port of Paris handles twenty-six million tons of freight a year, equal to a million truckloads.

With all that, the people who live and work on the Seine reject the geographers' term *fleuve*, the French word for a river that feeds into the sea. Instead, the Seine is *la rivière*, which is supposed to apply only to gentle inland waterways. Sequana was a lady, Seine people insist, and so is their river.

～～～～～

If you live on the Seine, you are constantly asked two questions: Isn't it damp? (The answer is yes) and Where do you get your croissants in the morning? (The answer is: At the bakery). Occasionally, some kindred spirit has a third: When are you going to die and leave this to me?

It is agreeable, as the French say, to take a candlelight cruise without leaving home. You can go away for a weekend and not pack. Your morning alarm is those ducks quacking. Friends visit without coaxing. My pal Barbara Gerber fled a Stockholm winter and dropped into the nearest deck chair. When a *bateau-mouche* passed, she flung out her arms and yelled, "Envy me."

But there are drawbacks. A boat is not a great place for

people who tend to drop their keys. When you're all dressed up with someplace to go, you don't want to crawl around your engines looking for car keys that slipped through the gearshift slot on the wheelhouse floor. Sleepwalkers, too, ought to think twice. Life afloat is like living in a small apartment, in a zone of frequent, quiet earthquakes.

This key business can be serious. Once my friend Gretchen and I rented a van from a hole-in-the-wall agency just before it closed for an extended holiday weekend. The next morning, at 6 A.M., we assembled furniture and another couple for a long drive south. I put my briefcase on the deck table, placed the keys atop it, and went below for a final check. Gretchen, meanwhile, was loading the last stuff. She called down through the hatch: "Was there something on your bag that might have gone clink on the deck and splashed in the water?"

For half an hour, we fumed like furnace flues, cursing fate. Then we quietly pleaded for a miracle, and one happened. Double-checking, I found that I had stupidly hung the van keys on the hook where my car keys should be. The Seine had swallowed the keys to my Peugeot, and I had an extra set of those. One is not always that lucky.

Jilly Faraday, a neighbor, dropped her key ring into the Seine: boat, car, the works. She called the *pompiers*, the river firemen who get bored waiting for real disaster. A frogman poked in the muck fifteen feet underwater. He found the keys.

Boats are also not the best places to teach an old cat new tricks. The lesson was made manifest in 1992 when a Marin County cat took up residence aboard *La Vieille*. Already slightly embarrassed by her name, Princess the cat had a few adjustment problems, one of which was that she fell into the river. No one knew it until she jumped back through a porthole onto the bed, her fluffy long hair matted and stinking, and produced a plaintive meow.

She was on penicillin for two weeks. All we know for sure is that cats, when pressed, can do the backstroke as well as chin-ups, and that Princess had run through eight and a half lives.

But then there is the secret life of the Seine, a separate *arrondissement* of the spirit. For years, when I watched the Seine from above, I treasured the river as a lovely but inanimate path through the center of the most thrilling settlement I knew. It took moving onto it, having it seep into my bilges and turn my underwear green, for me to realize that it was alive, a settlement in its own right, peopled by an elaborate class system of citizens who pledged allegiance to it.

Where else in Paris can you love thy neighbor? Late one night, I was washing dishes in the galley and heard someone bellowing my name. It was Olivier, who lives just aft, setting off in his little red boat with a load of nubile friends and his habitual shit-eating grin. They were off to the mysterious Ile d'Amour upriver and around the bend, accessible only by water. He just wanted to wave good-bye. John D. MacDonald's character Travis McGee insists that the *Alabama Tiger* hosts the world's longest permanent floating party. He obviously does not know Olivier.

～～～～～

Close to the madding crowd, Paris wakes to fumes, snarls, bent fenders and coffee splashing on silk ties. Olivier de Cornois, however, grins so wide you'd think he was crazed except for that glimmer which suggests he knows why he is smiling. "Ahhhh," he says each morning to anyone close enough to hear, breathing deeply and showing an extra molar on either side of his grin, "the river."

Scion to a sugar-aristocracy family from Picardy, Olivier fell for the river in 1970. *"J'ai flashé,"* he puts it. He'd been living in an apartment on the Rue Vavin in Montparnasse, studying drama, and fighting with his neighbors over loud parties; it is not clear whether the parties were theirs or his. But one night he went to a small orgy on a large boat and never looked back.

"My life has been paradise ever since," he told me one morning, grinning that grin which suggests Captain Blood on the way to bury doubloons. He lives on a red runabout that bobs like a cork in a dishwasher anytime something serious churns past. He paints for the few odd francs, but lives, essentially, on nothing. The Seine is his only love, except perhaps for women of tender age, and for riding his motorbike while standing up on the seat.

Olivier is tall and spare, with a rugged, handsome face and a shag of curls. He yells endearments at passing women, the kind that get your arm broken in California, and a lot of the women seem to like it. One of them married him.

For a brief time, Olivier and his much-younger wife were a model of bourgeois bliss. They had a daughter and moved ashore. "You know, the bouncing, the tight space, it's not so good for an infant," he said at the time, as if trying to convince himself more than me. When I next saw him, his crazed grin had matured to a beatific beam. He explained to me how it felt to nurture a tiny girl, and his eyes watered.

A little later, a touch of rue flavored his smile. In his forties, he was finding it hard to boogy all night and change diapers in the morning. But he was trying. Then I went away for a long time and came back to find him living alone on the boat. He was almost the old Olivier again, up with a grin, a few turns around the quai standing up on the motorbike, and a sacred thoughtful hour on the park bench under the trees in the late afternoon. But not quite.

I asked no questions, but soon enough the news came. Olivier's baby had died. His wife was with her family. He was back to his first love, the Seine.

At the time, Olivier was tied up behind me, next to a steel-hulled *péniche*. This is a 126-foot barge, the standard French workhorse. Its master is Philippe, a perfect neighbor who was not wild about my writing this book. When I told him the title, he recoiled: "But if you write about it, it's not secret. Be sure to tell them about floods and leaks." I resolved to spare his privacy, just as anyone aboard *La Vieille* is schooled not to see into his uncurtained windows. In France you can do it.

"Please understand if I do not seem to see you when we look at each other," Philippe said when we first met. I loved him instantly. Two boats tied alongside are like Siamese twins, and I am no Rotarian. Imagine the perils of proximity. You cannot get to my boat without walking across the bow of Philippe's. He can't leave the quai unless I go first.

Carefully, like a couple of porcupines sharing a den, we found a happy symbiosis. I don't sand my rails when he is sleeping in. He shrugs when I park my car on his hose during his shower. Every so often he comes aboard to dislodge debris about to tear off my port-side prop, a hazard I tend not to notice, and he mutters in English: "Unaware. Completely unaware."

You never know. The other Sunday, he emerged blearily at 5 P.M., unwound six feet of hung-over party victim, wandered below to get my guitar, and announced, in G, "I'm a little red rooster."

My neighbors began to settle along the quai in 1960s when few people lived on the Seine. By now, the old-timers know the river's every mood and who sells the best rope and the cleanest fuel. One barge has a rose garden worthy of Versailles.

Depending on the season, early morning on the quai produces a trickle of joggers—once Madonna and goons trotted by—or a few diehard lovers or a Dutch camper that sneaked through the gate. But you will always see Bernard, Captain Jacques's sidekick, and his burly German shepherd. Bernard will be in a greasy black seaman's cap and blue coveralls. The dog will be drooling.

Bernard was one of those *clochards* who live under the bridges, friendly trolls of a time-honored class of Parisian bums. In *Boudou Saved from Drowning*, a classic film about the river, Michel Simon plays a *clochard* who is saved from the Seine. Bernard, however, was saved by the Seine. One morning, Philippe gave him a few francs to clean up in front of his boat. Then another neighbor hired him, and so did someone else. Soon, Bernard had a steady job working for the port, and his bum days were behind him.

One of life's pleasures is a chat with Bernard as he leans on his broom or scratches his dog's ears. It's too bad I can understand only one in every ten words of his Gabby Hayes delivery.

A lot of characters along the river have only walk-on parts. Someone is always making a movie, or modeling underwear or uncorking a primal scream. It seems that a section of the Seine is reserved for every proclivity, and our quai is for lovers. Mostly, old-fashioned pairs stroll past. But one particular bench in the trees is noted for world-championship brazen coupling.

When I moved in, we even had a neighborhood swimming hole. This was the Piscine Déligny, a clean-water pool by the Quai d'Orsay where women displayed their breast implants and men showed each other most of their private parts. It was the last survivor of the *bateaux-bains*, floating pleasure spots that the Germans banished in 1942 as navigational hazards and needless frippery. For a century and a half, Parisians hurried to the sheet-metal beach, frolicked in the water, and ate lunch under umbrellas.

One morning in 1993, an hour before its scheduled yearly safety inspection, the Piscine Déligny sank like a stone. It had rested on three floating tanks, like barge hulls, linked by cable. For no apparent reason, the one nearest shore filled with water. Firemen could not detach the other two before the weight of the first capsized them. Immediately, the rumors flew: mafiosi did it; insurance played a part; someone was disgruntled at something. Paris lost its favorite swimming spot but gained a major mystery.

〰〰〰〰

As the lyricists have it, Paris makes love to the Seine. At least, the city embraces its waterways like nowhere else on earth. New York ignores two rivers. London turns its back on the Thames. Comparisons with Venice are more than hyperbole. The Canal Saint-Martin loops deep into the Right Bank, carrying barges past chestnut trees and dramatic old landmarks to the Ourcq and Saint-Denis canals. From these, you see a Paris that most Parisians would swear vanished decades ago. There is the hulking Grands Moulins de Paris, which made the flour for bread no one could match. And the Hôtel du Nord, which gave its name to another film classic. When Arletty leaned from a bridge and rasped to Louis Jouvet, *"Atmosphère, atmosphère . . .,"* Parisians cried a river. The city's Grand Canal, the Seine itself, winds among parks and fancy mansions you reach by crossing water.

Venetian waterways are public thoroughfares, but their edges are jealously guarded. Vaporettos carry gawkers past private landings and closed wooden doors. But you can get off a Parisian Bat-O-Bus at any stop and walk along like you own the quai. On the upper level, *les bouquinistes* offer best-sellers from the 1930s and travelogues of Timbuktu from open-air stalls. Down below, you can converse amiably with corn-fed tourists off the bus or play AIDS roulette with the rough trade. You'll hear French and English and Japanese, but also Catalan and Lapp and Dari.

On the Ile Saint-Louis or the Ile de la Cité, you can walk by the river and peer into mysterious worlds when someone swings open any of those massive double doors. At 17 Quai d'Anjou, for instance, Baudelaire and the *club des hashishins*—a play on *assassins*—met to smoke dope and plot the discomfiture of stuffy citizens. Rilke and Wagner and Delacroix were regulars; Hugo took a few hits and dropped off to sleep. Balzac didn't inhale.

Today's bohemians still gravitate to the river. So do most other Parisians. If most moored boats are people's homes or cargo haulers, and you approach uninvited on pain of death, others are there to be visited. Floating restaurants offer everything from tempura to tacos. By Notre-Dame, the *Metamorphosis* has been transformed from a sand barge to an Italian-style magic theater.

Down any quai, you can let your imagination run wild. Ask a few questions, and people are likely to misinform you about neighbors they hardly know. They guess by default; etiquette frowns on their prying in any obvious manner. Also, affairs are seldom as they seem. The Doges' Venice was straightforward as a Boy Scout troop next to a Seine-side boat community. People on the river by and large treasure their status as characters.

❧❧❧❧❧

Among the Seine's colorful cast is *La Vieille*, that cranky but lovable aging matron with whom I spent a rough first night when I moved onto the river in July 1987.

La Vieille was built from Burmese hardwood and English hardware at the turn of the century as an admiral's gig for the Royal Navy. Driven by a steam engine, she plowed her deep V-shaped hull into heavy seas as flag officers pottered about their fleets. Doubtless she had a rich, noble history: seamen rolling depth charges overboard at lurking U-boats, daring rescues in the North Sea, the Dunkirk evacuation— that sort of thing. Doubtless.

All I know is that after World War II, someone turned her into a motor yacht. She had lot of new names. The first was *Namouna*. Another evoked a port in Andalusia, an arid stretch of Spain not unlike my home country in Arizona. One of her names, I was told, meant "freedom" in Arabic. This appealed to me. When you can unplug a few lines and head toward anywhere in the world you have the fuel to reach, *Freedom* is a pretty good name to have painted across your fantail. But I prefer the nickname. *La Vieille*, like a lot of French terms, means whatever you want it to mean: the old bitch; your mother; or the woman you love.

The boat is fifty-four feet long and thirteen feet wide. Her hull of double teak planking over closely spaced ribs is solid as a mountainside. Deep below the wheelhouse lurk two BMC Commodore diesel engines, slightly modified versions of what powered London taxicabs in the 1950s. What used to be the engine room is a saloon, fitted out in mahogany cabinets and built-in benches. There is an aft cabin, a decent-sized galley and a head with a tiny tub, another cabin, and a fo'c'sle ("foxhole," as one friend kept calling it).

My friends, Paul and Jill, found the old girl moldering in a boat yard on the River Dart in the mid-1960s. Their knowledge of water was limited to baths and whisky mix. Nonetheless, they pointed her toward France and steamed up the Seine. When Paul and Jill signed over the boat, I went on a trip to give them time to wrap up the eighteen years they had spent on board. They left quickly, and the boat remained empty for weeks while the sun blazed down, preparing my welcome.

At some point, *La Vieille*'s deck had been laid in soft-wood planking, which was later covered with fiberglass sheets. This, I learned, is not such a great combination. If the air is humid, the decking swells and seals itself. When the sun bakes down, it dries out. Planks contract and fiberglass cracks, unless someone regularly waters down the deck. That July, no one did.

I went aboard in a raging downpour and found it raining nearly as hard belowdecks as it was up top. Deep cracks had opened everywhere. Fat drops splashed off the mahogany cabinets and the fancy folding table. The foam mattress was soaked in the aft cabin. All hatches leak a little; mine were streaming water.

Suddenly, I had a terrible thought: the deck would be leaking the length of the boat, pouring water into the bilge. I lifted the sodden carpet and pulled up a floorboard. The Seine was two inches below my feet. Like a maniac, I started to bail with a pot. Calming down, I pondered a call to the *pompiers*, a noble crew with sturdy pumps. Instead, I switched on both bilge pumps and waited. The level slowly dropped. I found a small dry patch, curled into a ball and slept until the rain stopped.

In the morning, I found the gift that Paul and Jill had left playfully behind. It was a huge wooden carving of the up-yours finger, yet one more treasure they had plucked from the Seine.

Upstream

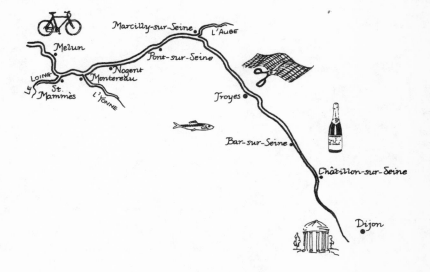

2 The Source

PAUL LAMARCHE, keeper of the Seine, scampered over the last traces of a vast Gallo-Roman temple to show me the river's source. He was into his nineties, quick, sturdy, with an elfin twinkle in his eye. Those old guys in Armenia last long on yogurt, but Lamarche thrives on the magical waters of the Seine.

"Look at this," Lamarche said, bending over a tiny stream trickling down a groove in the rock. He dislodged a stone and seized a waterbug, like a minuscule shrimp. "Any kind of pollution kills these things," he explained. "You won't find any cleaner water." He cupped his hands in the furry green moss and thrust his face into the cool liquid. I did the same. Water never tasted better.

The old man fell silent to let me ponder the past. Instead, my mind flashed ahead to the immediate future. I could imagine splashing water into guests' whisky aboard *La*

Vieille and mentioning casually that I had scooped it from the
Seine. A sadist's dream.

We were on the Langres Plateau in the Côte d'Or, up to
our ankles in red poppies and talking over the buzzing hum
of cicadas. Wild roses and columbines fringed the rocks, and
rich, fragrant grass hid little yellow buds. Lamarche first saw
this enchanted source when he was six. "We hiked down
from Chanceaux to say *bonjour* to the goddess," he said,
nodding toward a Rubenesque statue in a fake grotto built by
the city of Paris to honor Sequana.

The plaque says she was put there by Napoléon III, but
Paul knows the statue was replaced in 1928. Once water
spouted from her left arm, as though she were personally
filling the river, but in dry years the pressure was not strong
enough. Now water burbles ignobly from somewhere near
her feet. In any case, her cave is not the actual source.

"The river really starts here," Lamarche said, pointing to
a rusty grate by a few chunks of marble column, all that
remains of the biggest temple in ancient Gaul. "And there
and there." Water oozed from two other breaks in the rock at
the base of a low cliff, in a clump of trees. "Then it goes
underground and loops around to the grotto."

He was enjoying himself, poking holes in the first few
fibs the Seine's curators sought to perpetrate on the public.
The river was his life, and Sequana his beloved ancestor.
After checking out the world in the military, Lamarche
came home to Saint-Germain-Source-Seine, the village
nearby. In 1953, he settled into the old caretaker's farmhouse just below the grotto and opened the Café Sequana.
His wife, Monique, made omelettes and strong coffee. At
the source, Lamarche planted two willows, under which
picnickers can dangle their toes in cool water, and shaped
the small park. With money left over, he built the first

bridge over the Seine, a funny little miniature of the vaulted spans farther down.

These days, mostly, he and Monique tend their fields. The grotto is left open to the public and needs only a casual eye. But when anyone stops to ask, the old man seizes a fat iron key and shows off the real thing.

Lamarche took me to the gate and worked at the rusted padlock. For several minutes, he jiggled the key and muttered darkly. Finally, he worked it loose. My friend Jeannette, meantime, simply walked past the locked gate; the fence had long since collapsed. Inside, Lamarche showed us a heavy slice of column that looters had tried to roll into a pickup. He had run them off. "They've taken everything," he said, shaking his head at nonspecific sacrilege over the last two millenia.

The park belongs to Paris. After all these years, the source of the Seine, deep in the belly of Burgundy, is still a colony of the French capital. Napoléon III claimed it last century when such symbolism was pregnant with political import. Now, only a curiosity, the symbol still fits. When the river gets bigger, it is pushed around with Paris in mind. Downstream from Paris, it runs thick with urban waste.

Although Lamarche plants the flowers, trims the trees, and cleans up after slobs, what he likes best is talking to visitors. He wants people to get Sequana's story straight. Which is not so easy to do. The *Dictionnaire Etymologique des Noms de Rivières et de Montagnes en France* offers eleven lines on the name *Seine*. What they say, in brief, is that no one knows much. Next to a Ptolemaic name in characters my computer cannot approach (Sekoanas, in Roman letters), there is the Caesarian *Sequana*. This, via a string of variants used over the centuries, evolved into *Seine*. *Squan*, apparently, was a Gallic word meaning twisting, or tranquil, or both. The Romans added a few vowels. Later, French settled on a single syllable.

An eighteen-inch-high statue of the goddess has survived in a museum at Dijon. She is in flowing Greco-Roman robes, standing in a boat with a bow shaped like the head of swan; in the swan's mouth is a small round object, a pomegranate or a tennis ball. For myth spinners, it is a promising start.

〰〰〰〰〰

Archeologists, in fact, have put together a detailed account of the daily goings-on at the temple to Sequana. Reading it, I half-suspected that some clumsy printer had substituted pages from a modern guide to Lourdes. The Gauls' first temple was made of wood and clay earth, but Romans later hauled in enough slabs of marble and hewn stone for a vast religious complex. The waters trickled among high columns and past inner recesses reserved for holy business. Downstream, they widened into a pool where the masses took the cure.

Gauls, Romans and foreign tourists covered great distances, hobbling on foot or in fancy carriages. Priests received offerings in temple alcoves. Pilgrims sealed vows by pitching coins or jewelry into the water. Artisans fashioned replicas of limbs in need of curing, and they charged an arm and a leg. In bronze, wood, or soft rock, they depicted familiar-looking maladies—tumors, poxes and deformities—which the Seine was enlisted to heal. Souvenir stands sold kitschy statuettes; had transport been better, they might have come from Taiwan.

The temple thrived as a sacred health spa and also as a vacation getaway from a bustling Gallo-Roman settlement downstream started by a tribe of Gauls, fishermen and water traders known as the Parisii. *Par*, in Celtic, means boat. By then, the Parisii's capital on an island in the Seine, now the

Ile de la Cité, was rolling in resource. The settlement, as well as the region near Sequana's temple and the river that linked them, were at the crux of a new world taking shape.

About six centuries before Christ, and the Romans, the Greeks had found a more direct route to Britain than sailing by Gibraltar and up rough open seas. They needed English tin and copper to make bronze, buying it with Mediterranean wine. Greek traders followed the Rhône to the Saône until they ran out of river. Crews humped their cargo overland to the headwaters of the Seine. From there, it was only water to the Thames. The Greeks enriched not only the entrepôt region of Vix, not far from the source, but also Gallic villages clustered along the river.

Germans, meantime, carted their heavy metals from Spain, in exchange for honey, amber and furs. That required crossing the Seine. Wagoners settled on the Parisii's village, where flat rocks on either bank flanked an island made of silt. For much of the year, horses could ford the river; it was twice as wide then as it is now and a whole lot shallower. When the water was high, Gauls ferried the wagons across, for a price.

The island was perfectly placed. Forests hemmed in the river basin, and bandits cruised the few rutted roads. Anyone with a choice preferred the Seine—peaceful, dependable and free of muggers. And road convoys had to get over the river. Seven thousand strong, behind a stockade, the Parisii ran a bustling market and a mint that stamped gold coins. Politics were shaped by the watermen, the *nautes*, who ruled the wavelets until A.D. 52.

But after Rome conquered the British isles, Caesar realized he had to fuel his legionnaires there with home-grown olive oil. Like all other roads, he decided, the Seine would lead to Rome. His armies seized everything along the old Greek route. On their island redoubt, the Gauls fought back.

Caesar reported humbly: "Labienus exhorted his soldiers to remember their past bravery, their happiest combats, and to conduct themselves as if Caesar, who so often had led them to victory, were there in person." Romans routed the right flank, but the Parisii's general, Camulogenus, held the center. "All were encircled and massacred," Caesar wrote, adding that horsemen cut down those who fled. We have no Gallic version, but the battle was likely the origin of Parisian driving habits.

Having burned their town rather than leave it to Caesar, the Gauls started fresh on the island. On the river's left bank, a gleaming Roman city offered the usual colonial amenities: temples, baths, a theater, aquaducts, and stone streets, along with a port. Stone pillars and wooden planks made up the first Petit Pont. Gauls ran their own port on the island. The whole place was called Lutetia, a name that lingers today on a fancy hotel façade and a hundred other places.

The Romans built a temple to Jupiter atop a shrine to a Gallic god; Notre-Dame, on the same spot, now blots out both deities. By then, the Gauls had joined the invaders they could not beat. The *nautes* offered a statue to honor the Roman god and continued their lucrative river traffic.

Late in the third century, France was rearranged by the muscular Teutonic tourism that got to be a habit. Franks swept southwest from the Rhine estuary. They eventually settled most of the country, hence the name France. But Burgundians from the central Rhine, tall Wagnerian blonds with a power problem, made straight for the Seine. In A.D. 276, they trashed Lutetia, burning the Roman sector. Failing to dislodge the Gauls from their island, they moved upstream and razed Sequana's temple.

A Seine biographer, Anthony Glyn, reckons the Germanic invaders smashed the temple because they did not like female deities. In fact, centuries later, a monk named Seigne (pronounced "Seine") was sainted and recruited as patron of the river, which explains those impressive church towers at Saint-Seine-l'Abbaye, a few miles toward Dijon on the other side of the hill from the source. But he didn't take; Sequana has eclipsed Saint Seigne, whatever his role.

The Roman Empire was crumbling fast. In Lutetia, Gallo-Romans had shaped a new culture. Freed of Mediterranean keepers, they took the old name, Paris. And they looked mostly downstream, toward England and northern Europe, where trade was brisk. Wine from Burgundy and Champagne floated down the Seine. But not much came from beyond, overland from the Saône. Gradually, Sequana's shrine lost its pre-Michelin stars and slipped into the mists.

∽∾∾∾∾∾

I started my river journey on foot. This line might have carried some power in a Richard Burton diary, with chilling detail of treacherous porters and mosquitos the size of turkey buzzards, but walking down the Seine is not what you'd call hardship. In fact, I didn't go very far before I hopped back into an open car and followed the farmer's roads and narrow strips of blacktop to the first proper bridge across the river. A very short bridge.

My original idea had been a single journey, from first trickle to final rollers, in some form of conveyance. Paul Theroux suggested a kayak, the way he'd do it. Another old pro urged something more French, like a rubber Zodiac. Had I talked to Mark Spitz, I probably would have considered the butterfly stroke. But the Seine, often submissive, needs a minimum of conquering. To live her secret life, you've got to take it slowly, in various ways at different times. My exploring would take me among old books, into rusting engine compartments, and, as far I could go, into the thoughts of river people. More than a journey, this was a quest. I was after the soul of the Seine. Scrapping all plans, I simply set out.

The countryside is picturebook France, rolling, rich and rock walled. In its early stages, the Seine winds among fields and occasionally disappears in a brushy tangle. At any point, during the first few miles, you can hop across without getting your feet wet. Soon it widens into a respectable stream, snaking in even loops across fruited meadows. This is the deepest, greenest, richest heartland of Old Europe.

The Seine is formalized at Billy-lès-Chanceaux, its name on that enameled plate bolted to the stone bridge. It flows past a line of tile-roofed and shuttered buildings, the town hall and bourgeois homes, set on the cobbled quai as if the place were a busy port. Jeannette and I settled down to watch life. An ancient tractor clattered across the bridge. Some kids did a Flying Wallenda act over the water. A mother herded her toddlers homeward, a duck with ducklings. We laid out a lunch on the grass. It was less elaborate than Manet's, but we got the feeling. This was one lovely river.

Then we meandered downstream, stopping to sniff at kitchen windows and craning our necks over tumbledown stone walls to see gardens gone wild. Whenever we found a bridge, we crossed it and watched clear water swirling slowly around the pilings. If a side road climbed a wooded rise, we followed it.

France is particularly well endowed for this sort of sweet exploration. The Institut Géographique National (IGN) puts out a series of blue-bordered maps on a scale of one to twenty-five thousand. Two inches are devoted to each mile on the ground, enough room for street grids of hamlets and the shapes of château outbuildings. Each caprice of a streambed is traced in and out of green-shaded splotches. A practiced eye can almost pick out the places with cozy little cafés run by accomplished grandmothers, causing the practiced palate to moisten noticeably.

Thanks to the IGN, I could follow highways too insignificant for any color at all, doubling back to thwart dead ends and recrossing the Seine yet again whenever I liked the cut of a barn. There is a certain pleasant sameness in the river's early stages. As in much of France beyond the cities, most people are linked to farms or are shopkeepers who earn their living one baguette at a time. In terms of nature, however, all around is heavy on *luxe, calme et volupté.*

Hard times had begun to bite when I first tracked the river in 1992, and things were getting worse. The European Community, an imperfect union, bettered few lives. Farm subsidies plummeted, prices sagged, and agro-industry suffered. Other sectors stagnated, drying the national resource pool. Elsewhere, rural families were migrating to cities. The Seine's waters hardly shielded people nearby from the world beyond. But, I suspected, only desperation could dislodge many of them from their natural paradise.

Conflicting sensations came back, time and again, as I explored the river. Try as you might to avoid it, the Seine at its gentlest pushes you toward grandiose metaphor. It is a silver thread woven into a rich Old World tapestry, an inlay of precious metal . . . and so on. Then you turn another corner and find some architectural atrocity at the edge of a village gone modern. People are kind beyond belief, or porcine putzes. In microcosm, the Seine is France.

At Bar-sur-Seine, well before the boats start, Antoine
Richard fished for supper. His secret spot was just below the
picturesque wreckage of a wooden wheel that had churned
up electricity not long after Thomas Edison invented light
bulbs. A few days earlier, he had pulled out twenty-three
trout. A fireman in his twenties, Richard spends his down
time along the river.

The occasional French monarch dreamed of bringing
boats up this high. Under orders from Napoléon, engineers
once tried to dredge a channel near Bar and line it with rock
walls. But the riverbed is too porous in its early stages, and
the emperor's canal would not hold water. As a result, the
Seine's gently sloping grass banks are just about the way
nature wants them.

"Such tranquillity, beauty," Richard reflected, pausing
to let the scene speak for itself. Bright flowers climb mossy
village walls. Up the graveled road was a regulation church
with a pointy steeple. The cafés and shops had not changed
for generations and likely never will. Ah, the poetry of *la
France éternelle*. And then the other side. I asked about pollution.

"It's not too bad here," Richard said. "You can still catch
l'ombre, as far down as Fourchière." That was not so far
down. "Then it disappears." *Ombre*, a delicate white fish like
a trout, can't handle dirty water. Farther down, fishermen
have to settle for carp, chub, roach, bream, eels and other
hardy species. A few hours' drive from the source, the Seine
looked fresh and alive. But Paul Lamarche's tiny bugs
wouldn't stand a chance.

At Fourchière, a gas-station owner in greasy overalls
said that, in fact, the odd *ombre* still lurked in the river. He
eyed me carefully and added, "*Ici c'est une société privée.*" This
was confusing. *Société* can mean "association" but also "com-

pany." Had some business cornered fishing rights? The man explained, *"C'est reservé aux gens du pays."* Another two-way meaning: *Pays* usually means "country," and he might have been saying that only French people could fish there. He wasn't. The other meaning is "around here." He meant that the Seine, in that area, belonged only to Fourchière's people. But the bakery sold me bread.

Châtillon-sur-Seine is the first real town on the river. As in Paris, the water splits into two branches around an island of buildings in fitted rock that go back a half dozen centuries. But in Châtillon the channels are a coin's toss wide, and you can see bottom. At midnight, time tunnels you backward. Cobblestone streets, laid out for horses and slop buckets, echo footsteps. Rusty hinges hold up shutters in wood petrified with age. People have snapped off their lights, leaving only a flickering glow of street lanterns that might be oil torches. A fortified hilltop church stands above the river. From some angles, it is a brooding hulk. From others, it is a graceful sweep of towers and ramparts.

The river hairpins and eddies into a mystical pool under a rock outcropping. In fact, this is the Douix, perhaps the world's shortest river, and the first tributary of the Seine. The Douix gushes up from the cliff at rates approaching a thousand gallons a second. It boils over a natural fall of ragged rock. From source to mouth, it is one hundred yards long. In the darkness, it churns and rushes, blowing off mists. When the upper Seine was a highway, this had to be a Druid rest area.

∽∽∽∽∽

A number of years back, say about 50 million or so, when the Seine's bed was on the floor of a shallow inland sea, France was as warm as the Caribbean. Off and on during those

Paleocene times, waves covered a broad sweep of Western Europe, leaving islands of rich vegetation and small tropical beasts. Each dose of salt water lasted 2 to 4 million years. In between, the land dried and life forms nestled in the sediment to fossilize for the later amusement of geologists. Remains of two thousand mollusks have been found in the Paris basin, many of them dead ringers for the shells that get tossed out each night after a *fruits de mer* feast in Les Halles.

As time marched on, old sands and clays hardened into new formations. The limestone deposits that characterize Paris began in a subepoch called, naturally, Lutecian. Successive layers of gypsum, clay and sand already had taken shape by the Pleistocene epoch, a million years ago, when giant ice cubes elsewhere on the planet scraped slowly past and redecorated the scenery. Toward the end of the Quaternary period, the banks of the Seine were somewhat as we find them. Rich alluvial soil goes down yards deep on a sandy, porous base. In the heart of Paris, where wagons could cross once wheels appeared, hard calcified rock forms a solid foundation for a city.

A visitor today can sit on the bank under leafy trees and taste the fruits of this geological C.V. The chalky hillsides and plains produce grapes to kill for. And, above Châtillon, the northbound Seine flows into Champagne, where a monk named Dom Pérignon figured out a splendid use for them.

In these sorts of settings, one is well advised to husband the adjectives and go easy on superlatives. That said, there may be no place better than Vix, anywhere, to uncork a bottle and contemplate peace on earth. Two millenia after thriving as a crossroads of world trade, Vix has dropped from the map. Its ancient treasures—some gold and jewelry, but especially a stunning cast-bronze five-foot-six-inch-high Grecian urn from the tomb of a princess—are five miles away in Châtillon. The highway misses it by a mile. No one mentioned it to me; flashing by in the car, I saw a sign and hung a right.

Unvisited, Vix remains in a mossy-tile, preneon state, its falling-down walls half hidden in bursts of bright flowers. The Seine makes a gentle bend into the village and flows under three arches of a stone bridge. It is wide and clear as glass, with whorls of weeds under its rippled surface. In the falling light of dusk, fishermen in waders tie flies to their lines and snake them over the water.

For a while, I fussed with my cameras. By placing my car near the bridge, I could get high enough to picture the chipped "La Seine" sign, with a spray of red flowers in the foreground and the rich green far bank as a backdrop. After half a roll, I gave up. The power was not visual but spiritual, and every sense went into the picture: perfumes, ripplings and rustlings, balmy air you could feel.

A few couples, some young, some ancient, watched the bushy-haired man with Paris plates crawl over his car and twist into odd positions. Most quickly lost interest. They had come to see the river at sundown, a specialty of Vix that is now into its third millenium and shows no sign of losing its glory.

Approaching a man with a fly rod, I fished for quotes. Yes, outsiders were welcome to try their luck in the Seine, he said, and I was happy to hear it. Like picture-taking, words fell short. What could he tell me that I could not feel by sitting there quietly? Here in Vix, it all fell together: the cycles of geology, the waves of history, the link to modern times. Light was dwindling fast, and people were expecting me a long way down the road. I sat, and sat, and sat.

Energetic tourists, I found, can go deeper into the river. On this trip, I went from Vix on to Châtillon, back for a

second visit. Having gotten to know the river better, I
wanted to see what surprises it had to offer. Like a Cracker
Jack box, the Seine always delivers, but this time Sequana
surpassed herself: in a parking lot next to the shallow riverbed I found a dripping Belgian in a purple-and-yellow wet
suit, with full scuba gear.

"Are you going to dive?" asked the Belgian, a young
mason named Claude Chaslin, who, when I said no, looked
at me as if I were nuts. The Douix, it seems, is best seen
underwater. A low tunnel in the limestone face leads into a
deep subterranean pool. A rope and markers guide divers
farther along. Chaslin got out an elaborate sketch to show
me what I was missing. A short passage gives onto a towering chimney in the rock. Long galleries are broken by wells
up to sixty feet deep. Finally, a thousand feet into the rushing
water, boulders block the way.

〰〰〰〰

Past Châtillon and Vix, the river passes town after village,
and each relates to it differently. Mussy seems to be quietly
collapsing with neglect; the Seine is an innocent passerby.
Bar throbs with new buildings, heading away from the river.
Its old bridge supports a dilapidated but still imposing
wooden mill, once powered by water rushing underneath.
At Fourchière, the wide, shallow stream is the center of
activity, like a village square.

Dawdling as best I could, I made my way downstream to
where the riverbed gets seriously weird, and I learned the
tragic tale of Troyes. During fifteen centuries, rulers of
Champagne built a great city on wine and water. In each
epoch, their intricate canals were a technological wonder of
the age. Today, the wine is mediocre, and the water is gone.

Long before bubbles, Champagne country was a center

of Christian piety. In the twelfth century, a monk named Chrétien de Troyes wrote *La Queste de Saint-Graal*, forerunner to the legends of King Arthur's hunt for the Holy Grail. My own quest for a river spirit was a bit more modest, but this was promising ground.

Work on the river began with the Gauls and Romans, who tried to drain the marshlands. Tributaries fed meandering branches of the Seine, but the main channel often left boatmen in the mud. By the fourth century, the Moline Canal directed water into the river. In 1174, Henry the Liberal finished a cloverleaf of fancy waterworks. He diverted part of the Seine to beautify his palace, sluice waste from the city, and supply fire brigades. Linking fresh streams and old riverbeds by means of raised wooden aqueducts and dikes, his canals supplied millers, barrel makers and craftsmen. Also, they drew off stagnant water, opening new land for building.

Within a few centuries, Seine waters fed canals from forty-one sluice gates. Troyes had more canals per square foot than Venice. Artisans figured out the chemistry: parchment makers and tanners worked upstream, and textile weavers found that the acid left in the water bleached cloth to a white that made the city famous.

Count Thibault IV, a Middle Age nobleman who loved poems and horses and splendor, brought more glory. He held court at Provins, but Troyes was his international seaport. Each year, overloaded boats from all over France and beyond struggled up the Seine for the Troyes fair. The great sport was *joute*, river jousting. Colorfully dressed competitors balanced on the bows of boats, maneuvered by teammates, and tried to ruin each other's day with not-too-padded poles. Drowning was infrequent.

The city burned down in 1564 and was built again,

better. Its core is in the shape of a champagne cork, with the Seine at the rounded outer edge. Tall houses, timbered with exposed oak beams, overhang the narrow streets; medieval tax collectors measured only the ground-floor surface. Its cathedral and churches contain 10 percent of all the stained glass in France.

In 1847, Troyes's old dream was finally brought to reality. The Canal de la Haute-Seine ran shaft-straight for thirty miles to the confluence of the Aube, allowing barges to reach Troyes from the English Channel. This was a serious affair, patrolled by men with swords. Insulting a lockkeeper got a bargee hauled before the king's prefect. Four of its locks had hand-cranked gates, but the fifth was a guillotine, a precursor to today's huge metal gates that rise and drop at either end of the lock. That first year, the canal carried twenty thousand tons of freight. The total rose to twenty-six thousand in 1861, under Napoléon III, before plummeting because of war, neglect and competition from a new railroad.

Entering the city, I looked all over for traces of this grand canal, which had taken a Napoléon and forty years to complete. As it turned out, I was driving on it. Troyes today is lively and charming, redolent of every epoch of France's rich past. All that is missing is the river that built it. Troyes has buried the Seine.

Before going to Troyes, I looked up the number of city hall on Minitel, France's electronic phone book, which also offers thousands of other services, from buying a train ticket to finding amateur sex partners. Along with the number was an invitation to keep pushing keys. Troyes, the screen told me, was one of Europe's most beautiful cities. It was within three hundred miles of half the residents of the Common Market. Its willing labor force was skilled at intricate handiwork. Page after page explained the schools and investment codes. A list told who looked after sports, or culture, or building permits. The Seine was not mentioned.

Troyes flatters itself a bit. Much of it is beautiful. But it is also a faithful reflection of modern France: a fine old painting dabbed over in places with gaudy colors and set in a chintzy frame. Beyond the center, with original hand-forged nails and carved-wood fancywork, the edges are wide streets of nondescript apartment blocks, factory outlets and industrial slur. Parking lots sprawl around hideous *hypermarchés*, which are supermarkets but bigger and uglier.

Even in the old town, the feeling is more carnival than charm. A little wheeled train with a silly smokestack and an ad for McDonald's takes tourists around town. The Santa Fe restaurant describes its chile con carne as *"le cassoulet du cowboy."* Cassoulet is made with white beans and potted goose; the only connection I could see was flatulence. At the Oxford Tavern, I asked the proprietor about the Seine. He replied in the kindly tone that polite people use for dangerous cranks.

Jean Brangbour, in charge of tourism and Troyes's patrimony, labored nobly to push his city. "Well," he said, with a nervous hit of his cigarette, "we're within close reach of half of Europe if you don't count Portugal and Greece." Troyes produces half of the children's clothes in France. Big textile outfits abound: Benetton, Lacoste, Naf Naf. I asked about the city's famed dye plants, and he drew the cigarette to bright red. "They're cleaner now," he said. "Once you could see branches of the Seine in bright colors: purple, blue, red. Not anymore." That was something.

Soon he got into the spirit. "A few years ago, workers found some huge stones, bigger than this desk"—his desk was seven feet across—"when they were digging a foundation," he said. "They must have been for a platform for hauling boats out of the water." This was a mystery. The site was well north of where the canal stopped. Brangbour did not know more.

Poking around further, I found the Seine on the fourth floor of the majestic old city hall, in the dustiest of boxes on the farthest of shelves in the attic that houses Troyes's archives. Jean Lejeune, about to retire after thirty years of filing away records, seemed surprised at my interest but rallied to the cause. Soon I was immersed in parchment covered with delicate script.

"The Seine will be navigable to Châtillon," ordered an original copy of a decree signed Napoléon, Emperor of the French, in year XII of the Revolution. That was 1805. He gave his ministers six years to start passenger service from Paris to Troyes and beyond. Another document estimated the material needed, including 1,482 cubic meters of shaped stone. "I want Troyes to remember me and my visit," the emperor told notables after stopping off with Josephine on the way to Italy. Napoléon was finished before the canal.

Various attempts were made to keep the project going, including that abandoned work at Bar, but Châtillon was a long way up a narrow river. Instead, Napoléon's successors focused on the crucial part, a dependable water link from Paris to Troyes. The first boats reached Troyes in 1847. A few years later, Napoléon III threw resources into the project. Bonaparte's grandnephew, a great builder, saw river traffic in the future. But he also built railroads, and competition was bitter.

By 1868 merchants were already complaining that maintenance and other services on the canal were so lousy that traffic often stopped. "Given the vital importance to Troyes," reported the minutes of a May 13, 1868, city-council meeting, "authorities would take action . . ."

Over the following decades, the Seine came up often in the city's files. Much was written about La Bâtarde—the Bastard, a wayward branch of the river. Other branches divided the flow, a problem when the water was low. When the water was high, floods were another problem. All of this was eventually worked out. During the early 1900s, *péniches* carried grain from Troyes and brought in coal and gravel. After World War I, they grew scarce.

Lejeune's dusty archives did not say when the traffic stopped, or how much cargo was moved in the final years. It had been a while. Near Troyes, most of the emperor's waterway was paved over and forgotten. The last boat in town is a floating pizzeria trapped between bridges too low to clear a rubber duck. And some councilmen want to fill in this last vestige for parking space. I asked around to see what townsfolk knew.

"The canal was closed in 1984, but there is a plan to reopen it," one well-dressed gentleman on the street declared. This seemed hardly likely. In the cathedral, Eliane Hubert, seventy-seven and a Troyes resident since 1920, thought traffic stopped in the thirties. "By 1925, parts of it were already cut," she said. "We used to have the bridge of thirty-two steps that went over it." She paused to sigh at the memory. With lovely French understatement, she concluded, "It was agreeable back then."

In fact, a little barge called the *Dixit* brought sugar to Troyes in 1940. After it went back down the Seine, Lock 10 never opened again. The canal stayed opened to Méry, a third of the way upriver from Marcilly, and boats hauled out beets at a declining clip. In 1968, the final locks were closed.

I walked to the edge of the champagne cork. Just past a spirited game of *boules*—old men clicking metal balls on a grassy patch—a bridge crossed a pathetic little unmarked stream, weeds waving under its surface. "Is that the main branch of the Seine?" I asked a passing young man. "In principle," he said.

Taking one last shot, I stopped at a well-stocked used-book store. The young owner had a little of everything. He looked blank when I asked for something related to the river.

"You mean Troyes has abandoned the Seine?" I asked.

He shrugged. "Let's just say she is covered over."

3 Rolling on the River

WHEN ALL ELSE FAILS, Flaubert's Frédéric slinks back to memories of serene dalliance by the Seine at an idyllic town called Nogent. These days, Nogent does not look like anyplace for a sentimental education unless a young man's fancy turns toward nuclear power plants. Two looming concrete stacks, reflected in the river at dusk and illuminated at dark, remind all within miles of the downside of splitting atoms.

In Flaubert's time, the 1840s, a branch of the Seine coursed through mill wheels and rejoined the main channel in a boiling waterfall. Then it was tamed in an Eden of golden blossoms, roses, lily pads and ancient willows. "The horizon was defined by the curve of the river," Flaubert wrote. "It was flat as a mirror, with great insects skating on the tranquil water."

Today the river is still at work, but it is not grinding

grain. The nuclear plant sucks in water to make the steam that drives its turbines and also to cool its reactors. It produces 50 million kilowatt-hours a day, enough to electrify a small house for three thousand years. Under normal conditions, fifty gallons a second spill back into the Seine.

No one will make it go away. In France, three-quarters of all electricity is generated by nuclear turbines. The last American reactor was licensed in 1979; all fifty French reactors, except for two pilot plants, have been built since 1980. A fifth of the electricity is exported to neighboring countries.

At first, ecologists thought the Nogent plant's only pollution was visual. Then the Green Party traced radioactive algae in the Seine. The Greens said condensers containing alloys of zinc and copper also contaminated the water. Electricité de France, which owns the plant, made changes while denying any major problem. In 1993, however, Claude Brayer of the Greens called the plant the biggest polluter on the river. Each day, he said, it pumps twenty-seven tons of sulfuric acid into the main channel.

All of this causes little stir in Nogent. The plant employs 580 people, and the prevailing view is that hungry families are a greater worry than bream that glow in the dark. Surrounding fields are rich in wheat, barley and oilseed, but farming is no way to grow wealthy in modern Europe. Work is scarce. The dockside mill is closed, a rickety tin château of silos and precarious conveyor chutes.

Electricité de France officials hasten to insist that they are not poisoning the Seine. Government regulators who monitor pollution have yet to sound the alarm. By the time the river passes Nogent, it is stiffening with so much chemical pollution and bacteria that radiation is a secondary threat.

Reactors and rust aside, Nogent is not without charm.

Or sentiment. Among its half-timbered gothic and Renaissance buildings is a stone vault covered in ivy, the remains of Le Paraclet convent, where Héloïse and Abélard got back together in death. You probably know the story—in the twelfth century, Fulbert, the canon of Notre-Dame in Paris, hired Pierre Abélard to tutor his teenaged niece. Abélard, a poet of thirty-six, was not Fulbert's idea of the perfect catch. When he learned that the two not only were lovers but also had secretly married, he was seriously pissed.

Abélard sent his wife to Argenteuil to be looked after by nuns. Fulbert dispatched thugs to excise Abélard's testicles. Years passed, and Héloïse ended up as abbess at Nogent. When Abélard died, she had his body brought to her for burial. She died twenty-two years later, and sympathetic sisters opened the crypt so she could be placed next to him. According to unconfirmed reports from the scene, he arose to embrace her.

Time has rounded off the story's rougher edges. Close inspection suggests that Abélard might have been a womanizing rake who dumped Héloïse at the first sign of trouble. But no one is watching anymore. After the French Revolution, the couple's remains were reburied at Père-Lachaise Cemetery in Paris, still near the Seine, but in mixed company that now includes Jim Morrison of the Doors.

∾∾∾∾∾

I poked around Nogent because, for practical purposes, it is where the river starts. From Troyes to Nogent, navigation is mostly a fond memory, and this is part of a larger picture. Just as Troyes reflects a wider France, the Canal de la Haute-Seine exemplifies what happened to the waterways. Over the last century, willful neglect has pushed hundreds of miles of French canals to the edge of ruin, or beyond. The

Canal de Berry once linked the central canals to the Cher and the Loire, allowing boats to reach the Atlantic at Nantes from the Seine and the Saône. It was abandoned, then partly filled in. The Canal d'Orléans suffered the same fate. Even the fabled Canal de Bourgogne is in serious disrepair. Few captains venture with a load into the canal through the Burgundy backcountry. Between broken walls and leaky gates, they are never sure they'll get out.

In theory, the Seine is navigable twelve miles above Nogent. A series of shiny blue and white map guides, published by the Port Autonome de Paris in French, English and German, details each waterway in France, starting with the Seine. Navicarte Two fixes kilometer zero at just above the village of Marcilly, a few hundred yards up the Aube at the downstream end of the condemned Canal de la Haute-Seine. Unless you are in a rowboat, don't try it.

"Hah!" replied Bernard Gueu when I showed him the chart. I found him in rubber hip boots, emerging from the trees on an overgrown towpath at Marcilly. He was president of the local fishermen's association, obligatory to anyone who wanted to fish along twenty-five miles of nearby banks, and vice president of the *département* (state) of Aube. "I saw the last *péniche* in that channel thirty years ago," Gueu said. "It was stuck in the sand."

Traffic, he said, stopped at Conflans-sur-Seine, a few miles down at the end of a straight cut along the river to Nogent, but there wasn't much there, either. Although the river bottom grows firmer after Troyes, he said, you still couldn't count on the young Seine to hold water. With his finger jerking around the page, he traced five separate streams that branched off the main channel and skirted the large town of Romilly, opposite from Marcilly. They all rejoined farther down.

It was a chicken-and-egg problem. With such a feeble flow, only regular dredging and maintenance of canal walls could keep the river open. Brisk river traffic would generate enough funds for this. But, since there was no dredging or maintenance, there was no traffic. Troyes and towns along the old canal would have to see a need and lobby hard.

Gueu was not holding his breath. For a lot of people in Troyes, he said, the Seine was a gutter. The city fought for *autoroutes*, not canals. "Those dye plants turn the river black and kill the fish," he said. "You want to see? Just go upstream and look at what collects in puddles by the banks. Disgusting." I made a note to do that. Meantime, Madame Regnault was expecting me for lunch.

Madeleine Regnault, a fireball at eighty-four, lived alone with her relics in a crumbling château built two centuries ago when the Seine made the region rich. Back then, the forests near Paris had long since disappeared into roof beams and fireplaces. Timber kings far upriver cut logs and lashed them into gigantic rafts. The average *flotteur*, who manhandled these convoys day and night in all weather, would have sneered at Paul Bunyan. Profits were enormous, and Marcilly was bourgeois heaven. When coal torpedoed the market, merchants exported grain in barges.

A half century ago, Madame Regnault married into Marcilly nobility. Her husband was a traveler and bon vivant until he died in his eighties. Now, nearly blind, she has only a few dwindling treasures. Her prize is a diary penned in 1793 by an illustrious Regnault aboard the warship *Duquesne*, blocked by the British at Bizerte harbor in Tunisia. But someone had sneaked in and stolen forty of her hugely valuable prerevolutionary painted plates. The thief, well briefed, took only the cream. Fairly sure who was responsible, she concluded with a rueful laugh: "That is the last time I let an antique dealer visit this house."

Madame Regnault is no nostalgia-bound old lady, frozen in time and form. Not long earlier, bored at a stuffy dinner, she had local notables choking on their spoons with a rude play on the word *baiser*. Its meaning ranges from a peck on the hand to a poke in the hay. Still, she remembers what the river used to be, and her memories are among the treasures she carefully guards. She is not about to hurry along decline.

When I mentioned that Gueu last saw a *péniche* at Marcilly thirty years ago, she snorted. "Let us not exaggerate. I remember seeing one twenty years ago. Maybe twenty-five." Later, she allowed that the end of river traffic had drained the life out of Marcilly. The few shops closed down, leaving only a bakery and an inn run by a woman of eccentric ways. Remaining residents went to supermarkets over the bridge in Romilly, but she had no car. "It's true," she said. "We have lost something precious, and I miss it."

After lunch, we went to see the river. I walked ahead with Jean-Robert Villepigue, a yachtsman pal from Paris who had brought me to Marcilly. His father had been close to Madame Regnault's husband, and, all of his life, she was his adoptive aunt. As a kid, Jean-Robert spent every free weekend playing along the banks, and he wanted to show me his secret haunts.

A half mile up, we crossed a bridge over the Seine at the point where it meets the Aube. To the left, the Seine is almost black, a raggedy river with wild banks of tree trunks and undergrowth. To the right, the Aube is twice as wide, of a green so luminous it is as if it were lighted from below. It has a shimmering whitish cast from the chalky Champagne fields it crosses. In frenchified Latin, *aube* is white. Its banks are tailored, lined with summer homes and little fishing piers.

The rivers meet beyond a leafy spit of land, and they travel side by side, separate colors divided by a long sharp line. Far beyond, the waters blend to a fresh forest green. But for the Seine's longer bed and richer history, poets in Paris might instead be searching for words that rhyme with *Aube*.

From the bridge, up the Seine, Jean-Robert pointed to a tunnel in the wall of vegetation along the bank. Barely visible, its entrance was blocked by a half-submerged wooden dugout canoe. It was one of the dead branches of the Seine, a thoroughfare of Jean-Robert's childhood. "We used to paddle far up and imagine ourselves in the Amazon," he told me. "It was just like a rain forest, covered over in rotting vegetation, with swirls of insects and funny noises. It was a *merveille*."

Up the Aube, the abandoned first lock of the Canal de la Haute-Seine looked like a colonial outpost in Indochina that the jungle reclaimed. Heavy oaken slabs held back some water, but cascades poured through the cracks. The hand-crank mechanism was twisted and rusty. Jean-Robert once wanted to buy the lockkeeper's house, but it had since been demolished. We poked in the grass to find its foundations, archeologists probing the edges of Angkor Wat.

On the way back, the Seine delivered its de rigueur surprise. At a pier by a summer home, we saw a thirty-foot sailboat that had somehow knifed its keel through the silted channel. Farther down, the old Marcilly waterfront across the river was a ghost town of stately stone mansions with closed shutters. Along the road, I noticed a barrel-shaped stone hidden in the tall weeds, tilted askew. Looking closer, I found more stones and some rusted metal studs. They were the bollards that had allowed rows of *péniches* to be tied up alongside a wooden wharf that Jean-Robert used to visit as a kid. All other traces had gone, along with the warehouse and silo.

Leaving town, I passed the park under the old bridge to Romilly. A row of off-white stone pillars on massive bases lay off to the side in the grass. These were yet more bollards, extracted from the banks like useless wisdom teeth and left to await another purpose. Bleached by the sun, they looked like those chunks of marble column at the source of the Seine.

∾∾∾∾∾

A few miles below Marcilly, I passed some genuine ancient relics. Archeologists were digging at a Gallo-Roman site that was supposed to be the battlefield where Attila the Hun was beaten and sent home in shambles. Possibly. He had been in the vicinity. Saint Genevieve is still revered in Paris because she persuaded Attila to pillage elsewhere. I was preoccupied with a fresher mystery: Where did navigation start on the Seine?

I spotted a grain silo above the trees, parallel to the river, and found a back road leading to it. Next to it, the Conflans-sur-Seine lock was deserted. It was hand operated, the standard 126-foot length fixed by a far-seeing transport minister in the 1870s, Charles Freycinet, whose name still designates the garden-variety French barge. After some rattling at the lockhouse gate and an energetic "Allô," Jean-Pierre Cartier emerged, bare chested and bare footed.

He seemed delighted to have a little company. I asked how many *péniches* came through these days.

"Two this year—and three *yachts*," Cartier said. It was already late July, in 1993. "Last year, three *péniches* and ten *yachts*." In French river terms, a *yacht* is a pleasure craft— anything from the Onassis flagship to an outboard bumboat.

Cartier maintains the locks and cuts back foliage. His wife, Evelyne, is the keeper. She and two other women handle the five locks between Conflans and Nogent. It is a simple arrangement. If a boat starts the canal downstream, the keeper at that end goes into shock. Then she gets in her little Service de Navigation de la Seine sedan and follows it along to crank the gates open and shut. When the boat comes back down, Madame Cartier does the same.

Locks are free of charge in France. A yearly river tax was imposed on *yachts* in 1992, but that hardly begins to cover the cost. In eighteen months, five *péniches* at Conflans carried away eight hundred tons of colza, an oilseed—forty truckloads. Money is a problem.

On the books, the canal's depth is 1.8 meters, nearly six feet, comfortable clearance for a loaded *péniche*. But a converted houseboat had just come through drawing only 1.25 meters. Picking through silt and sandbars, it took all day to cover the ten miles to Nogent. The sailboat I saw at Marcilly scraped upstream with a 1.2-meter draw. It was stranded until winter rains swelled the river.

Somehow, Cartier said, engineers scrounged enough money to dredge the first section of the canal from Nogent to Marnay. After that, no one could justify the expense. In the natural course of things, the end was only a matter of time.

I made a last stop on the canal. At Pont-sur-Seine, the charts showed the Bridge of Sighs, and I was intrigued. The town turned out to be a jewel, yet another walled settlement by a collapsing château, built upon river wealth that had vanished. No one had heard of the bridge. When I asked in a grocery store, aging women shoppers gathered to discuss the subject, surprising themselves at how little they knew about the river their medieval bridgehead once controlled. "It's funny," the owner concluded, "the Seine is just over there, but we hardly pay any attention to it. It used to be a lot of fun, watching the *péniches* go by."

Cartier had given me directions. I turned off the highway at the château wall and drove through a cornfield to a dirt track onto a short span of rusty girders. The canal lazed below. Weeds poked among the old rocks, a reminder of what would happen if anyone stopped making regular rounds to whack them back. Planking on the bridge needed attention. If I'd had a month or two to spare, I could wait for a barge to pass. But the bridge was aptly named. I sighed.

❧❧❧❧❧

The Nogent lock, at 45 meters, is bastard-sized. It is longer than it has to be for Freycinet *péniches* yet too short for much else. Farther down, at Bray-sur-Seine, maximum length doubles to 90 meters, allowing room for tug convoys or those big self-powered barges from the north. And at Montereau, fifty miles from Paris, the capacity doubles again to 180 meters, big enough for a Spanish Armada.

Like the Aube at Marcilly, the Yonne at Montereau is a bigger river than the Seine it feeds, broad and purposeful. A small school holds that it is the real source of the river that winds on to the sea. The thought is troubling. Paris would not be the same if its thrilling watercourse were pronounced *yawn*.

Until joined by the Aube, the river carries the first of its *noms-de-fleuve*, the Petite-Seine. Farther on, augmented again by the Yonne at Montereau, it is the Haute-Seine until Paris. Then it is the Basse-Seine to Rouen and, finally, the Seine-Maritime to the open roads.

But there is only one Seine. At the top, by Marcilly, the beauty beguiles gently. Those forgotten inlets, lushly overgrown, suggest primeval jungle with nothing more importuning than low-powered mosquitos. At the bottom, when salt water surges in and ocean freighters dwarf the barges that seemed so huge, the romance remains. In between, it can be stately and wild all at once.

Just beyond Nogent, tourists stop at the Château de Motte-Tilly, imposing and perfectly proportioned, with classic, clipped gardens. Milos Forman selected the place as backdrop for his film *Valmont*, which explored yet again the dangerous liaisons of noble perversion. More interested in the river, I nosed around out the back gate. The Rue de Seine veers left off the village's cobbled main street. A block later, it is only two dirt wheel tracks through deep grass, shaded by trees. The port is a patch of sand, empty but for a few crude wooden boats that might have carried wine barrels back from the old Troyes fair.

Having gotten this far, I saw that the Seine in its earlier stages was true to its character in Paris. It was predictable until you tried to predict it. If you looked, there was always a secret. It could jolt your adrenaline flow, but it seldom stood your hair on end. White-water maniacs can have their Devil's Gall Bladder or Rip 'Em Up Rapids. In French, fresh water translates to *l'eau douce*—sweet water—and that's how I prefer it.

Past Nogent, the river was deep enough to be ridden, and it was time to get into the current.

∞∞∞∞∞

Almost any riverboat has three electrical circuits: the 220-volt system for use in port; the 12 volts, or 24 volts, for essentials when under way; and the charge that crackles on board the night before when you prepare to leave at dawn. I explored much of the Seine in *La Vieille*. In real terms, one boat equals another if your purpose is gawking over the side. But this was a thrill the dimensions of which I could never have guessed.

Pérignon, the red-nosed monk, must have felt this when bubbles first collected in white wine, as he had calculated they would. When the first head rolled neatly into the basket, M. Guillotin likely experienced a similar *frisson*. My achievement was of somewhat less moment but, Jesus, it felt good when my house pulled away from its lot.

Without fail, visitors ask, "Does it move?" or, worse, declare: "But of course it doesn't move." Defending the old girl's honor, one is tempted to harsh retort. The truth, however, is that it didn't move much. The previous owners loved the boat, and the fact that it was a boat, but they thought navigation a costly bother. I inherited a floating apartment. It took a lot of costly bother—physical reeducation and moral rearmament—to bring *La Vieille* back in sync with the Seine. But she made it.

We flushed the water tanks and put in pumps. Running lights were decrudded; cabin lights were rewired. We messed with the engines and gears and fuel system. From stem to stern, we added, subtracted, and multiplied. Then we loaded up on flags, maps, and dorky dishes with anchors on them, made by people who understand too well what I'm talking about here. Cash registers rang in Paris, London and New York, and it was worth it. We had dressed up a dowager, poured her a drink and took her dancing.

I, of course, was another problem. Reared in Arizona, I could drive a horse. Brought by occasional circumstance within range of artillery, I could drive a four-wheel anything smartly across open ground. But here was thirty tons of deadweight, which, when you spun the wheel, kept on going in the same direction.

In fact, any idiot can drive a boat. You merely point it and move the throttle. To go backward, you shift to reverse. Avoiding the big stuff is as easy as not walking into a wall. That was lesson one. Lesson two was just as simple: Only an idiot believes lesson one.

Captain Jacques was my training wheels, and a cooler, more patient hand does not exist. Early on, we took a run up a narrow channel of the Marne. Relaxed after a sunny lunch on deck, with crew and company dozing in torpor, I told Jacques that I'd take it on in. He nodded. We cast off without incident, and with my mariner's eye, I chose a slightly wider spot to swing *La Vieille* around. A textbook maneuver: port engine forward, starboard aft, ease up the throttles. The boat turns on a *centime*.

I drifted toward the tree-fringed bank and turned the wheel hard. She began to come around, sort of. Just then, a police boat shot by on its afternoon rounds, throwing a serious wake. The boat dipped, and I felt a hint of shudder. "Bottom," observed Jacques, with the inflection of a Smoky Mountain grandpa remarking on the sunset from his rocking chair. He was kind enough not to add: "A few more centimeters, and you'll break the prop if you don't wreck the god-damned boat." With a deft pirouette, I ceded him the wheel.

After lesson three, it gets tricky. At the helm again, I avoided what looked like some whirling water to port and eased to starboard toward a stone quai on the opposite bank, with hefty bollards for tying up big boats. It ran a long way along shore, inviting visitors.

"Not there," Jacques said.

"How can you tell?"

"Water lilies."

Sure enough, almost invisible little lily-pad shapes waved under the surface; not far below were rocks and sands. Neatly skirting Charybdis, I was delivering us to Scylla.

If you're lucky, the river is marked with buoys or posts in the water. For big obstacles, there may be a *duc d'Albe*, a great wooden structure similar to those on which some past Spanish tyrant affixed his torture victims. Often, however, you're not lucky. Seine boatmen know the river like Mark Twain knew the Mississippi. Sometimes, simple physics is a clue. Silt gathers at the outside bend of a curve, and you swing wide. Other times, things are as they are simply because Sequana wants it that way.

Locks are a particular challenge. The concept is simple enough. One gate closes, and the other opens. Boats enter, and the open gate shuts. Water spills in or out until it reaches the level of the next section of river. You rise or drop up to fifteen feet at an impressive rate of speed while your crew keeps you steady with ropes looped around bollards above the lock wall. Deep grooves worn in the stone testify to how many boats have gone before, each straining and groaning in the rush of water.

In a regulated world with overbearing authorities trying to look out for everyone's safety, locks are a refreshing change. You're free to do anything you're dumb enough to try. And if you don't do something dumb, you may not get through. When heading upriver, someone has to scamper up slimy iron rungs set in the wall, hopping off to catch a first foothold as the boat floats past. Someone else has to fling up the ropes, trying not to miss and get an end caught in a prop. Others scramble to shove fenders between the boat and the wall. Going downriver, getting off is easy. But, when finished, there is a perilous climb down.

The leeway is wide if no one else is in the locks. When double barges cram into the tight rectangle of churning water, however, adding to the turmoil with their prop wash, the fun begins. Slackness on a rope can bounce fragile wooden timbers against the unforgiving mass of a steel hull.

Lockkeepers, often retired bargees, are a quirky lot. They can hold the gates a bit longer to squeeze you in, or they can slam them in your face. You might wait an hour, or more, for no apparent reason. In principle, pleasure boats hold off until all barges have placed themselves in the lock. But lockkeepers often operate on a first-come, first-served basis. It helps to know them and say a kind word over the VHF. Mostly, you learn patience or quit the river.

One afternoon, the lock at Maisons-Alfort was acting up. Gates would not open, and then they would not close. We held off forever, idling in the mouth of the Marne, waiting to rejoin the Seine. The radio had no explanation or apology. Finally, the doors swung open, and the light went green. Once inside, we waited. The gate eventually closed, and the water dropped. Then we waited. And waited.

Suddenly, I remembered why I was there in the first place. I had no sand to haul to Gennevilliers. My lights worked. Once the gate opened, no more locks separated us from home. So I watched the river.

Floating crud had collected at the edge of the rapids just over the lock wall. Hanging on to *La Vieille*'s bowline, I peered down to see why the stuff was emitting bubbles. The water thrashed mysteriously and calmed again. I kept staring. Suddenly, in a great geyser, a fish broke the surface and rolled in the air. I don't like to exaggerate these things; let's say it was the size of a small donkey.

Again and again, Moby Carp leaped and dove in the tasty garbage. I thought about getting the boat hook but dismissed the idea. Jeannette's last view of me would be me yelling, "Arggh," roped to this monster, and disappearing into the roiling Marne. When the lock door finally opened, I was sorry to move on.

My sentimental education continued a few weeks later, when we came back through the Maisons-Alfort lock into the Marne. This was only a twenty-six-butt trip; in the ashtray, I counted twenty-one mashed remains of the non-filtered Gauloises that habitually dangle from Jacques's lip, and factored in 20 percent more for those he flipped over the side. About eight hours. After reaching the ability to solo, I brought Jacques along whenever I could. He was good company, a rich lode of lore. And, on the river, you never know.

The ship's pleasant company included a sister, my surgeon–ballet dancer nephew and two pals from Colorado. The trip was flawless, a steady chug on a smooth river. The first lock gates were open, and we breezed through. The second lock was no harder. The air had a refreshing bite. Light was soft, dappled by fluffy clouds over a rising sun. We drank warm coffee, then cold beer, as the sights slipped by. Gaily painted *guinguettes*, garden taverns where couples dance away sunny afternoons, dotted the banks. Willows wept, and we laughed.

Jacques was expansive. As we passed through the darkened Saint-Maur tunnel, a half mile long with a few feet to spare on either side, he had me scribbling in my notebook.

"When you see that red light, believe it," he said, with the guffaw that seldom occurs before a few Heinekens. He meant the traffic light at the mouth of the one-way tunnel; once red, it might stay that way for half an hour. "One time I came through here in my *péniche*, and the guy coming the other way said to go on ahead, no one was behind him. I got halfway through and saw I was headed into the middle of a sculling race coming straight at me."

A flotilla of popsicle-stick boats, each crewed by four

terrified rowers, was barreling full tilt into the monster steel bow of a sand barge. If Jacques's boat had been bolted firmly to one side, and the water had been dead still, there might have been enough room for them to squeeze by single file. Under the circumstances, even if a scull managed to slip past, a churning prop would likely grind the crew to carp bait. Even stopped, a barge could bounce off one wall, smashing anything in its way against the other. Jacques was cool.

"I stopped as close to the wall as I could get and used a rope to guide them past, one by one," he said. "It took a long time, but they all made it safely. The police could not believe what had happened. They kept asking me, over and over, why I didn't stop at the light. I came that close to losing my license." He showed me how close by holding a thumb very close to a forefinger, and he guffawed again. "They kept me all afternoon."

But we had no incidents. Unlike the last time, kids did not piss on *La Vieille* from the bridges overhead. (This, I was told, is nothing personal. Sometimes arrested children of advancing years amuse themselves by dropping eggs, tomatoes or pots of paint on boats below.) When we started up after for a lovely barbecue, I decided this was a charmed voyage. Jacques tapped his finger on the starboard oil gauge to draw my attention. It read zero.

What the hell, I thought, if I've got to lose an engine, I'd rather be in a boat than a plane. We continued on with one propeller. The boat was slower and harder to handle, but it chugged along without difficulty. Suddenly, the pitch changed. Jacques tapped another instrument, but it wasn't necessary. Even a boob like me can recognize a clutch slipping, on its way to marine heaven. The short version is that we got home safely, even comfortably. Eventually.

4 Riders
of the
Long Days

NO BARGEE LOOKS SEPARATELY at the Seine any more than an osteopath messes only with the spine. The Rhône is bigger; the Saône and the Marne link France to the rest of Europe. Taken together, the five thousand miles of French inland waterways reach three seas via a network of astonishing variety. Yet for reasons as much spiritual as actual, the backbone is the Seine.

Coming downstream from Nogent, your choices begin at Montereau. A hard left takes you on the Yonne, into the lush edges of Burgundy. Pleasant cruising brings you past Sens to the fine old city of Auxerre. Then the Canal du Nivernais heads you south through fairyland forests toward the Loire Canal. If you have the time, you can take the Saône and the Rhône to the Mediterranean, ready to follow the old Greek route to Piraeus.

Farther down the Seine, a left at Moret-sur-Loing leads

into the Canal du Loing, lock after lock of placid beauty. Old trees and stone-fronted hamlets line the towpath until Montargis and the Canal de Briare. Here you cross a canal bridge: your boat floats in the air along an ornate Gustave Eiffel aqueduct over a gorge, passing over Louis XIV's seven stepped locks at Rogny. Then, after paralleling the Loire and following the Canal du Centre, you are on the Saône.

From either direction, you can eventually turn right near the mouth of the Rhône, past the medieval port of Sète and onto the seventeenth-century Canal du Midi. After new sights and more river, you're at the Atlantic.

When you approach Paris, the option is to the right. The Marne leads up into Champagne, to Epernay, and beyond to the Moselle and the Rhine. In fact, the Yonne and the Loing can also head you toward Germany, where a new canal ties the Rhine to the Danube. The missing link—which Charlemagne dreamed of forging in 793—now connects thirteen countries. With inclination and fuel, you can breakfast on the Seine and, months later, beyond Vienna, Budapest and Belgrade, dine in Constantsa, Romania, on the Black Sea. Unless you go to Prague.

The pull is strong at any of those junctions, but it takes a long time to run out of Seine. You do not, for example, want to pass up Moret-sur-Loing, the impressionists' way station, where Alfred Sisley starved to death over the last twenty years of his life. The medieval bridge Sisley painted is still there, leading to stone gates and cobbled streets. Like so many river towns, Moret was built to reveal itself best from the water.

One summer morning I drove through Moret wondering what had become of the charming place I had seen while gliding into the Canal du Loing. Crappy construction, bristling with billboards, masked the tower gates and church spires. I beat my way through town until traffic stopped dead. A road crew was at work, leaving one open lane but no one to arbitrate among drivers from both directions who demanded to use it. I sat, boiling over along with my radiator. Then I noticed the name of this street from hell, which represented the modern chaos impressionists sought to avoid: Rue du Peintre A. Sisley.

My purpose in Moret was to leave it. I was headed for neighboring Saint-Mammès, a thin line of picture-book buildings on the water. For normal people, it is barely a blip on the radar. Saint-Mammès, however, is upriver capital of the bargees, the itinerant river tribe known as *les voyageurs aux longs jours*, riders of the long days.

∞∞∞∞∞

The quaiside buildings are mostly *marinier* bars and shops that supply passing boats. Bargees tie up out front the way horsemen used to throw their reins over hitching posts in the old American West. Time does not exactly stand still in Saint-Mammès, but a hundred families afloat cling desperately to the hands of the clock. Seeing little future, they are trying at least to hold on to the present. I made a beeline for the Café de la Marine.

I am hooked on establishments with something nautical in their name. This goes back to Madame Grente and her Café de la Navigation in Saint-Jean-de-Losne, the bargees' town on the Saône. I wandered in by chance one day and asked for a sandwich. "We don't serve food," she said, in a neutral tone that also could have meant "We don't serve land creeps."

Then I went back with boat people she knew well, an American couple with a converted Dutch barge. She did not serve food, in fact, but she explained where to buy especially toothsome brioche. After an hour, my friends drove off, headed on a long trip. I walked to my car and could not find the keys. I had a flash: my pals had scooped up my keys by mistake. Madame Grente saw me panic and asked why. When I told her, she handed me her own keys and car papers. "Try to catch them," she said. "Good luck."

When I gave up and came back, I found my keys in the passenger door. I felt like an idiot, but one with a comfortable sense of belonging. This is what tribes are about. Beyond her own generosity, Madame Grente respected the code. Though a stranger, I was indirectly among her number, capable of being trusted and deserving of all necessary aid.

At the Café de la Marine in Saint-Mammès, I found a likable Tugboat Annie named Denise polishing glasses. She did not look as if she would lend me her car, but she was helpful.

"Things are not exactly brilliant," she said, when I asked about bargees. "The crisis has got everyone, even land people," she said. "But this . . ." To finish her sentence, she tossed me the *liste des tours*, a movement sheet put out by the Service de la Navigation office, which controls all freight charters. At the last thrice-weekly session, where brokers offer cargo contracts, 5 boats were signed up. Another 101 kept on waiting.

Most *péniches* are mom-and-pop jobs, run by families who have been on the river forever. I would be exploring their economics at Conflans-Sainte-Honorine, which is Saint-Mammès writ large. Here, I wanted to get a feel for how bargees saw the future. For the time being, the facts were simple enough. Breaking even was already a victory. It was 10 A.M., and regulars began appearing for their breakfast beer. Some ignored me, an obvious alien. Others bought me *pastis*, happy that someone seemed interested.

"The river is a village, a mobile village," explained Roger
Mayer, Denise's companion, a burly man with a bristling
mustache. "Whatever happens anywhere on the water, we
feel it here." He bought the bar in 1985 when he saw the
writing on the hull: For Sale signs everywhere. He was a
sixth-generation *marinier*, and he had put in a quarter century. The joint has been a fixture of the tribe forever. Rather
than leaving the life, he is a mooring point for others still
afloat.

Village and *tribe* are not figures of speech. For a century
and a half, bargees have married among themselves, talked
their own language and sent their kids to the same tribal
boarding schools. Friends may exchange a few words, disappear for six months, and then, when they end up in the same
lock, pick up the conversation where it left off.

For marriages, families bring their boats from halfway
across France or from Holland and Germany. Funerals are
more pressing. Whoever is in port stands in as pinch-
mourners for relatives who are too far away. If someone
stumbles onto a windfall, some of it goes into church-run
charities for others who suffer calamities.

In their element, these water people have extra senses,
like Indians who felt the ground to pick up the distant thundering of buffalo hooves. I'd seen this on the river. Before
land people even notice a far-off boat, a bargee knows its
direction from the mustache of water at its bow or the boil of
its props. Like braves who prove themselves with bow and
arrow, eleven-year-olds can slip a *péniche* that measures 5.1
meters across into a lock no more than 5.2 meters wide.

Ordinary kids learn about Aesop's fables and the Hundred Years' War. On the water, they're told of the winter of
1930: Someone steering a convoy turned too sharply at the
Port-à-l'Anglais lock, smacking the *Marolles* into a piling and

heeling it over; the *Dulong*, crushed by the *Quo Vadis*, sank like a stone; the *Papillon* also split open and foundered. A young woman aboard the *Marolles* drowned, along with a pilot who tried to save her.

Generations back, *péniches* were towed *à la bricole*: men, and often women, wore woven harnesses attached to ropes, and they pulled their barges along. Then horses made it easier. In bargee talk, *"les longs jours"* used to be the free-lance haulers who hired out their horses. They rose at 4 A.M. to feed their teams and get them in place. When the day stopped at dark, they worked to 11 P.M. rubbing down the horses. Now everyone's days are long. Man and wife take turns at the wheel. There is maintenance, cleaning, loading, planning. All of it forms a bond, a different way of seeing things.

Not having been introduced as I was at Saint-Jean-de-Losne, I was extended only partial confidence. Someone taught me the trick to turning on the men's room light so I didn't have to piss in the dark. But I wouldn't have gotten much farther anyway. Few people are in the tribe who are not born to it. Bargees learn the trade from their grand-fathers.

"That's the problem now, the kids," said William Quievy. "Most of them go to school, and they don't want to go back to the river under these circumstances. Who can blame them?" His own two teenaged sons, however, would not leave their boat if forced at gunpoint. Frédéric, sixteen, put it simply: "I hate school, and I love the river. It is a wonderful life. Why change?"

I worked the bar hard for words to explain the river's draw. Neither in Saint-Mammès nor anywhere else later could I find my quote. Partly, it is because bargees are seldom great talkers. They communicate by silence, or half thoughts they need not finish, or a burst of clipped jargon on the radio. But, more, it is because there is no explaining it. Like gypsies, cowboys or foreign correspondents who ignore their electronic mail, bargees suffer from *la bougeotte*—the inability to stay in one spot. But *suffer* is the wrong verb. Most of them love this curse.

"It's always different. You never know," Jacques remarked once in a wistful mood. "Once I got a load of wine, and it wasn't very good stuff. I'll tell you, 250 tons can reek something awful. It stank up everything. The last thing I wanted to do was drink wine." He has gotten over that. Then he told me about carrying unbagged fertilizer, and pesticides, and all the other reasons he had loved the life.

You can get a sense of the feeling from the names people paint across their bows. Mostly, these evoke some faraway fantasy, a state of mind if not a place. Names range from *Apaloosa* to *Zambezi*: *Koh I Noor*, *Excalibur*, *Gondola*, *Titantic*, *Graceland*, *Boss*, *Top Gun*, *The Guy*, *Le Release*, *Safari*, *Yukon City*, *Volga*, *Java*. There is *Arizona*, *Kentucky*, and some other states, not always spelled right. Or *Notre Rêve* and *Ma Pensée*, *Flipper* and *Baby Tonga*, *Diablo* and *Styx*.

William Quievy's tug is called *Maracaibo*, and he is obsessed by the place. He acquired two other tugs and called them *Caraïbes* and *Antilles*, just to keep the same neighborhood. When I told him I once worked in Venezuela, on the shores of Lake Maracaibo, he peppered me with questions. Six people who promised to send him postcards had neglected to do so. I am a poor bet for such promises myself, but I resolved to come through. Quievy seemed happy with the fact that he was not likely to get to South America on a bargee's earnings. Mostly, he wanted the dream.

Before I left the bar, I told Roger I'd be back aboard *La Vieille*. Where, I asked, did visitors moor?

"Just tie up to a *péniche*," he said, gesturing broadly to the quai outside. "Anyone will let you. It is a code of honor. You know, we squabble among ourselves like a bunch of old ragpickers. But the minute anyone is in trouble or needs something, we hang together. That is the code."

Outside, rows of *péniches* looked disturbingly spiffy. "Whenever you see a boat that's all freshly painted, with everything neat and perfectly in place, and all the wood sanded and varnished, be careful," Jacques had warned. "That means the owner has too much time on his hands." He knew. If you carry coal to Poissy and then hurry to pick up sugar at Gennevilliers, you've got a hell of a lot of sweeping and wiping to do in the hold. But, Jacques had added, it's an even worse sign when a working *péniche* looks too cruddy. "That means the guy can't afford paint, which is as important as food."

But a quick sampling made plain that it wasn't over yet for the river tribe. Four *péniches* moored side by side were blazing with color, each flying lines of bright flags from wheelhouse to bow. There were beer logos, pennants from fuel suppliers, signal flags and a huge ensign of the city of Paris, a gold lion on a scarlet field. Balloons and crepe-paper pom-poms covered the boat nearest the quai. From the antenna mast, a large blue dummy was hanged by the neck, the symbolic French groom. This was a village wedding.

The *péniche* belonged to Jean-Marie Leclerc, and he was trying to sell it. He wanted what amounted to $65,000 and almost certainly would not get it, despite its excellent Baudouin engine. He was host to a friend's wedding. Like Leclerc, the friend had left the river. But he had already sold his boat, and even an ex-bargee does not marry on land.

Jean Bonnevie had not sold his *péniche*, nor had he left the river. At thirty-five, a fifth-generation *marinier* with regulation tattoos and polished incomprehensible speech, he was not about to quit. The days were long, and the work could be a supreme pain in the ass. Bonnevie faced the same numbers as everyone else, with the same long wait for a load and the same black future. When I asked why he kept on, he gave a little shrug and smiled to himself.

"I'll keep at this," he said, "for as long as they let us stay alive."

⧼⧼⧼⧼⧼⧼

At Moret and Saint-Mammès, it is hard to tell where the water stops and the land begins. Everyone seems connected to river life. "I ran a *péniche*, and so did my father and grand-father," said Garry Droissart, who now runs a cab and dreams about the old days. We found him at the train station and kept him for the grand tour. "It was great while it lasted."

When we told Droissart we had to catch a boat but did not know for sure when it was coming, or where, he solved the problem simply. He took us to an inn on the Loing. Two-thirds of the way through a fluffy fresh omelette, our boat came past. We drove to the first lock into the canal and hopped aboard.

We were meeting the *Occitaine*, a Dutch-style *péniche* we had helped to relaunch in Lyon. It was based at Saint-Jean-de-Losne, on the Saône, but we had last seen it docked for a month a few spots down from us in Paris. It was yet another rust bucket when Captain Hazel Young and her pals got their hands on it. In its new life, it was an itinerant showroom for a line of soaps and beauty products. Above and below, it was a work of art.

A young carpenter had paneled the main saloon in glass-fronted cabinets and drawers, like an elegant shop of the Belle Epoque. Then Alain Vagh tiled the whole damned boat. Vagh, a lovable lunatic, earlier had tiled a Jeep Wrangler—everything but the rubber on the tires—and a Steinway piano and a cowboy hat and the bathroom in my little Provence house. Vagh and his wife run a booming business making fine tiles, but he got bored easily. Doing a *péniche* was a challenge.

The *Occitaine*'s steel deck was covered in swirls of small reddish fired-clay rectangles, his trademark. Contrary to the assurances of every old-timer who looked at it, it held up perfectly. You could drop an anchor and chip nothing. The master cabin had a tub big enough for a hippo, and the guest-cabin shower spurted from three directions. Both rooms were done in ceramics—aquamarine, rose pink, and touches of trim in darker tones.

But Hazel was more colorful than the decor. She and her guitar-player husband, both American, had had a boat in Amsterdam. "I went to Holland in 1979," she said. "I saw all those boats and just freaked, like when I saw Provence at eighteen." They moved to Paris and fixed up a barge. When her husband wanted to sell it, she had to choose between him and the river. As anyone who'd met Hazel knew, that was no contest.

"Can you imagine any better way to live?" she asked, beaming in the (tiled) galley, washing dishes. Hazel is a Cordon Bleu chef, and her pizza is famed from the Seine-Maritime to the lower Rhône. Her friend Jean-Luc Brouic was driving the boat, also beaming, with Jimi Hendrix's "Band of Gypsies" on the wheelhouse speakers. He said almost the same thing, his grin never dimming: "I love this, going slow through *la nature* at the pace of life. I'm doing what I love. How many people can say that?"

If it isn't always that easy, Hazel added later, it is almost always fun. She rose early for the usual hauling and hewing.

Boats demand a lot of small, tedious jobs. On the canal, she flung ropes and cranked open lock gates. The family crew ate three times a day, not counting hazelnut brownies in between. Washing up was constant. Something always needed fixing.

"Last trip, a friend brought her three-year-old daughter, who kept watching me," Hazel said. "Finally, she said, 'You never work. All you do is cook and clean.' Her mother talks on the phone all day, writes things down, goes to a job. The need to go to work in some organized way is ingrained in her. Poor kid."

Once on the Canal du Loing, boats waited at locks for hours in both directions. These days, underworked keepers regard two boats a morning as a heavy load. At one lock, we picked up Maurice Vicq, gray haired and squinting behind glasses, who simply wanted a ride. He steered to the next lock like a little kid on his daddy's lap. Vicq was a victim of *déchirage*, and he was suffering.

Déchirage is a hard and accurate word. It comes from *déchirer*, "to tear up," which is what scrap dealers do when they take apart a boat for its reusable materials. It is also what happens to a bargee's papers and, therefore, his spirit. Forced to quit the river, Vicq accepted a government indemnity to give up his license, a program to reduce the number of working *péniches*. He lived aboard his rusty *Vercors*, but he was not allowed to take it anywhere.

"I used to carry wine from Paris to Sète," he said, recalling the old days where barges frequently worked their way from the Seine to ports on the Mediterranean. It took three weeks or more. "I had to stop because of my wife, who was getting very sick." His eyes squinted more, and they moistened. "She died of cancer. I haven't much to do now. Navigation was my life."

Vicq still cannot get used to the sight of so many *péniches* clustered on riverbanks. "When I saw a barge stopped," he said, "I always wondered what was the matter."

Hazel drew a bleak picture of willful neglect by officials who favored rail and road. From the beginning, she said, the state-owned railroads undercut rates to wrest freight from the river. As soon as a new canal opened, train tracks paralleled it. Their bridges crossed canals at minimum height. Captains often have to take apart their wheelhouses to get past. Some have broken propellers because they loaded too much ballast so they could squeeze under the low bridges.

"We're living the end of an epoch," she told me. "Kids aren't taking over—no way. They stay in boarding schools and come out on the weekends, but they don't have the old pride. They don't want to be thought of as marginals, gypsies. You see the old ones sitting in bars, alcoholic and heartbroken. They tried to fight the system but ended up fighting among themselves."

Hazel figured it was worth the fight. A lot of exceptions offered promise, like Jean Bonnevie at Saint-Mammès. On the river, you can spot the young couples on working barges: they put cages atop their cargo holds so young kids can play in the fresh air without toppling into the water.

Boats like the *Occitaine* put fresh energy into the river, strengthening the hand of the few powerful people who defended a disappearing way of life. If a hard-pressed government was going to pour money into the water, it needed a good reason; tourism in all of its forms was as good a reason as any. And if the canals were dredged and the locks refurbished, freight orders might follow. A lot of old bargees didn't see it that way. To them, pleasure boats were obscene. Their dilettante captains fouled the waters.

I had seen this on other trips. On a Saône canal, a friend

headed his converted *péniche* into the narrow passage of a single-lane bridge and saw a loaded barge coming toward him. In such cases, right-of-way goes to whoever gets there first, with an edge toward the downriver boat. My friend usually gave way to working barges anyway, but this was clear-cut. To stop and back up, he risked smacking the bridge. If the other guy was doing the speed limit, we'd be through before he even had to slow down. When we passed, a bovine Belgian stood in the bow waving her fist and bellowing curses until she was out of range.

But this time the mood was mostly jovial. Hazel and Jean-Luc signal optimism to the old-timers who know them. They are part of a new generation that struggles to save classic old boats from meltdown. "We've cried at the sight of some of these beautiful old boats waiting to be scrapped," she told me. Under the *déchirage* program, once a boat is scheduled for the junk heap, it cannot be sold. The trick is to move fast, find loopholes and apply pressure. "They call us Greenpeace," Hazel said, chuckling over victories so far.

Friends of theirs run floating hotels, carrying happy tourists to places they could never see by land. Others restore *péniches* for anyone lucky enough to find mooring space. At Saint-Jean-de-Losne, the *Occitaine* joined with forty other boats in an association to promote river traffic, convincing large companies to move cargo by boat. Between 1991 and early 1993, tonnage on the Saône increased by 37 percent.

Every lockkeeper knew Hazel or pretended he did. She ribbed them mercilessly, about their disturbed naps or their tight budgets. At one lock, the double gates took twice as long to open because there was only one handle. "I see," she said. "They only give you two handles a year, and if you drop one in the water, you're out of luck." That might have been true.

Jean-Luc explained the logic of the river. I asked about a sign with a circular arrow and a line through it.

"It means no turning around," he said. "Once you start, you go to the Saône and come back a month later."

But what if you have to get back quickly to Saint-Mammès?

"You turn around."

It was December, the trees stark and beautiful. Once, we tied up near a house where Camille Pissarro painted, just another forgotten impressionist shrine. At nightfall we threw a rope around a tree, laid down a gangplank and bicycled off for fresh groceries. Sleep was blissful. Early in the morning, we drank coffee in the clean, crisp air. The next afternoon, we got off. Hazel and crew were going on forever, but I had to catch a train and go to work. She said good-bye with the same look as when she told us about the little girl who looked forward to life in the office. Poor fools.

5 The Edge
of Paris

THE LAST LOCK INTO PARIS is eight hours past
Saint-Mammès, at Port-à-l'Anglais. During the 1970s,
Jacques waited in line two days to get through. Coming
down in *La Vieille*, we found the door wide open. We had the
basin to ourselves. Not long before, the gates stayed broken
for four days, and lockkeepers cranked them by hand, the
old way. This was not so surprising. The tonnage is a little
different, but probably more vessels used the Seine above
Paris a thousand years ago than do today.

Past Port-à-l'Anglais, this backwater nostalgia vanishes
fast. To the unsympathetic eye, the Seine near Paris is an
anonymous industrial wasteland, an ugly sprawl of concrete
yards, abandoned factories, discount emporiums and glassy
megablocks of cheap office space. Tugs scoot among rusting
barges, which sink toward the waterline with loads of
crushed rock. Dredgers haul up dripping, stinking black

mud. The river is wide, busy and about as uncomely as water can be.

Steaming toward Paris, I noticed a beat-up *péniche* moored among others in a small floating slum. Laundry obscured its name, but I could make it out: *L'Atalante*. This was the name of a film, the bargeman's *Gone With the Wind*. Just pronouncing it can moisten a weathered eye.

In *L'Atalante*, Dita Pardo marries a barge captain, Michel Simon, and sets up a home afloat. Her world is 126 feet long, populated by a stern, jealous husband who likes his bright lights at a distance, and by his battered old deckhand, a lovable lout who talks funny. One night, drawn by the secret life of the real world, she sneaks away. In the morning, she realizes her mistake. She loves *L'Atalante*, the river and even her husband. She hurries home to find the boat gone.

For much of the film, she searches for *L'Atalante*. The deckhand hunts her down in the low life of the cities, in grounded bargees' haunts, where the separate worlds meet.

In fact, such a search likely would have been much quicker. "It could take less than a day to find out where a boat was," Jacques said, when I asked about those days. "People telephoned the lockkeepers if there was a death in the family, or an accident. These were mostly old *mariniers*, and they knew everyone. They kept track of who passed through, and they could calculate how long it would take to get to the next lock. Word passed from one boat to another."

Now the big locks are automated and impersonal, with keepers high up in glass booths like air-traffic controllers. But you only have to snap on the VHF radio to see how little has changed. Old pals still keep up on gossip. The log of passing boats is kept more faithfully than ever. With the help of radio and mobile telephones, finding *L'Atalante* would be a snap. For most old riders of the long days, this is a mixed blessing.

~~~~~

For Paris boat people, the troubled waters just upstream from the city—*amont*, in French, as opposed to downstream, *aval*—are a golden gateway. You can spend a lifetime of weekends on runs up the Seine or the Marne. When there is a little extra time to spend, there is always something to hold your attention.

In June, on the Île de Berceau off Samois-sur-Seine, for instance, there is the Gypsy jazz festival to remember Django Reinhardt, who lived in Samois until he died in 1953. For a few glorious days each year, the place is overrun by the converted and the curious. Gypsy families travel halfway across Europe. Jazz lovers come across oceans.

I went years ago, long before my Seine addiction. It was one of those extraplanetary experiences. A few earnest tourists want to know when Django is scheduled to appear. Another sort of visitor is too far into a chemical orbit to notice whether he appears or not. And a devoted few will swear that he is there already onstage, doing a guitar backup for Elvis.

Just below, by the Bois-le-Roi, you can prowl through the nineteenth-century artists' colony of Barbizon. Millet, Corot and Théodore Rousseau worked in lovely homes by the water, and some of these are open to the public. Around Melun, and closer toward Paris, posh mansions crowd the Seine, with gardens sloping toward little wooden docks.

For a longer look at a different world, turn up the Marne. About the middle of the 1800s, Parisian sports bought striped swimming costumes and straw boaters, took the new train from the Gare Saint-Lazare to Le Pecq or

Chatou, and hired canopied boats called *canots*. When not posing for all the impressionists lurking about, they ate huge meals of fish and white wine, while flirting with women of relaxed virtue. That was the Seine in another age. The closest thing to it now is the Marne on Sundays.

The stripes are gone, if not the whole bathing suit. Rather than *canots*, people rent ski boats by the half hour. But plenty of sailboats are around, and so are a few *guinguettes*.

As German troops learned the hard way in World War I when defenders piled out of commandeered cabs, the Marne is a short taxi ride from Paris. Once along the river, weekend revelers can hire or hitch a ride on the water. By boat, a Marne ride takes much of the day. Depending upon how far you go, there are locks, canals and a tunnel. It is a lovely trip.

Along the Marne near Paris, houses are not ancient old, just weathered and well-enough built to have come from another time—say, a century ago. Their gardens tumble down to the water. Moss softens the banks. Heavy tree branches angle downward into leafy tunnels. At regular intervals, café terraces are shaded by awnings in that rich French red, a few shades lighter than what is in glasses on the tables. Around marinas and town docks, the water is dotted with pleasure craft. Just occasionally, a *péniche* barrels through this playground, in a hurry to do a little work.

∞∞∞∞∞

At some point, the Marne takes on a life of its own, separate from its sister Seine. It is darker and deeper, bringing chocolate-colored water from the mountains of eastern France. No one agrees where it changes personality. As good a spot as any is Marne-la-Vallée, where a foreign rodent with buttons on his pants has placed on French maps something that is delicately labeled *Royaume Enchanté*, the Magic Kingdom.

Some 150 million years back, Euro Disneyland was Jurassic Park, a favorite stomping ground of the long-necked, pin-headed diplodocus. Much later, Marne-la-Vallée was within hunting range of the first humans to inhabit the Paris basin, hairy humans with lousy posture who appeared about a half million years ago. Little is known about these early people. But archeologists have found extensive traces of settlements that date from the last ice age, about seventeen thousand years ago.

Magdalenian hunters camped along the Seine at Pincevent, near Montereau, in the late ice age as the river's bed was taking its final shape. Earlier earth movements had shifted the Loire in one direction and the Seine in another. The river was broad but shallow, and Pincevent was its best ford. Once a year, reindeer migrated across the Seine, and the Magdalenian cavemen were waiting with flint spearheads carved from nearby cliffs. A more permanent community settled later at Bercy, where the Marne meets the Seine.

In 1991 and 1992, near where the Marne joins the Seine, workmen tearing up the quai for riverside renewal unearthed a fleet of Neolithic dugout canoes. Three were dated at about 4500 B.C., each skillfully carved with stone tools from a single oak tree. One was sixteen feet long. Altogether, archeologists found fifteen hundred objects, from a hunting bow to soup plates. And they also discovered an old channel of the Seine, off to the right, filled in about the fourth century B.C. With all of this, they put together a fair idea of what Paris was like before the Parisii.

At the time, the Seine was an archipelago of islands, with several channels. At low water, the river was barely three feet deep. When it rose, it flooded dry land in the middle. The Stone Age settlers of Bercy picked the bank with a better command of traffic on the water. That was the left bank. Today, Bercy is on the right bank. The settlement did not move, but the river did.

∽∽∽∽∽

My favorite secret spot within easy reach of Paris is the Ile d'Amour, a tiny Marne island of giant trees, a sandy beach, and the mysterious ruins of a brothel. The charts show a large Ile d'Amour on the main part of the Marne that heads on up into Champagne country. That is not it.

The island is on the way to nowhere, down a dead-end branch of the Marne past the port of Bonneuil. Purists say the moldering shell of a terraced building might have been a mere *guinguette*, for drinking and dancing, where sex was not regularly practiced. Whatever its past, there is sex in its present. Empirical evidence attests to this fact; only the hardest of entwinable souls would not take the plunge in such lush and leisurely surroundings. "I want to give you more love," someone had scrawled in English. A nearby drawing offered graphic detail. It is also an excellent spot for innocent reverie or revelry. Another inscription, in French, said, "Thanks for the memory."

The French treasure the religious holiday of Pentecost, usually in May, which celebrates the Holy Spirit's descent on the apostles. It is a long summer-warm-up weekend. Some people go to church, but Paris boat dwellers go to the Ile d'Amour. Long-dormant *péniches* cough to life and head upriver, low in the water with party food and wine. Musical instruments and sound systems are set up on decks. The first arrivals tie up to trees, and others moor alongside until they choke off the narrow channel.

A Saturday-night party spills from boat to boat. Designated drivers are not necessary. To go home, a happy drunk need only drop through his hatch. People who avert each other's gaze while tied together in Paris fall about in laughter. Others lie on their backs far from the loudspeakers and watch the stars they can't see at home.

No one leaves on Sunday. The Maisons-Alfort lock is closed for the holiday, and there is nowhere to go. Instead, potluck delicacies sway on overloaded camp tables. The music gets mellow in the warm afternoon. Children make friends from other boats in the old way. These are houseboat people, not really pure tribal stock. But when a kid learns patience with proverbs like "A watched lock never opens," he needs pals on his own frequency. It is the sort of place and time that makes all present remember why they put up with mildew in their socks drawer.

We went to the Ile d'Amour a week late. I was in some fragment of Yugoslavia and missed the party but did not want to miss the venue. Getting there was half the fun. Along stretches of the Marne, gaily painted summer homes, some of them mansions left from a noble age, sit back among luxuriant gardens. Weeping willows touch at either side of little inlets. Boats slide in and vanish. Spring flowers blaze in orange and red. It was Sunday, and the minifleets were in the water: ski boats, sailboats, paddleboats, kayaks. But the island was nearly deserted.

Captain Jacques was smitten. He wandered slowly around the wreck of a building, an open-fronted broken shell with masonry and wire hanging from its beams, and silently calculated how long it would take him to restore it. On the water, above the flood line, reachable only by boat, it was a retired bargee's dream. My friend Dev gazed at the soaring maples, with visions of syrup and board feet of lumber dancing in his head. It was a pancake-loving artisan carpenter's dream. We watched water birds and butterflies, and we wondered how long we could stay before anyone thought to start looking.

When we first arrived, a lone *péniche* flying the skull and crossbones lay moored to the trees, the only spot where we could dock. Slowly, we hove alongside. The tacit rule in such cases is that one boat ties up to the other, but the young woman having breakfast on deck hadn't heard of it. She scowled mightily and willed us to vaporize. I couldn't blame her; clearly, we were disturbing her peace. The next time, however, it might be the other way around.

The man with her knew the etiquette. He got up without a pause and walked over to catch our line. The day wore on, and we sent over a small load of chili. Finally, the Ile d'Amour worked its magic. We parted friends.

Paris

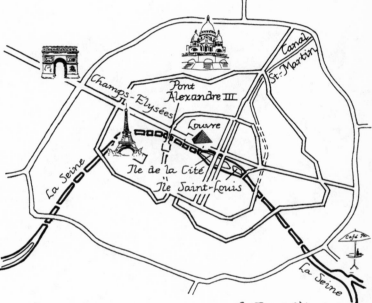

Arc de Triomphe • Sacré-Cœur • Canal St-Martin • Champs-Élysées • Pont Alexandre III • Louvre • Île de la Cité • Île Saint-Louis • La Seine • Café PM • La Seine • Le Port à l'Anglais

6 Paris-sur-Seine

THE SEINE, at Paris, is more than beautiful. Poets and neo-impressionists shift their attention to it as the mood strikes. But it is also the main character in the lives of 8 million people. Three-quarters of Parisians' drinking water comes from the river. And a lot of their industrial poison and raw sewage empties into it. You do not have to jump off a bridge to commit suicide, one engineer observed. The backstroke is enough.

A French study on public hygiene, unearthed by a sewer-loving North Carolina historian named Donald Reid, observes: "The urban physiology of excretion constitutes one of the privileged means of access to social mentalities." By that measure, Paris is full of shit.

For weeks after that California cat tumbled off my boat, she lazed around like a zombie. Antibiotics picked her up, and then she'd drop into relapse. The vet explained it: each time she licked her fur, she poisoned herself again on die-hard Seine scum.

A glance at the river suggests its level of crud. Just what floats past *La Vieille* over any five-minute period is enough to put you on beer for life. Worse, of course, is what only scientists can see, and they shudder at the real dimensions. "If the Thames was this filthy," one British analyst observed, "there'd be a raging scandal." The Thames could not be so filthy. London is close to the estuary, which flushes away urban effluent. But the Seine is much fouler than it needs to be.

Each day, three hundred thousand tons of noxious substances are dumped in the river, legally. Old-style factories are grandfathered against more stringent controls. New polluters make deals. Unfathomed amounts of prohibited poisons flow past the few officers deployed to stop them. Fines are cheaper than refitting. The Seine is a cocktail of lead, chromium, copper, and way too much zinc and iron. The cadmium level is 95 times normal. Mercury is 134 times what it should be. There is ammonium and arsenic. Farms add nitrates and phosphates from fertilizers, along with lindane and high doses of PCBs. Then there are compounds that elude testing.

The Greenpeace specialists who found bacterial pollution at Paris to be one hundred times higher than the European Community norm for safe swimming were not optimistic about the near future. If you don't expire, you risk salmonella, other gastric horrors, conjunctivitis, or skin and mucous infections.

"The water is disgusting," said Jean Allardi, among the few scientists on the case. With a smile of tender concern, he added, "But it's a wonderful river."

Allardi works at a private research facility called

CEMAGREF (Centre National du Machinisme Agricole, du Génie Rural et Eaux et Forets), in a charming wood building in deepest Paris. He is also part of an environmental hit squad, known by the acronym PIREN Seine, which coordinates the work of laboratories, universities and assorted specialists. He is a fish man, but his work of twenty years has been finding ways for a huge city to coexist with a small river. With a shock of silver hair, an easy grin and bunched-up energy, he is a scientist-advocate from Central Casting.

The good news, he said, is that the situation is getting better rather than worse. In a few years, the river added three to four milligrams of oxygen per liter. I didn't know what that meant either, but it made Allardi pretty happy.

"No one will fight to save an open sewer," he told me, eyes alight with passion. "When people see progress, it will be easier. The government is starting to fix up the quais, with promenades and parks. Once more people take a closer look at that water, authorities will have to do something fast."

An official body called SIAAP (Syndicat Interdéparte-mental pour l'Assainissement de l'Agglomération Parisienne) has been slogging away since the mid-1970s. In the 1990s, it is spending nearly $2 billion over five years to treat more wastewater, raise oxygen levels and reduce pollution. It seems that milligrams of oxygen per liter is the scientists' measure of life support. When it drops below three, only mutant monsters get by. Above seven, there is a chance for salmon. The Seine is somewhere in between. In twenty years, SIAAP says, its work has brought the number of fish species around Paris from three to thirty.

When half of those fish died in the summer of '92, SIAAP scrambled for something new. The experimental units that pumped bubbles into the river at critical points created pockets where fish could gather for a gillful of fresh oxygen. Engineers, happy with the result, planned to install huge tanks and pumps along the Seine. But in France, nothing is quite so simple; you don't just set up bizarre contraptions along a river. Conflicting institutions and interests first must go to war. Oxygen tanks might be dangerous. Jurisdictions overlap where land meets river. Navigation might be affected. Pumping scheduled for 1993 was delayed indefinitely.

Meantime, economic decay is helping the Seine. Some serious polluters have gone out of business, closing their aging factories. As manufacturing stagnates, fewer wastes are generated. A shift to different activities means new equipment designed to reduce contaminants.

Any fisherman can confirm SIAAP's impact. In fact, the Seine's muddy bottom is now alive with the mysterious *silure*, or wels, a Danube catfish that grows to the size of an alligator. When I asked Allardi about it, in a conversation that whipsawed from pollution to poetry, he leaped from his chair toward a rack of ancient leather ichthyological encyclopedias.

"Listen to this from the sixteenth century," he said. " 'The *silure* is very voracious, and in one known case the stomach of one was found to contain a human head and a hand wearing two gold rings.' " A later reference mentioned a small person inside a *silure* along with a quantity of gold jewelry. Allardi figures the Midas obsession reveals archaic imagination. The *silure* has gotten a bad rap. Nonetheless, various people have seeded *silure* since 1970, and they have flourished. Some, he said, are eight feet long. Yet another reason not to swim in the Seine.

Altogether, forty species of fish are native to the Seine, and another twelve were introduced. After Montereau, they begin to drop out. More damage to river life has been done by dams and canals than by pollution, although nitrates and phosphates are killers. By the time the Seine reaches Paris, nine fish out of ten are *gardons* (chub) or *chevaines* (roach). There are also carp, bream, eels, bleak, perch, pike and the flavorful *sandre*, the perch-pike. Taming the rapids has all but wiped out barbel, but other fish survive because rough water under the lock barriers freshens the river.

When I asked Allardi whether Seine fish were edible, he laughed. "In most places when you see a fisherman, the question is always, 'Are they biting?' Along the Seine, you ask, 'Are you going to eat that?' " Analyses show contamination in fish caught below Paris, he said, but levels are within the guidelines for human consumption. "Most fisherman throw fish back, however," he said. "It's a question of ethics. They fish for pleasure."

I asked if I was likely to catch anything in the calm waters off the stern of *La Vieille*.

"Yes," Allardi said. "A ticket."

You can't just go fishing in France. A license is required, as in most places. But to qualify for a license, you have to join a fishermen's association. In some places, this is easily enough done at tackle shops. In others, only locals can belong. Just as well. Who wants to catch something called a roach?

∽∽∽∽∽

The harrowing Greenpeace report in 1991 was followed by other studies on the state of the Seine. Even for those of us whose interests seldom wander into hydrology, it is riveting stuff. Many of the worst offenders were farther down, and I made a note to check them out. In Paris, the main problem is all the people.

A vertical bar graph showing comparative river flows

looks like a ski jump. At the top is the Amazon, averaging 207,400 cubic meters a second. The Mississippi is 30,800, and the Danube, 2,720. Down at the bottom, right where the skier leaps into space, are the Seine and the Thames, with piddling flows of 300 to 400. But the same sort of chart showing population density along the banks is nearly the reverse. The Amazon drops almost out of sight. The Seine and Thames are smack at the top.

Each day, the city of Paris draws off 2.6 million cubic meters for its water supply, nearly equal to the flow at the Pont-Neuf. This is pumped at staggered points along the Seine and its tributaries. Only 2.1 million cubic meters are treated at three stations before being piped back into the river. The other half million cubic meters go back as raw sewage. That's just part of it.

The sewers of Paris were built last century when the stench in the Seine grew unbearable and Victor Hugo needed a setting for *Les Misérables*. Since then, the city has grown by 7 million. Much has been paved over, adding runoff to the inadequate sewer system. When it rains, gutter water and backed-up sewage run directly into the Seine.

In the summer, the river is low and hardly moving. Flow can drop below 75 cubic meters a second, a fifth of normal, or one four-hundredth of the Mississippi's volume. An oily film chokes off its ability to breathe, lowering the oxygen level. A hard rain can be catastrophic. That was why, in 1992, that thousand tons of fish floated belly-up.

Since Paris has no storm drains, overflow reaches the river every which way it can. And torrents gush through *les égouts*, the celebrated sewers, to a spot forty miles downriver: the treatment plant at Achères.

〜〜〜〜〜

At the Ambiance Marina in Achères, I chatted with the owner, an elderly gentleman named Jean Goujon. He knew the treatment plant was a quarter mile upriver—the stench would not let anyone forget it—but said he did not give it much thought. No, he said, the hundred people who keep powerboats in his marina don't think much about it either. I thanked him and walked to my car. On the way, I noticed a shop window full of water skis.

"Excuse me," I said, returning to Goujon's office. "Do a lot of people ski around here?"

"Yes," he said.

"But what about the sewage?"

"And you were sent by whom?" he asked.

I mentioned what engineers at the plant had just told me. When it rains in Paris, their capacity is overwhelmed. Twenty to 30 percent of what comes in goes back into the river with no treatment at all. At best, sewage is only partially treated, reducing chemicals and bacteria to "acceptable levels," nothing that you'd want to wash your German shepherd in.

"That is not true," he said. "All of it is treated."

When I mentioned my sources, a chief engineer and his deputy, Goujon frowned, a little concerned. He knew them both.

"They told you that?" he asked. Then he thought for a minute and concluded: "People ski in that water all the time. I never heard of anyone getting sick."

Goujon was right about the skiing. On weekends, boats cut carefree circles on the brown water. A large windsurf club operates nearby, also downstream from the pipes. He was wrong about the sick part. Just thinking about it made me want to barf.

Achères is no backyard filter operation. It is the second-largest purification plant in the world; only Chicago's is bigger. According to Allardi, its overflow can go over 25 cubic meters a second, equal to half the river's flow rate at that point. That, he said, can be greater than any of the tributaries on the Seine.

The obvious answer is more and bigger treatment plants, but cost is only one obstacle. "Ecologists who scream about the filthy water don't want us to add more capacity because that will take up more land, and the stink will reach even farther away," remarked an Achères engineer who would probably get fired if I named him. "You can't win either way."

Another answer is separate storm drains for Paris to channel rainwater away from the Seine. It would mean tearing up the city and spending kazillions of francs. That, a SIAAP official remarked at one point, would be like building a twenty-five-lane freeway for the two days a year in August when all of France is on the road.

Yet another solution is the path of least resistance: send clothespins to Rouen. Once the water clears Achères, it is not a Paris problem.

A more constant flow of the Seine would certainly help, not only to dilute waste but also to control flooding. Any doubts on this score were dispelled in 1910 when the heart of Paris was underwater. Since then, the Seine has starred in one of those grand watershed plans that work until nature decides to do something else.

The simple means of regulating the Seine is a system of *biefs*, adjustable sluice gates atop dams alongside the locks. These help when winter rains and melting snow push the Seine into a torrent. But there is more. Three large reservoirs draw off water from the Seine, the Marne and the Aube, storing 800 million cubic meters to be released according to need. More specifically, the need of Paris.

The balance is fragile. Each year, more upstream banks are paved over, and new buildings cover land that absorbed water. Drainage spills into the river. If a hard storm lasts too long, the Seine can rise five feet in two hours. A nasty mountain winter can send dark water churning down the Marne. With runoff into the Aube and the Yonne adding to the mass, the Seine overspills its banks.

And this can work in reverse. In 1942, Allied planes bombed the lock at Suresnes, blowing the *biefs* at the downriver edge of Paris. The Seine emptied. Amid all the familiar sights of Paris, boats sat on the mud in an apocalyptic nightmare, stranded in a morass of flapping fish out of water.

∽∽∽∽∽

Paris is much more agreeable above the surface. To know it well, one starts on the Seine. Romance languages invest spiritual powers in the verb *to know*. Simple jobs are fobbed off on the workaday *savoir*, like *saber*, in Spanish: to know some specific fact. But *connaître*, as the Spanish *conocer*, suggests a familiarity that reaches the soul. For this, in Paris, you need some quality time with Sequana.

The first time I saw Paris was after living there for three years. It was early on a spring Sunday when the flowers were up and the Parisians were asleep. In a battered, topless Peugeot, with no radio to mask the city's few fitful sounds, I set out from Saint-Germain-des-Prés on an urgent errand. I crossed the Pont du Carrousel, into the Louvres garden for a left turn up the Rue de Rivoli toward the Place de la Concorde, my milk run to the office.

Speeding along, I glanced to the left and stomped on the

brakes. The beauty was paralyzing, and I'd never really noticed. A miniature Arc de Triomphe was lined up perfectly with Napoléon's grandiose arch at the end of the Champs-Elysées. Halfway down, past the rich Tuileries foliage, the Concorde obelisk was centered like a gun sight. And there was all the rest. Each slate rooftop had a geometric purpose. Every scarlet tulip was a carefully placed brushstroke on a giant canvas.

I got back in the car and did Paris. The errand could wait. I swung back and forth from one bridge to the next, savoring each detail and cityscape. Doubling back, I headed down the Left Bank express lane under the Pont des Invalides, hurtling along like Anthony Perkins in the last scene of *Phaedra* except that I was dum-ta-dumming the music myself. The roadway flung me back to street level at the Eiffel Tower, deserted and lovely in morning pink. Then I stopped in the middle of the Pont d'Iéna to look back at this city of light.

No one had thrown this place together one piece at a time. For two thousand years, people who loved it had shaped it with style and grandeur. Always they worked around a central theme, a languorous, life-giving, treacherous, life-taking river. I had enjoyed Paris up until then. Finally, I realized what all the fuss was about.

Ten years later, I saw the city again for the first time. I was at the wheel of my old wooden house, steering among the thirty-five sets of stone or steel arches that span the Seine from one end of Paris to the other. By then I had seen most of it from car windows. Walking, I had savored and smelled it. This time, from the inside out, the way its settlers had lived it since those Stone Age boatmen at Bercy, I could feel it.

From either direction along the river, with a basic guidebook, a cocked eye and a little imagination, you can find the past, present and future deftly blended together.

If you start upstream, the old wine quais at Bercy suggest the first *raison d'être* for all that followed; the Parisii, rivermen and traders, knew their priorities. Today, by the ancient Bercy landing, the vast glass box of a new Ministry of Finance holds the keys to France's treasure. At Seine level is a dock for the minister's speedboat. Parisians, down deep, are rivermen and traders.

From an unusual angle, familiar sights roll by: thrilling stone facades of the Ile Saint-Louis; depending on which fork, Notre-Dame or the towers of Conciergerie, where Marie Antoinette and lots of others waited for the guillotine; the Louvre and the Gare d'Orsay; picturebook bridges; that sweeping tower put up for a world's fair by Gustave Eiffel, who also invented garter snaps and enabled silk stockings to defy gravity.

An unexpected Paris unfolds when you look close. Under bridges on the island quais, colonies of homeless huddle in desperate camps. These are not the fabled *clochards* who people French literature, lovable bums who cadge pocket change as a style of life. They are the flotsam of a society headed for trouble, economic wreckage hanging on for dear life. Graffiti visible from the river captions evolving attitudes: a new nihilism, a tinge of punk power, a humor-flecked rap commentary on troubled times.

Coming upstream from the world beyond, the view is different. Your opening scene is a Statue of Liberty, far more modest than the one in New York Harbor, but a perfect replica; it was presented by the American community not long after France gave the original version to the United States. The buildings are new, the nondescript skyscratchers of Beirut-sur-Seine, where rich Levantines live; the Nikko Hotel, full of Japanese; the round and weird quarters of Radio France. From this approach, the Eiffel Tower comes first, Belle Epoque before Middle Ages. By the time you pass the Ile Saint-Louis, you're back in time, caught up entirely in a sense of place. Then you glance ahead and gasp in surprise. You're in China. A four-story pagoda looms from the river, the Quang Dong Hotel, on the peninsula formed by the mouth of the Marne. The Seine will do that to you every time.

For the patient, a boat down the Canal Saint-Martin inches along, lock by lock, under elms and iron balconies. The canal begins with a lock across from Austerlitz. You cruise an eerily lit tunnel under the Bastille and thread through forgotten parts of Paris to the Canal Saint-Denis and the Canal de l'Ourcq, built by Napoléon to keep heavy traffic from overtaxing the heart of the city. In summer, you bake. But as the boat drops down behind iron gates, you're cooled by the spray of thousands of mussels clinging to the wall. At full speed, two miles takes three hours.

Nostalgia oozes from the banks. Bouvard and Pecuchet got to be friends along the canal, offering Flaubert a backdrop for his satire of the Parisian bourgeoisie. When boulevardiers affected canes and the first open Renaults frightened the cart horses, this was where Paris played. Among featureless concrete apartments, the old façade on the Hôtel du Nord recalls the atmosphere of sweet bitter times gone by.

∽∽∽∽∽

For old photos of the Seine and its canals in Paris, there is the Hôtel Carnavalet museum in the Marais. Medieval maps and detailed diaries offer the facts of earlier history, a feel for the river's dominance of old France. But for a sense of the timeless beauty, to see a Seine that runs deeper than the settings around it, you've got to go to the train station.

The Gare d'Orsay was built at the turn of the century when Paris transformed itself into something new. The tower went up, and Trocadéro appeared across the river. A graceful single arch spanned the Seine, flanked by soaring gold statuary, between Les Invalides and two new ornate exposition halls. A short way down, toward Notre-Dame, the city built a railway terminal of equal grandeur. Carved stone climbed four stories to rosettes, a handsome clock, and iron fancywork domes. Chiseled over soaring doors were the names of cities it promised: Orléans, Angers, Nantes, Brest. When World War II ended, the station welcomed returning prisoners—the largest repatriation center in France.

After the war, no one wanted trains so close to the old center. Tracks were removed, and the Gare d'Orsay moldered quietly. Sometimes it held an antique fair. Developers hovered like buzzards, eyeing the land. It was to be razed, replaced by a modern hotel. Instead, it became the world's greatest repository of impressionist paintings, a shrine to the river.

In the 1860s, when out-at-the-elbows renegades abandoned old schools and took their easels outdoors, the first thing they saw was the Seine. Along with country riverscapes, impressionists pictured Paris. Paul Cézanne painted a before scene of the wine quai at Bercy. Paul Gauguin captured the Pont d'Iéna fifteen years before that tower of Eiffel's which artists hated, when the Right Bank was a gentle slope of pastel-colored homes with gardens. Later, Camille Pissarro showed the Louvre from Notre-Dame, its stolid shapes softened by shafts of light.

From Armand Guillaumin, we learn that factory pollution is nothing new. In 1873, his view of Ivry was a backdrop of stacks spewing smoke. With a series of six paintings as graphic as news photos, Alfred Sisley depicted the 1874 floods that inundated the town of Port-Marly near Paris. Farther downstream, Vincent Van Gogh painted the Seine in his last desperate years.

Everyone had a crack at the river, even Toulouse-Lautrec, whose tastes ran more toward flesh than flowing water. But the strongest sense comes from the gang of three who were obsessed with the light at Argenteuil: Monet, Manet and Renoir. Each painted sailboats and bridges and trees. But for every canvas, the model was Sequana. She was an expanse of shimmering gold. She was dark and mysterious, emanating blues from unknown depths. Her mood changed often, but her character was constant. The impressionists revered light, and she personified it.

These days, Argenteuil is an industrial slum, its gardens abutting the concrete walls of cheap high-rise housing. Other old locales, closer in and farther down, have gone the same way. Yet a few hours at the Gare d'Orsay can offer enough clues for you to find what is still there and probably always will be.

On a bright warm day, for instance, Jeannette and I drove along the Seine at Gennevilliers, a Paris suburb even closer in than Argenteuil. Everyone knows it. Gennevilliers was where Manet painted his soft-porn picnic, *Le Déjeuner sur l'Herbe*. One imagines Eden before the fall. From a tipped-over basket, peaches and cherries spill onto lacy underthings. A naked lady aims her toe between the legs of a reclining gentleman in a pasha's turban, and another man attends. A second nymph approaches. But the eye lingers on a fifth subject, a luminous pool of water that beams radiance deep into a virgin forest.

Gennevilliers today harbors the Port Autonome de Paris, a thousand acres of working docks, oil tanks, scrap heaps, coal piles and abandoned slips where corroding barges float on fetid water. To approach the river, we threaded our way among stark ugly warehouses, past rusted rail spurs. In the middle of the worst of it, facing a tin-roof cement plant with smokestacks, a painter dabbed color at a portable easel. His subject was something else entirely, enchanted water reflecting light, in pastels and gold, off old stone and through tall trees.

"I love to come here to paint," said Gérard Mahieu, explaining his canvas. "This is Brittany, a village I just visited, but I came here to finish it. I can always keep my subject in my head, but I need the light of the Seine. I don't see all that ugliness over there. It doesn't matter what is on the banks. It is a beautiful river." When I revealed my mission, he rummaged in his trunk for a map. With great enthusiasm, he stabbed his finger at bends in the river to show me spots that painters loved the best: Louveciennes, Pontoise, Chatou, Bougival. I thanked him but did not need to make notes. I had been to the train station.

〰〰〰

A little poking around will reveal what else lurks along the river. There is, for example, the Salvation Army navy. At a distance, it is a docked barge in those unmistakable shades of yellow and purplish red, lit by those ubiquitous faltering, underpowered fluorescent bulbs, ready to save any souls in sight. Except that it is afloat and in Paris, and its shield says, "Armée du Salut," it is a familiar sight. But not up close.

The boat was designed by Le Corbusier and built in 1926, a gift of a wealthy society matron. It is a nighttime refuge for the indigent. They get no lectures or bass-drum concerts; it is supper, bed and out in the morning.

Down a little way is the float-up police station, base of the Brigade Fluviale, which gives speeding tickets and pokes under bridge pilings for missing persons. Except that their half-dozen squad cars have no wheels, they are not much different from what you might expect. Early in the morning, you'll find a fair number of officers on the pontoon landing, joking over coffee, their own version of Dunkin Donuts. *La Fluviale* is a branch of the Paris police, a rescue squad and patrol with roots back to the 1600s.

Before there was much to leap from, and pistols and pills were only moderately lethal, despondent Parisians had only the Seine. Others fell in by accident; bridges toppled, boats collided and sank. The day's latest technology helped gendarmes save lives. In the eighteenth century, they used a leafy American plant propagated by a Frenchman named Nicot, believed to counteract asphyxiation. Each police post had a *machine fumigatoire*. When drowning victims were pulled from the water, their rescuers, as the saying goes, blew smoke up their ass.

A first aid manual noted: "One may replace the *machine fumigatoire* by using two pipes. The stem of one is inserted with caution into the *fondement* of the person taken from the water. With the two bowls pressed one against another, someone blows the tobacco smoke via the stem of the second pipe."

One hundred years ago, the police were equipped with one rowboat and ten rescue dogs that refused to jump in the water. Today's *Fluviale* of about fifty river cops was set up in 1900 as a security force for the world's fair.

If *La Fluviale* keeps order, the *pompiers* put out the fires. More often, they zoom up to a sinking boat, shove powerful pumps into its depths and slap on emergency patches. Their reputation is mixed. One veteran bargee scowled when I mentioned them. "I broke down in the middle of Paris and was drifting dangerously," he said. "First, they wouldn't come. Then they didn't even know how to attach a tow cable. Useless. Don't use my name, or they'll let me sink next time." My own experience runs contrary to this, however. Whenever I call, the firemen seem happy to plan a training exercise around yanking the branches and plastic crap from my propellers. That requires submersion in the Seine, which is more than I'm prepared to do.

Along both banks and on out of town, one surprise follows another. On a curve by Notre-Dame marked as dangerous, no mooring allowed, the Calife Café serves drinks to a lively crowd. Next to it is a floating puppet theater, and a troupe of riverborne magicians. Another *péniche* offers opera. Farther down, the big restaurants start, and they continue on past Paris. The Shogun's speciality is self-evident. At El Mariachi, someone might rim your margarita in sugar if you're not careful. Quai Ouest is Jimmy Buffett style. In Neuilly, there is a restaurant on a submarine. The B.B. Antillais in Saint-Cloud smells of island spices and vibrates with Caribbean drums.

Some of these eateries are only coincidentally on the Seine. Once inside, you can forget where you are. But others are part of the subculture. After polling my neighbors, I picked one to sample. I might have gone to dinner at the Péniche in Neuilly but instead chose brunch at the River Café.

Le River is a large barge by the Pont d'Issy, on a murky branch west of town. It overlooks a forested bank with ferns and flowers to the waterline. From another angle, factory stacks fume smoke. Sunday brunch can fill all five hundred seats, but I found a table on the aft deck. Eyes closed, I'd have known where I was. Ducks quacked furiously over my shoulder. A breeze delivered the fresh if slightly fetid scent of home. Also, I smelled varnish. Nearby, someone was at work on his classic *péniche*. His neighbor sanded a fine old wooden barge, the kind that was pulled by horses, with its bow in rich yellow.

The food, as the French say, allowed itself to be eaten. Eight courses began with tuna terrine and olive tabbouleh, moving on to fancy eggs with forest mushrooms and so forth. Had I spent an extra $150 on bubbles, it would have included Cristal Roederer. Patrons seemed less interested in eating than in the Paris sport of *regarder les têtes*—to watch and be watched. An unofficial canteen of a nearby television network, the café is favored by the celebrated class. Men wear the uniform of French cool: a well-cut jacket, Levi's, no tie, no socks. Women are high-tone casual.

The bread was scented with the perfume of the person who had sliced it. I later spotted the likely culprit: a hostess in a halter and designer Daisy Mae cutoffs with flowers embroidered on what was left. She was seating Lolita and her little sister. Both wore strangulating shorts and tank tops. One of them was masked by a black satin baseball cap pulled low and fiery red lipstick. The other wore Converse De Luxe high-top basketball shoes and a lot of gold. A long message was engraved on her belt buckle, but I decided against leaning close enough to read it.

The River Café opened in 1990 and, after a rocky start and a change of owners, took off among boat people with a few extra francs to blow. One speciality is *mille-feuille d'artichauts et sandre mariné, sauce aigrelette*. *Sandre* is the tasty perch-pike that optimists say is reappearing around Paris. My guess is that they buy it at the market.

On a island across the narrow channel is the Parc Saint-Germain, a patch of green in the midst of cement plants and cheap office blocks. I never knew it was there, but obviously a lot of others did. Its stage was huge, and posters announced performers at its summer festival: Jerry Lee Lewis, Chuck Berry, Bo Diddley. And Kid Creole and the Coconuts, Ile-de-France music champions.

The next island is a Museum of Post-Industrial Calamity, open around the clock, with no guides or visitors and not many windows. The Ile Séguin was settled by Louis Renault, a Henry Ford with table manners, who made his first car there in 1898. His factory turned out millions of those round-nosed Dauphines that so many Americans loved and all the fancy sedans before and since. The island plant had a great advantage. Barges loaded cars at the gate and hauled them cheaply to Rouen and Le Havre. When new roads began competing hard with the river, barges were not an asset to a truckmaker. In 1992, hopelessly antiquated and with no room to expand, the plant closed.

But what now? During the 1980s boom, the twenty-five-acre island and flanking land on the banks was worth nearly $2 billion. In 1993, no one offered more than $400 million. To turn it into anything else, or to tear it down, would cost additional fortunes. From a distance, "Madame Séguin" resembles a long white ocean liner. Up close, it is a white elephant, sick beyond recovery, with no one to haul it away. Plans were studied, but time dragged on. The old carcass remained where it was, rotting away on the river.

I passed the Ile Séguin one morning with Jacques and noticed the opposite left bank. As if to match it, a line of abandoned *péniches* hugged the shore. One had burned. Others were simply left to rust away and sink. When I pointed them out, Jacques looked over and shook his head. Then he turned away and said nothing until we approached the Suresnes lock.

⧉⧉⧉⧉⧉

The bridges of Paris look pretty much alike from a bus window. At river level, each has a story, a personality and an artistic flourish. The Pont de l'Alma, for instance, promises little on top, a wide greenish gray metal suitable for the heavy traffic it distributes to the Champs-Elysées, the Champ-de-Mars, and a dozen other directions. But underneath lurks the *Zouave*. He is the only survivor of four sculpted soldiers, who represented the army branches that beat back Germans at the Battle of Alma in 1856. The others vanished in 1972 with the old stone bridge.

Lyrics fete the stone-faced colonial soldier, a North African Berber in flowing cape and fez. He is the sentry of Paris in flood. The river is fast and dangerous when it wets his spats. If water leaves a ring around his neck, banks are awash. God help Paris if it reaches his mustache and laps at his beetled brow.

Two bridges upstream, the Pont Alexandre III needs no subtle scrutiny. Four winged horses rear up atop high columns on either side. All are plated thickly in gold. Thirty lampposts flank the bridge, each with three glass globes set in ornate metal. Cherubs and bearded gods highlight sweeps of iron scrollwork. The bridge was centerpiece of the 1900 Paris world's fair, meant to outshine the 1889 exposition that produced the Eiffel Tower. As before, the fair revolved around the Seine, but the new theme was to hide high tech behind fancywork. The 354-foot arch was the longest single span of its time, its gentle angle unheard of in its day.

Alexander III, a particularly foul Russian czar, hated France for flaunting a past in which peasants dabbled in regicide. But he hated Germany more. Since a Franco-Russian alliance might have discouraged Kaiser Wilhelm—it didn't—he is immortalized by the gayest, gaudiest structure in Paris.

The Pont Alexandre III still symbolizes France's grandeur. Just before the bicentennial of the revolution in 1989, President François Mitterrand rode across the bridge and noticed that the great horses had gone green with age. He murmured to an aide. Night and day for weeks, workmen shot gold flake with high-powered pistols. Four years later, no one wanted to tell me how much gold that took. But the horses gleamed as intensely as in 1900.

Just off the bridge, past the grass and lime trees, is Les Invalides, built by Louis XIV as a veterans' administration hospital. Now it is a well-stocked military museum, heavy on the Middle Ages but with everything else down to Napoléon's socks. The imperial remains lie behind, under the golden dome, by an inscription reading: "I wish that my ashes rest along the Seine among the people of France I loved so much."

The Pont-Neuf, meaning New Bridge, is the oldest. Henri III placed the cornerstone in 1578. Henri IV walked across the pilings on a rickety plank in 1603 and galloped his horse over the finished bridge in 1605. He died by it ten years later, stabbed by a fanatic when his coach stalled in a Paris traffic jam.

The king saw his bridge as an early beacon to beam French radiance toward the less civilized. It was an engineering marvel, at three hundred yards the world's largest and the first to be integrated into the city around it. Architects aligned its two spans with the triangular Place Dauphine. From inside the *place*, cozy and shielded from wind, the bridge leaves an open window on the Seine. Henri IV stands discreetly to the side. Balconies like ships' prows overlook the Louvre. The parapet is rimmed by 341 stone faces, either royal courtesans or people on the sculptor's shit list. One tests one's intimacy with Paris by trying to identify them. And one seldom gets any right.

Today, the bridge is still wide enough for Paris traffic, high enough for river barges, and solid against caprices of the Seine. Engineers fixing it up in the 1990s found only minor damage. After four centuries, even perfectly hewn rocks wear away at the edges. Taken together, it is some package. Which is why Christo gift-wrapped it in fabric and cord in 1985.

The Petit Pont, fifty steps long, has been where it is in a dozen different forms since the Romans built an arch over the Parisii's ford. Gauls had burned the bridge when legionnaires approached. That got to be routine, like a turtle pulling in its head. When enemies threatened, the Petit Pont was sacrificed, and the Seine was a moat.

In 583, the flimsy bridge did in the Count of Tours, Leudaste. He had irked Queen Frédégonde, who was apparently a howling bitch. One Sunday, he asked for pardon, kneeling at her feet at a church where Notre-Dame now stands. She scowled and he backpedaled out the door. When she emerged with the king, he offered flowers. She called the guard. Leudaste drew his sword but, overwhelmed, fled to the Petit Pont. A rotten plank broke his leg. Frédégonde had him treated. When he was healed, she had a guard tie him to an iron bar and beat his head into pulp.

In the twelfth century, the bridge was set in stone, but it collapsed eleven more times because of currents, ice, or leaky pilings. The fire of 1718 brought an urban renewal, blotting out houses on the Petit Pont. It was at the heart of Paris when Abélard slipped across it nightly to see Héloïse. It still is.

〰〰〰

A walk along the Seine begins, almost by historical decree, around the Petit Pont. For starters, there is Notre-Dame, with a plaque out front from which all distances in France are measured. (Paris street numbers start at the Seine.) The Ile de la Cité, the start of it all, was ravaged by Baron Haussmann but remains thrilling. On the Left Bank, everyone has a favorite corner. Along the Quai des Grands-Augustins, the oldest intact waterside street in Paris, is Lapérouse restaurant. Mirrors in the private salons still bear centuries-old scratches from courtesans who checked out the diamonds their companions offered over lunch. Nearby, there is Shakespeare and Company bookstore and flophouse, a quirky reminder of the long-past literary scene. It is run by George Whitman, a goateed free spirit with a tongue of flint and a heart of gold—or, on occasion, vice versa.

A little imagination can restore the medieval waterfront, a stone cluster of bridgeheads and turrets, alive with street-level shops and upper-story apartments occupied by people who did not have to take out the trash. One princess of Burgundy was noted for her orgies in the Tour de Nesles, after which servants tossed plates, goblets and unwanted lovers into the Seine.

Slightly downriver, the best view of it all is on the Pont des Arts, a footbridge from the Institut de France, seat of literary glory, to the Louvre, a high temple of art. Years back, a gentleman writer asked a *clochard* under the bridge why so many derelicts camped in that particular spot. "We feel more at home here," he replied. "One's dreams have more distinction."

But nothing says Paris and the Seine like the Ile Saint-Louis, possibly the most beautiful island in the world. Its only palm trees are hidden on fifth-floor terraces, and sunbathers on its beaches have to settle for cobblestones, not sand. Tastes vary widely, but before making up your list of favorite pieces of land surrounded by water, stroll its streets on a Sunday morning when the shops have opened but the crowds have not arrived.

The fish guy with the little white mustache used to post a sign: "Deliveries on the island and on the continent." He finally took it down. Too many people thought he was kidding. I realized how much the place was a country village the first Christmas I lived there. Monsieur Martin, the baker, offered to cook our turkey in his bread oven. Later, Monsieur Turpin, the fruit-and-vegetable man who knew each tomato personally, helped a friend make me a birthday present. He grew a fat pumpkin with my name on it. And a heart.

On the island, I learned that someone has to give you instructions to get along in France. For months, we looked out the window at lines winding around the block for a cone of Berthillon ice cream. On freezing December mornings, housewives from Rouen stood patiently with tourists from Roanoke. Surely, I asked an old-timer, there must be a better way. Of course, he said. Walk inside and buy a small brick of the stuff. It's much cheaper, and there is never a line.

If the *Zouave* on the Pont de l'Alma is a quick gauge of Paris in flood, the real measure is taken at the Ile Saint-Louis. A tall vertical marker is implanted along the Quai de Tournelle, near the short stone span where you can gaze in awe at the back of Notre-Dame and walk a few steps to eat yourself into a stupor, and into poverty, at the Tour d'Argent. The normal mark is 2 meters. At 3.59 meters, it is considered too high. At 4.03, traffic stops. When it reaches 6, it is disaster. During the 1910 flood, water rose to 8.48.

After leaving France for a while and moving to the boat, I came back to the Ile Saint-Louis only sporadically. Each time, I found some new outrage. A snooty art gallery had bought out the last family hardware store within reasonable range. Now you had to go to Paris for your nuts and bolts. I'd loved the place. I always forgot and helped myself at the light-bulb rack, hoping to spare madame a trip across the shop; invariably, she glared as though I were trying to swipe sixty watts of silver. Monsieur always boomed, *"Bonjour, l'ami,"* and asked what he could solder, shave or shorten as an unpaid favor.

This is how cities work, of course. When the well-lit, well-stocked bookstore went in, people remembered the loss of their favorite blacksmith and coal vendor. But how many galleries does a little village need?

Until the early 1600s, the Ile Saint-Louis was all cows and grass, and it was called the Ile de Notre-Dame. Part of it was a separate island, Louviers, where lumbermen landed their logs. Like a glorious housing development meant to last, most of it went up at once. These days, little plaques on walls tell you which illustrious tenants have stopped there since, from Voltaire and Baudelaire to obscure film critics who impressed their landlords.

Coming downstream, the first building on the island, across from the one with the small gatehouse we would all kill to own, is perhaps the richest in lore, the Hôtel Lambert. Le Vau built it for a wealthy gentleman who had a hand in Louis XIII's finances. Rousseau dallied there with Madame Dupin and Voltaire with Madame du Châtelet. Prince Czartoryski acquired the Hôtel Lambert in 1830 and it became the Poles' paradise. Chopin was a regular. During World War II, the Resistance used it to shelter Allied airmen shot down in France. Then the Rothschilds moved in.

When I first moved to Paris in 1977, I visited an American correspondent friend in the Marais. "Come on," he said, "I want to show you something." We walked to the island. "Up there," he said, pointing to a wrought-iron balcony ablaze with flowers. It was off a wing of the Hôtel Lambert, facing the Right Bank. "I turned it down. It was for rent, but I just couldn't swing it." The poor guy was despondent, and I could see why. We strolled along the rest of the Quai d'Anjou as it curved gently to follow the Seine. As we walked down the dark quai, something I wouldn't do armed with a shotgun in most cities, we saw gold playing on the water.

∽∽∽∽∽

Every moment, these days, the river is different. At first light, when the current is low, it is dead calm, murky opaque glass. By the Pont Alexandre III, the only ripples are the wakes of a mother duck and the ducklings thrashing their tails behind her. Heavy moist air refracts the early colors, an impressionist's dream. Birds caw in the trees. Cars on the quai have not yet begun to drown out the snores of bums on the benches.

Invariably, the first bit of traffic is a heavily laden barge barreling flat out for the locks. Gates open at 7 A.M. sharp, at either end of Paris, and the first to go through has every chance of leading the pack all day long. Even at the pace of a *péniche*, time is money. By breakfast time, channel ten on the VHF is alive. Bargees exchange the night's news in clipped phrases that land people can barely understand.

Closer toward noon, the radio is all business. The little *Lutèce*, full of tourists, wants to turn around and warns a giant *bateau-mouche*, which is booming along behind. That sort of thing. By afternoon, the river is rolling like a calm sea, churned up by every sort of propeller.

Péniches go by at irregular intervals, different but alike. The small touches are routine: a woman in an overwashed dress sweeps the deck; a small car hugs the aft deck; wind ruffles the petals of geraniums in a pot. Across the bow, each barge is painted with the name of someone's fondness or fancy.

Tugs—or pushers, as the French know them—chug past behind four sand barges lashed together at the corners. Familiar shapes turn up often. The *Cher*, a skinny, short barge, delivers diesel fuel the way horse-drawn wagons used to haul coal. The outboard-powered *Belgrand* heads toward a choked-up bit of river installation that needs its attention. Gray police launches lumber up and down. When in a hurry, the cops flash past in their *Miami Vice* runabouts. Firemen in frogman suits use rubber dinghies for the small stuff—clearing props and poking at dubious hulls. The fireboats are not much bigger, no more than floating cannons. They don't have to carry water.

A motley mix of private craft weave among the barges: boxy rent-a-boats taking families to the canals; stubby sail-boats with English or Dutch markings and cheery crews eager for a meal on shore; elegant yachts with stepped masts and gleaming hulls, captains drawling on radio like pilots landing at a busy airport. On weekends, there are cabin cruisers, Zodiacs and the odd kayak.

The barges trail off at dusk, but tourist traffic swells to a tide. One after another, sometimes three abreast, boats of different sizes from a half dozen companies cruise past, droning tape-recorded patter in most living languages. Each blinds nighttime strollers with its long rows of reflector searchlights. By midnight, most have stopped. At 1 A.M., when the lights go out on the Eiffel Tower, section by section, top to bottom, the Seine is calm again. With a few odd lights mirrored gold on its surface, it is of a beauty words cannot approach.

High water changes all of this. In the early morning, the

river boils brown, surging noisily and hurling debris against the bows of moored boats. The ducks have gone to Miami Beach. Working barges may still navigate, but the captains are too busy to chat on the radio. Tour boats are winnowed down to only the small ones, which can still make it under the bridges. When the water gets seriously rough, they stop, too.

This happens mostly in winter, or when the spring is still cold. Wind whips down the quais, all but deserted except for a few people hurrying by in turned-up collars. It is a wonderful time, wild and thrilling.

The river is at her best in June, when the nights lengthen and the current is always at peace. Varnish is fresh on the boats. Soon, on July 14, Bastille Day, the water will flash with fireworks. Long-planned vacations are about to happen. Tourists are streaming in, but the hordes are still beyond the gates.

On a recent Friday night just before the summer solstice, the Seine exuded magic. It was one of those perfect evenings, clear and fresh, where you wear a short-sleeve shirt and wonder vaguely whether to put on a sweater. Up over the stone wall, on the real-world level, we could see the tops of tents set up for the annual Fête de Musique. Pleasant sounds wafted on the balmy air.

Near the gold-statued bridge, the village was alive. My neighbor Jillie, a movie wardrobe lady, zoomed by in her open Volkswagen with a cheery wave. On every boat deck, someone was barbecuing veal chops, dipping artichoke leaves, or sipping Veuve Clicquot. At 9 P.M., with the sky still bright blue, the lovers' bench was already energetically in use.

Olivier thrust his illuminated grin into the open hatch. "Do you have rice?" he said. "I have a beaut-i-ful *rôti*, a

beaut-i-ful *salade*, and no rice." He was speaking Olivier
English. "I have just come back from the Atlantic, beaut-
i-ful. I have five beaut-i-ful girls for dinner, but no rice." He
added, unnecessarily, "I am so ah-pee. Very ah-pee."

The river churned with traffic. During a brief lull, two
river cops in their hot rubber patrol boat cut high-speed
doughnuts in the water. They roared in tight circles, skidding
into turns, and, goosing the throttle, shot halfway into the
air on the backstretch. They were good. Both were grinning
like idiots. A training mission, no doubt.

One after another, the boats came past, and we settled
down to watch the parade. First, the giant *Normandie* filled
the horizon with its massive white hull, starting its regular
cruise from Paris to the estuary at Honfleur. Philippe, the
captain, blasted us a brief recital of "Frère Jacques" on the fog
horn. We honked back, with a can of compressed air, and the
crew—Loic, Bernard, Karin and a cheerful dishwasher
whose name escapes me—waved until they were out of
sight. The *Lutèce* was next, with its distinctive green stripe,
dirty white hull, and nasty little wake. Then there was the
one we call Darth Vader, a purple-jowled, violently lighted
monster of a *bateau-mouche*, trailed by its partner in ghastli-
ness, the Neon Cockroach.

Following fast came the *Louisiane Belle*, powered by
diesel-driven screws in spite of its fake paddle wheel and silly
fold-down smokestacks. We could hear the next boat before
we saw it. *Don Juan*, the handsome lady-killer of a dinner
cruiser, may be the noisiest thing on the river. It was a classic
1930s yacht, all white and trimmed in rich teak. The elegant
Bretagne we could smell, its star-worthy galley blowing delicious scents out the porthole. Next was a floating outdoor
café, complete with globe lamps on posts, the *Europa*. And all
the rest: the biggest new boat of the Bateaux Parisiens, with a

logo that is either an Eiffel Tower reflected on the water or a cancan dancer with a broken leg; the *Eiffel Star*, looking like something between a waterborne Concorde and a black suppository; the silver and red *Château Gaillard*, a barge turned fancy dining room; more *bateaux-mouches*, gigantic covered platforms that can carry a thousand people at a time.

The air throbbed with sound. Accordion tunes spilled over the high wall from the festival tents. The *Canotier* slipped by, a floating party, blasting bullfight music. One of the dinner *mouches* behind it blared a roller-rink rendition of "Smoke Gets in Your Eyes." On the quai, a saffron yellow Saab convertible skidded to a halt and disgorged six smiling people, clearly ready to the make noise all night on the neighboring boat. As the late dusk finally darkened, the orange lamps snapped on above the Pont Alexandre III. Boats on the river switched on their nav lights, red at port and green at starboard. The only word was *magic*.

Used to the Seine's surprises, we thought we had seen it all. Then a large launch came by, painted, "Bateau Ecole." A scrawny guy perched in the bow. He wore blue tights, a red cape, and, on his chest, a large red *S*.

Far in the distance, a siren moaned. For all we knew, Paris was burning. But that was another world. We were caught up in the Seine, and we were ah-pee. Very ah-pee.

7 Walking on Water

''A H, MY FRIENDS,'' Nicolae Karamzine wrote to his Moscow newspaper, "never have I approached a city with such excitement, such curiosity, such impatience." At twenty-four, he was among young Russians who had come for springtime in Paris. That was in 1790, soon after that Bastille business. Once in Paris, he was crushed: "Narrow streets, dirty and muddy, with foul-looking houses and people in torn rags." Then he saw the river.

"The decor transformed totally when we reached the banks of the Seine," Karamzine wrote. "There were magnificent edifices, houses of six stories, rich boutiques. What a multitude of people! What a tumult! One carriage races after the other. Every second someone yells, 'Make way! Make way!,' and the throng ebbs and flows like an ocean. This indescribable noise, this marvelous variety of objects, this vivacity of the people all threw me into a spin. It seemed as if, like a grain of sand, I had fallen into an abyss and was sucked into a whirlpool."

Karamzine picked a lively time to visit. His description might have fit the city at any time from the early Middle Ages to halfway through the nineteenth century. But Paris was especially crazed in the late 1700s. There was, for instance, that mad scramble in 1783 for front-row seats to watch a guy from Lyon walk across the Seine at the Pont-Neuf without using the bridge.

On December 8, Paris was still aflutter at the exploits of the Montgolfier brothers. Before the king at Versailles, they had sent a sheep, a duck and a rooster into near space, airborne for several moments in a basket hung from a balloon. Science knew no bounds. That morning, the *Journal de Paris* carried a letter under the heading "Physics." From an anonymous Lyon watchmaker, it announced the discovery of *sabots élastiques*—springy clogs—which allowed their wearer to bound across water.

With modest understatement, the inventor said the discovery was the result of twenty years' time and expense. Each shoe was no more than a foot long. They worked on the principle of weight distribution and rapid forward movement, like a stone skipping over the surface. Properly tuned, he said, they could allow the wearer to cross the Seine fifty times in an hour at its widest spot. The writer begged temporary anonymity, for fear of ignorant derision, but offered a demonstration on New Year's Day. He would cross the Seine and come back again on the condition that he would find two hundred gold coins waiting on the bank. For sport, he promised to walk faster than a horse could canter on the Pont-Neuf above him.

Paris went nuts. Nobles and ranking churchmen demanded private boxes in the grandstands that city officials hurried to build. People besieged the newspaper for more information, with no success. Public subscriptions mounted fast; investors outbid one another. Soon the price of tickets soared out of sight. Royal circles talked of little else.

With everything in place, ten days after the letter was published, the inventor was still lying low. On December 22, editors of the *Journal de Paris* announced that they had lost touch with the mysterious watchmaker. It was a hoax. Some people got their money back, but ranking nobles refused to admit they had been had. Instead, they transferred the funds to a charity that bought fathers out of debtors' prison so they could be home with their families for Christmas.

∽∽∽∽∽

It is an old writer's trick to praise an author and then steal his best stuff. I found both of these gems in a rich tome called *Les Inconnus de la Seine* by Simon Lacordaire. Apart from a sharp ear for irony, Lacordaire seems to have a superhuman ability to endure the Bibliothèque Nationale, France's fabled look-but-don't-touch repository of wisdom. I also learned much from a lovely book, *The Seine*, by Anthony Glyn, a slow ramble down the river. And, like me, both of these authors must be indebted to Jacques Hillairet, who has traced the origin of every street and most buildings in Paris.

Over time, I spent a lot of afternoons waiting for librarians to allow a fleeting glance at rare texts. Fat volumes in the corners of friends' boats filled in details. Such eminent voyagers as Henry James and Robert Louis Stevenson have written about the Seine. More recently, Carey and Julian More produced a handsome photo study. But it seems every old-timer I meet has old lore to pass along. Picking up history along the Seine is as easy as snaring plastic waste. It is everywhere.

One July 14 evening, for instance, friends crowded aboard *La Vieille* to watch fireworks and frolic. Facts were not on the evening's menu. But France was broke that year, and the display was padded with historic narration over loudspeakers. Words are cheaper than skyrockets. Tess Bitterman, eleven, declined another Coke, her mood dampened. "I gotta go study for a history test," she grumbled. In America, kids keep track of only centuries. The French digest two millenia.

Since those first Greeks in boats, what happened along the Seine has shaped much of the Old World. Europe's course was set by the Mad Merovingians, the Capetians, François I, a pile of Henris and Louis, and a pair of Napoléons. After the Gauls, this parade was led by an axe-wielding, fork-tongued mass murderer named Clovis, the father of France, who made Paris his capital.

Clovis and his Franks ran off rival Germans. By brute force and poison in the family goblets, he built a kingdom from the Rhine to the Pyrenees. His wife, Clotilde, a noble Catholic, steered him to the church. No fool, Clovis saw the power Christianity represented. He defended it fiercely without reading the fine print. When a warrior smashed a holy chalice, he did the same to the guy's head. Needing a well-situated base, Clovis moved onto the Parisii's island in 508. Over three centuries, Merovinginan kings fortified the island into a citadel. One of them, the redoubtable Dagobert, strung abbeys down the Seine, the castles of God, to extend his reach to the English Channel.

The dynasty changed with Charlemagne, a Germanic emperor of a refined nature who ruled from Provence. When he died in 814, rival heirs scrambled over his grave for power. But he left style and order. France was a Latin-based Western European culture, with engineers, a clergy and tax collectors. Whatever else squabbling kings managed to hold, they clung to the north and the river that ran through it.

In 855, the Vikings redecorated Paris. They returned the next year to sack and burn what was left. Charles the Bald got fed up. His masons and carpenters swarmed over fourth-century Gallo-Roman walls, already reinforced by Merovingians. The Grand Châtelet and Petit Châtelet loomed at either end of the Notre-Dame bridge. Pilings barred the main channel like stone sentries. When Vikings returned in 861, pillage was damned hard work.

Nordic hordes came prepared in 885: thirty thousand warriors in longboats, armed with catapults, battering rams, towers, everything but high-powered speakers to blast rock music. They broke open both Châtelet fortresses, but Paris held. Charles the Fat struck a deal. If the Vikings abandoned the siege, they could roll their boats past town on logs and continue up the Seine to what they really wanted: wine from Burgundy. The Vikings stopped raiding, but stone ramparts grew higher.

For a thousand years, Paris strangled the Seine and suffered for it. Heavy high walls sunk into the riverbed. The skyline was jagged with pointy towers, crenellations and turrets. Bridges on closely spaced pilings spanned the Seine like picket fences, mills and water wheels blocking their narrow arches. Boats clustered in two dozen ports. Artisans found new uses for the river, narrowing the channel. Filth piled up in the shallow water. Each new ruler added his imprint in stone.

Until 987, Paris alternated between capital and outpost, depending on whose fiefdom dominated. Then warring nobles united behind Hugues Capet, the duke of Paris, a descendant of Robert the Strong, who had beat back the Norsemen. Three hundred years later, the Capetians left a

France that swept from the English Channel to the Mediterranean, ruled from Paris. And they spilled a lot of fresh blood into the Seine.

Normandy under the Vikings was a worrisome neighbor. A Norman named William the Bastard annexed England in 1066, creating a superpower that controlled the business end of the Seine. Kings in Paris had to beg favor. In the 1180s, Philippe Auguste chose muscle. He put up new walls around his capital—some still remain behind the Panthéon—and also the Louvre fortress. The Seine was locked up at night by a thick chain stretched across to the Nesle Tower. Philippe Auguste squared off against Richard the Lion-Hearted, but the English duke of Normandy expired early, and his chicken-hearted brother was no match for the French. Soon, Normandy answered to Paris.

With the Seine secure from mouth to source, Paris boomed. Its lords were the watermen. Until the twelfth century, boats used the old Roman port on the Left Bank and the Gallo-Roman docks behind Notre-Dame, both on the narrow branch where currents were easier to handle. But the channel was choked with collapsed bridgeworks, silt and garbage. In 1141, the Water Merchant's Guild bought a chunk of Right Bank marsh and set up the Port de la Grève opposite the Ile de la Cité. And in 1170, a royal charter gave them a lock on river traffic. Only card-carrying watermen could move cargo in Paris. Their cut was 50 percent of value.

The monopoly lasted five centuries, and no one has yet to shake the boatman's belief that he owns the Seine. The Paris coat of arms bears a ship adapted from the watermen's seal, vaguely like a Viking drakkar. Under it is the motto *Fluctuat nec Mergitur*. That is, Slapped Around by Water but Unsinkable.

As Paris grew, the water often slapped hard. Two days

before Christmas of 1596, the Pont-aux-Meuniers crumbled, tossing tall houses and their inhabitants into the roiling current. The king had given the bridge to church authorities, who did not bother to inspect its pilings. A dozen floods soaked Paris. In 1658, the Seine's highest known current washed much of the bridge away.

Even at normal levels, water rushed down the Vale of Misery—the narrow stretch along the Right Bank between the Pont Notre-Dame and the Pont au Change. The two bridges were close together, but their central arches were out of line. Downstream boatmen routinely smacked into stone, unable to maneuver with rudimentary rudders. Upstream boats had to be hauled against the current by straining laborers who named the towpath the Street That's Too Long.

Finally, in the 1860s, Napoléon III freed the Seine. His minister of grandeur, Baron Haussmann, made broad boulevards of the city's twisting back streets. On the river, he swept away the whole lot. Ancient walls came tumbling down. The Palais de Justice with its Conciergerie was spared, but most was demolished. Bridges let the river through, without eddies and backwashes. Heavy barges from the north threaded their way behind Paris to the Canal Saint-Martin. Spaces opened along the river.

But, in a sense, Paris turned away from the Seine. Parisians could swim in it. It still sluiced away their sewage. The water hens remained—laundrywomen who beat shirts on the rocks and took no lip from anyone. Passenger boats plied the river. But ports moved to the edge of town. Tanners and millers and smithies went to work elsewhere. The Seine, still the principal artery of Paris, was no longer pumped by its heart.

∽∽∽∽∽

No one paved the Paris streets until, one day in 1185, Philippe Auguste opened a window and was rocked back by the
stench from the putrid mud below. Thick stones, more than
a yard square, were put down on the main drags. It took
nearly five hundred years to lay smaller paving stones on
most city streets. Roadways were concave, with sewer gutters in the center, so that passing coaches splashed filth on
passersby.

Philip the Fair's Paris of 1300 was still clustered on the
Ile de la Cité, though protected by the Louvre. On twenty-
five acres, two-thirds of its present size, the island packed in
a bustling city: a palace, gardens and fields at the downstream end, and Notre-Dame with its cloisters at the other; in
between, Hôtel-Dieu hospital, the market, a forest of bell
towers over eighteen churches, and four-story houses were
wedged side by side on thirty to forty unpaved winding
streets. Much later, when Haussmann turned loose the bull-
dozers, twenty-five thousand people were evicted.

Seine water grew progressively more fetid. The Bièvre, a
little Left Bank tributary, was so polluted by tapestry makers
that it was later bricked over as a sewer. Wells were dug on
the marshy right bank, but kings, nobles and churchmen
got first call on their trickle of water. By the time of the
revolution, the common rabble were allowed a quart a day
per person of well water and all they could scoop from the
Seine.

Engineers had not worked out sewage, so architects put
open toilets on staircase landings; that, I fear, is the origin of
those quaint exposed iron sinks in old buildings, between
apartment doors. Pipes quickly backed up, but nature's
needs did not diminish. Each morning, people emptied
night-soil buckets out the window. In the evenings, butchers
slopped blood and guts into the mess, kicking the bloated

flies into higher gear. Parisians merely averted their eyes and numbed their olfactory senses.

The much-mourned Piscine Déligny had roots in the malodorous Middle Ages. At baths known as *les étuves*, Parisians had themselves washed, shaved and plucked. Then they stretched out to rest in lounging areas. Soon, deluxe service reached previously neglected parts of the body. Magistrates forbade messing around, but no one paid any attention. As the streets were risky, gentlemen often stayed the night, reveling by the lapping waters of the Seine. In 1399, a wet blanket ordered separate *étuves* for men and women, with strict codes for operators. Nothing changed. To this day, the French like to mingle the pleasures of bath and bed, which may explain why *baigner* and *baiser* are so close in the language.

Before the twelfth century, the Seine was twice as wide as it is today, with treacherous shallow spots. Encroaching walls defined the channels. Islands formed an archipelago. Today's Rue de l'Université was a channel separating the Left Bank from the Ile de Maquerelle, the duelers' island. Plague victims were buried in mass graves there. They were joined by eleven hundred Huguenots fished from the reeds, all murdered in a religious score settling and dumped in the Seine. Later, Louis XIV populated the island with evil-tempered swans from Denmark, and it became the Ile des Cygnes.

In medieval times, frequent riverside spectacles broke the routine. One morning, fourteen English prisoners from a battle at Pontoise were brought to the Pont au Change, bound hand and foot. No one would pay their ransom. With ceremony, they were stuffed into weighted sacks and dumped—where else?—into the Seine.

〜〜〜〜〜

As Paris drifted from Middle Ages to Renaissance, the quais were raucous and pulsing with life. Men wrestled wine barrels, grain sacks and hay bales from barges to wagons. Women pounded linen on the rocks, dragged off buckets of flopping fish and humped stacks of firewood on their backs. A class of lumbermen waded in the river to manhandle islets of logs that were floated downstream. Water wheels creaked and groaned. In the din of hammers, horse hooves and market wails, discourse was by shouts.

On festival days, the Seine was ablaze in color, with jousters in the bows of boats flying banners. Mostly, the river was a floating free-for-all. Narrow passages were choked with *moulins-nefs*, mills mounted atop wooden hulls. Sunken boats pierced with holes held live fish for the market.

Each *quartier* had its purpose or specialty. Tanners worked together amid an unworldly stink. Flea markets met regularly on the same spot. Foreigners stopped at the Pont au Change to be fleeced by money changers. But millers were sprinkled along the Seine and its tributaries, wherever they could find a free spot where the current was strong enough to turn their wheel without tearing it off its axis.

Nobody loved the millers. Customers accused them, usually accurately, of mixing horse feed in with good wheat. Boatmen fought a running, losing war to keep mill wheels out of the narrow channels through Paris. Millers squabbled among themselves over lucrative business. And then, around 1650, there was that year during which Parisians greeted every miller they saw with a howl of laughter and a hearty "To the ring!"

One hot summer day near the Place de Grève, an over-fed miller, having cooled off with too much Burgundy, declared in a loud voice that his rolling belly was merely an illusion. Someone challenged him to prove it by slipping through a large iron ring—a boat mooring—on the nearby quai. Certainly, the miller replied. A banker was designated to keep track of the bets.

The miller, apparently, had heard that if you can get your head past a tight space, the rest will follow. He began with a triumphant grin. Shoulders followed with some difficulty. Intense wriggling got his thorax through the iron. When he got to his stomach, he was in tighter than a champagne cork. In a vise grip, the miller could barely breathe. He turned a shade of purple from strangulated circulation, the blazing sun and fear. All of this, of course, brought a delighted, roisterous crowd.

Laughter grew louder as the miller moved less and less. After an hour, the crowd got bored with the inert victim. A bystander volunteered to get a file and free the wretched miller. No way, a peace officer insisted. The ring belonged to the city, and no one was cutting it without approval from the watermen's chief. City Hall was not far away; permission was granted.

Work started, touching off another round of merriment. The miller already exuded an odor of barbecue, and the heat and sparks from filing singed his exposed flesh. He howled like what became the proverbial stuck pig. Regularly, he was doused with buckets of Seine water. The crowd loved it. It took an hour to free him. The miller staggered home to a resounding chorus of "*A l'anneau!*" To the ring.

A year after the incident, a delegation of exasperated millers insisted that the chief of police outlaw the phrase and jail anyone who uttered it. Tallemant des Reaux, who published this account in 1834, did not say what the chief decided.

∾∾∾∾∾

The character of Paris changed with the Pont-Neuf. It reached from the permanent flea market at the Quai de Conti on the Left Bank, home to Europe's swiftest cutpurses, to the Ile de la Cité. Then it continued on to the gates of the Louvre. Regal convoys could sweep from the palace, stop off at Notre-Dame, and canter off to the western woods.

The bridge tied together the elements of what was getting to be a beautiful city. Nothing was just decoration. The horse that dominates the Pont-Neuf, for instance, was cast in Tuscany to carry a statue of Ferdinand de Médicis. Horse and rider were sent to France by Ferdinand's son as a gift for Marie de Médicis, wife of Henri IV. The boat sank on the way. By the time Ferdinand was fished out of the water, the king had died. After twenty years, Louis XIII decided to put his own father on the horse. In the revolution, *sans-culottes* tossed him in the Seine. Louis XVIII ordered up the present rider, using bronze from two unneeded statues of Napoléon.

Under an arch near the Right Bank, Henri IV built La Samaritaine fountain, a grotesque wooden contraption with a clock, which made navigation even more dangerous. But it brought a steady supply of water to the Louvre and some of its neighbors.

The new crossing starved another unloved class of parasites, the ferrymen. In need of cash, an early king had sold hereditary patents to a few operators. Thus protected, they charged high rates and hired untrained kids to do the work. Routinely, boatloads of passengers ended up in the Seine.

As soon as it went up, the Pont-Neuf attracted every sort of snake-oil artist, sneak thief, minstrel, seer or pusher. Among them was Grand Thomas, the puller of teeth. Lacordaire describes him as gargantuan, kitted out like a war elephant in scarlet robe, golden trappings and a heavy long sword. He worked from a wagon near the Henri IV statue, bellowing rhymes that boasted of his services. His rap went something like:

> *Big Tom, with his fancy boots,*
> *Is the pearl of charlatans.*
> *He'll cure you of your aching tooth*
> *By yanking it out by the roots.*

On the Pont-Neuf, a saying of the day promised: "At any hour, you're certain to find a nun, a white horse and a whore." That last category grew so numerous that, in 1647, police rounded up cartloads and sent them to America.

That's not all that went to the New World from the Seine. By 1629, twenty-nine *bouquinistes* were installed on the new bridge, amassing an inventory of leather-bound books that captivated Thomas Jefferson when he lived in Paris more than a century later. He shipped home mountains of them to begin a Library of Congress. Later, when Americans built a home for their presidents, it was made partly from white blocks cut from the limestone honeycombs under Montmartre, plaster of Paris. American ships loaded them as ballast after dropping cargo at the French capital.

Larger vessels on the Seine signaled the end of most floating enterprises moored to the shore. Among the last to go was the leech pound. Doctors treated patients by bleeding them, and they relied on the insects to help them out. Police enforced rigid standards, raiding pharmacists who harbored nonregulation leeches. Vast quantities of little suckers were held as evidence aboard a barge off the Ile Saint-Louis.

The *poulets d'eau*—the Seine's redoubtable water hens—held on until the twentieth century. These women ran the *bateaux-lavoirs*, giant boiler-mounted barges on which they did Parisians' laundry. They worked like slaves every day of the year, except when the Seine was too icy for the finger-powered rinse cycle. But they pioneered women's liberation, brooking no direction from a man's world. It took four generations of bureaucrats to get them off the river and, more than officialdom, washing machines delivered the final blow. Mooning, that California surfers' salute, was a specialty of the Seine. To punctuate a heated exchange, a *poulet d'eau* turned her back and exposed her *fondement*.

By the revolution, France had amassed wealth from colonial trade, wherewithal that was invested into a city that Frenchmen regarded as the center of the world. This post-Renaissance flowering was part of a continual process of refinement with roots going back to the first Franks. Under Clovis, Parisians knew their city was the focal point of human enlightenment. *Plus ça change.*

∽∽∽∽∽

This sense of history, and attachment to the river, is why every new flourish is debated in public, for months or years. If it is something significant like a glass pyramid outside the Louvre, the president pores over each detail as the kings did. Once built, it takes Paris a decade to pass lasting judgment.

From time to time, someone attempts an atrocity on this priceless Paris ensemble. Hitler wanted to burn it at the end, but he never even managed to shell it properly. John Dos Passos, a wartime volunteer French soldier, watched a round explode harmlessly in the Seine; Parisians scrambled with nets to scoop up the stunned fish.

In the 1970s, Paris nearly suffered from an inside job. President Georges Pompidou started a grand Left Bank Expressway. It would take some room from the river and obliterate its old embankment. Part of the Quartier Latin, together with the charm of Quai Voltaire and the Gare d'Orsay, would go, along with traces of the Romans and God knows what else. It would run six miles. "It is necessary to adapt Paris to the automobile and sacrifice a degree of estheticism," the president remarked.

Pompidou died before much got done. The new president, Valéry Giscard d'Estaing, paralyzed the project. He froze the national government's share of funds, leaving Paris unable to pay the rest. Mayor Jacques Chirac, running for president against Giscard, railed against what he said was holding up progress. This was an act of "demagogues and incompetents . . . one of the worst blunders of our time."

Twenty years later, traffic still jams, but no one is sure how much a freeway would have helped anyway. In 1992, the United Nations Educational, Scientific and Cultural Organization proposed to protect the banks of the Seine as a world heritage site, putting them in a class with the Pyramids and the Parthenon. This time, Chirac beamed his accord. We must, he said, protect a unique treasure.

It was Chirac who spiked a more recent threat, in 1989. A Paris ad magnate, playing on the overlapping jurisdictions on the Seine, secured dubious authority to put huge illuminated billboards on ninety-six *péniches* along the river in Paris. Advertisers paid $120,000 a week for the privilege of scarring the riverscape. "One can hardly imagine a worse blight," the mayor said, promising to eliminate them. But they would not go away.

Interviewed in the trade paper *Médias*, entrepreneur Michel Halimi was asked about the many people who complained. "These are mostly politicians, at the moment of municipal elections," he explained. "As for Parisians, we have made concessions: there are no more *péniches* at the foot of the Eiffel Tower, or in front of the Musée d'Orsay, the only places on the river where they can really spoil the view."

In fact, he said, only the Transport Ministry could issue a decree banning the billboards. What with one legal nicety or another, that would take at least a year. Then we would have two years to comply. By then, who would care? "Ten years ago advertising on the Champs-Elysées provoked a real scandal," he concluded. "Today, no one notices." Right.

Chirac managed to close enough loopholes, and opposition rallied against the floating monstrosities. They vanished.

8 Life on the Quais

BEATRIX KOSTER WOULD NOT OBJECT to being described as ladylike. Dutch-born, French-bred, American-educated, she handles herself with grace and aplomb, speaking of gentle subjects in a soft voice. She seemed out of place, therefore, dangling by one arm from a ladder over a raging river, and grasping a bag of groceries to her bosom with the other arm. It was no particular trauma. Beatrix was merely coming home at high current.

It was February 1988, when you needed a boat to get to your boat. Beatrix had punted without incident across a flooded quai to the *Nahuilhuapi*, tied up near the Pont Sully. She caught hold of the boarding ladder. As she reached for the groceries, the dinghy took off in the current.

"I was hanging with one hand, and my legs were kicking in midair over the water," she recounts to friends, with a laugh that gets louder as the memory fades. No gymnast, she figures that dropping the groceries to free her other hand would not have helped much. That left screaming at the top of her lungs over the wind-whipped river. A guy on the next boat heard her before too long, thus cutting short her favorite Seine story but probably also saving her life. He pulled her and the groceries up on deck.

I was in New York at the time, watching television. Peter Jennings said a few words about the latest victims of the world's whims, and I discovered I was one of them. The camera panned my flooded quai, and there was *La Vieille*, looking like she was back at work in the North Sea. I had left her moored with some slightly frayed lines, which the current had stretched tight as E-strings. "They don't break when they're taut," Captain Jacques had said. "Only when they are jerked." Jacques would know. I prayed for no jerks.

By the time I got back to Paris, the flood was a muddy stain three feet up the stone wall across a wide parking apron. People took pleasure in describing the size of logs that had slammed into *La Vieille*'s hull and wedged under the keel. "She was lifted half out of the water," someone said. Damn, and I missed it.

But I did not miss them all. There is nothing like lying in your bunk and hearing a dull boom that shivers your timbers and then rat-a-tats in your ear like a crazed woodpecker. It is no particular problem. You put on a yellow slicker, hang over the rail and point a flashlight downward to illuminate your glasses as they tumble into the current. With luck, some rudimentary knowledge of physics (water pushes stuff downstream), and much awkward straining with a sharpened boat hook, you can usually dislodge the log. Then you wait for the next one.

What the river teaches newcomers, I was amazed to learn, is that you are on your own. It is not exactly crossing the Pacific solo in the *Kon-Tiki*. More, it is a time-eating lesson in uniqueness. Only one guy on the river can haul wooden hulls out for drydock. The man who built the battery charger retired to Bournemouth last May; if you can find him, he might answer questions by phone. No one still makes the right kind of fuel filter, but if you look hard enough, you can find probably the last one left. In emergencies, however, you had better know where to shove the plug.

My own education was, at best, a challenge. To help, I had Manik and his Sri Lankan navy—until I was able to shake free.

∽∽∽∽∽

You had to feel bad for Manik, standing there that fateful morning, fighting to keep rue from tinging his habitual smile. He saw me with a varnish pot. Though he took it like a gentleman, the eyes were a dead giveaway. I was painting solo; God only knew if changing a light fixture unaided might be next. It was as if his golden goose had keeled over from a sudden stroke.

Manik, an affable, even lovable Sri Lankan with a lot of kids and two Russian wolfhounds, always reminded me of *Green Acres*, that television series in which a city type buys a farm and finds an army of crafty locals to help him. For a price. In the Seine version, the head sucker-plucker was a credit to his class. When I offered to pay handsomely for him to clean and paint chunks of metal ballast under the floorboards, he knew he had a live one.

Manik's day job was ambassador, or commercial attaché, or some such, but he made his fortune on the quai. He did decent work and would roll out of bed before dawn in an emergency. He was intelligent, not dishonest and a good soul. Somehow, however, he always came out ahead. Once, for example, I ended up with two extra high-tech batteries a mechanic brought from England. Manik asked if he could borrow one briefly. Much later, my car battery died. No problem, I had two spare power packs in my workroom. Well, actually, I didn't. Er, Manik? The smile and shrug.

His business vocabulary was limited to "three thousand five hundred francs." This was not a bad deal for an engine overhaul or brain surgery. For painting a small surface, it was steep.

On that black morning with the brushes, Manik realized I would soon figure out that it did not take all of June, and four indentured laborers, to varnish the railing. He also suspected that I would think it was fun.

In the end, I outfoxed myself. All I saved was some money, and any boat will find a million other ways to suck your wallet empty. I missed Manik when he went off to nibble greener twigs. He comes around now and again, but as friend, not bandit.

Of course, bandits are hardly in short supply on the Seine. Nor, for that matter, are Robin Hoods and every gradation in between. Ordinary people tend to fear the river. One emergency doctor refused to treat a sick friend until she dragged herself onto the quai. "I have a wife and kids," he said, explaining why he could not risk his life by stepping aboard. A drunk plumber invoked a union rule to extract an extra eighty dollars for working in unsafe conditions. A separate class of people fill the vacuum.

To trade with Cyrano Lasalle, you need not leave the water. His shipchandlery is the *Excelsior*, a converted *péniche* that has been moored near Austerlitz for a quarter century. It is best to catch him in the right frame of mind.

"I wouldn't touch one of those things," he declaimed, voice rising fast, when I showed him a Visa card. He meant all plastic. "You use that and the minister of finance knows everything you do, everything about you, everything . . ."

When he paused for air, I remarked that the minister of finance needed only binoculars to know what he was doing. The *Excelsior* was directly across from the Treasury's new quarters on the Quai de Bercy. He grinned and told me what time the minister arrived for work that morning and when he left for lunch.

I next saw him alongside *La Vieille*. He also runs the *Cher*, that gas station that comes to you. His help was on holiday. "Quick! Quick!" he barked, when I stopped to inspect our bumping hulls before tying his bow to mine. He hopped on board and peered into my fuel tank, dropping ash into it from the half-smoked cigar in his mouth.

"A hundred liters," he grumbled, when I told him to stop. "That's not worth the trip." I chose not to remind him that had he stopped, as agreed, the day before when he passed by, an extra trip would not have been needed. Instead I took another two hundred liters, which I'd regret if we had to remove the tank when I went into drydock. He has a way about him.

Lasalle, with hair slicked back in the old style, is the sort of person depicted in a loving portrait by Dutch filmmaker Joris Ivens, *The Seine Meets Paris*. That was in 1957. It was a string of grainy images in black and white set to a poem. The credits were simple: "There are no actors in this film, only men and women and children who love the Seine."

Ivens showed the whole range of river people, lingering long on bare-chested dockers loading wine and rubble, cranking enormous wheels and bending fat ropes around hardware of another age. Most striking were the sketches of proper Parisians at leisure on the cobblestone quais: a man in a tie washed his car; women in sensible shoes rinsed out tubs of laundry; kids splashed in the water. And the photographers' models were all clothed from toe to teeth, in prim hats.

Today, the portrait would come out a little differently.

∽∽∽∽∽

On the Quai Saint-Bernard, architects Xavier Esselinck and Yves Bour used to fall behind in summer. Instead of drawing, they would gaze out their window at beautiful women sunbathing naked. After a while, friends circulated the rumor that the curving lines of neo-Parisian architecture were inspired along the Seine. Both came to the river in the mid-1970s, looking for a cheap place to live. They found themselves in a different world altogether and helped pioneer a new age along the quais. The rule, they found, was that there aren't really any rules.

"This is France, but it's not Paris," Esselinck told me one morning on the deck of *La Vieille*. Everyone knows that, in its figurative sense. He meant for real. "Paris stops up there," he explained, pointing to the plane trees along the sidewalk overlooking the quai. "Down here is the Seine. It is administered by the Voies Navigables de France, but everyone wants to get his oar in. Paris has nothing to say about it."

Functionaries will argue, however you define it. The VNF, a nineties remake of the old Office National de Navigation, is a public body under the wing of the Ministry of Transport. It makes the rules. The cops, the Brigade Fluviale of the Paris prefecture of national police, enforce them. Paris spends $2 million a year to care for the bridges. The city is charged with preserving the stone embankments, declared world heritage sites by UNESCO. But who manages the water and its flood fringe?

Esselinck's *péniche*, the *Alma*, is moored by the Pont de Sully. Within the space of a few yards up the bank, a half dozen jurisdictions overlap: the VNF levies taxes; Parks and Gardens patrols what is planted, but Streets and Garbage cleans up any mess; river cops keep order within shouting distance of the bank, but then regular gendarmes take over. And the city of Paris sends a demand for lodging tax to the mailbox on shore.

Not that this is new. In *Sentimental Education*, set in the 1840s, Flaubert wrote: " 'But do you imagine the press is free? Do you imagine we are free?' said Deslauriers passionately. 'When I think that you have to fill in anything up to twenty-eight forms just to keep a boat on the river, I feel like going off to live among the cannibals.' "

The difference is that when Essenlinck and Bour settled on the Seine, that was like living among the cannibals. Now authorities are demanding to see all twenty-eight forms properly filled in, stamped, and, above all, paid for. From eccentric marginals who melted into the decor, river people are getting to be seen as a privileged few, enjoying a luxurious free ride.

"The VNF has said flatly they want to see survival of the richest so the river moorings produce as much tax as they possibly can," said Esselinck, eyebrows bristling under a shining bald pate. "That's what gets me. First I'm some kind of gypsy, a squatter not worth thinking about. Suddenly, I'm a Rockefeller who spits money. I may be worth more, but I earn the same."

By the time new rules came into effect, the character of the quais was changing. Yves Bour bought the *Elza* for the equivalent of four thousand dollars in the early 1970s. Now, with rights to a scarce mooring spot, a *péniche* might bring a half million. The temptation is great for a first-generation boat person, no longer happy to be penniless and no longer twenty years old.

Accountants who rule the river decided that boats should be taxed like apartments, assessed at so much per square foot, comparable to land space near where they moor. They wanted about twelve thousand dollars a year for a hole in the water. Owners point out that apartments do not sink when they spring leaks. Land people are not liable to turn a key one morning and discover they've got to spend a year's salary on a new engine. In winter, apartment dwellers do not have to pole their way home in a dinghy.

Old-time boat people feel akin to homesteaders who fight Indians and dig out stumps only to find that they've got to sell out to some rich carpetbagger who can afford to pay an outrageous property tax. Getting started was not exactly easy.

Esselinck hit upon the idea while walking past a For Sale sign on a *péniche* near the Ile Saint-Louis. He stopped at the neighboring boat, Bour's, and asked about it. Bour warned him off the deal, the first step to a very close friendship. For months, Esselinck prowled docks in France and Holland looking for his boat. Finally, sent by a broker to a village in Belgium, he found the *Alma*.

"It was perfect—the lines, the space, the condition—and I loved it," he said. "Then I went to the engine compartment. The motor was huge, a monster, thirteen tons, pistons five feet high, sort of a cathedral designed by Jules Verne. It was something called a slow-cycle engine, and I'd never heard of it. I figured it was too old, too unwieldy to be reliable. Rats, I thought. This kills the deal."

Reluctant to give up the *Alma*, Esselinck decided to learn more about its bizarre power plant. He spent a long night hanging around mariners' bars in the area. The Brons *régime lent,* he discovered, was an antique Rolls-Royce of engines, infallible, unstoppable, liable to last through his grandson's lifetime. It idles at a hundred revolutions a minute, a tenth the normal speed. "There's only one still around," an old-timer told him. "It's in the *Alma,* but the owner will never part with it." The next morning, Esselinck forked over earnest money.

To allay lingering doubts, he set a condition that the captain deliver the boat in Paris. "That way I'd know for sure," he said. "If the guy hesitated, I knew he would be worried about the motor. He huddled with his wife for a minute and came back grinning. 'You know, we haven't been in Paris in twenty-five years, and we'd be thrilled,' the man said. 'Could we bring my wife's parents?' I had a boat."

For a week on the canals and rivers from Belgium, Esselinck learned how to work on a 1930 Brons motor. He also learned, for the first time, how to drive a *péniche.*

Like others in the rapidly growing New Captain tribe, he spent every spare franc on wiring, plumbing, painting, paneling and fittings. Unlike many, he got to know every bolt belowdecks. Once he took the *Alma* to the Brons factory in northern Holland. "They met me with open arms, possibly because of my beautiful Dutch first mate," he said. "The whole motor got rebuilt. Only one piece wasn't in stock, so they got out a lathe and made it."

It will be tougher next time. The factory has gone out of business. Hardly any modern mechanic has even heard of a Brons. "Come to think of it," Esselinck reflected, "if anything happens to me, I don't think there's anyone who knows how to start that engine. I suppose I'd better write it down somewhere."

∽∾∽∾∽∾

In those early days, Keystone Kaptains terrorized the Seine. Boat people, now the height of cool in laceless Top-Siders, were just getting started in the early 1970s. Few went through as much trouble as Esselinck. They could pick up a hulk in Amsterdam for nine hundred dollars, praying it would float. After a simple test aboard a little outboard, they could get a license. Then they barged down the Seine, side-swiping bridges and bouncing off walls.

Now settled communities cluster on the Seine in Paris. Arsenal, just inside the first lock of the Canal Saint-Martin, is popular with smaller boats. It is near the Bastille, on the site of a medieval cannon and powder factory that accidentally blew itself halfway to Lyon. The port is calm, protected from the Seine's waves and currents. But it is almost part of the city around it.

The Port des Champs-Elysées shelters fifty boats, from the footbridge to the Gare d'Orsay to the Pont de l'Alma. Some have been there a quarter century, seldom venturing out to cruise, and then coming home quickly. One has a rose garden to rival the Bagatelle's. Another has a movie star.

Other boats are tied up in the center of Paris, some as permanently as mooring goes and others in a precarious state. Farther downstream, a line of boats are comfortably installed along the Bois de Boulogne and the banks of Neuilly. What they lack in city lights and excitement, they make up for in tree-shaded country comfort.

Altogether, perhaps six hundred converted *péniches* and other large houseboats dock around Paris, two hundred of them in the city itself. But the early thrill of taking the pad for a spin is getting to be rare. A new class of owners lives on the water.

"If I had to guess," Esselinck said, "I'd say 10 percent of the boats are capable of moving, and 10 percent of those are owned by people who can pilot them."

Like New Yorkers, boat people link spirits only when faced with common calamity. In the 1970s, the calamity was Paris mayor Jacques Chirac. Before Chirac, boats tied up wherever they found space, and the Seine throbbed with life. "I don't want Paris to look like Hong Kong," the mayor announced one morning; he levied taxes and laid out stringent rules for permits. War raged. Petitions went around. Boats carried banners reading, *"Sans péniches, Paris pleur-niche."* Without barges, Paris weeps.

Early in 1979, barges blocked the Seine. Boat people simply cranked up their engines and chugged their living rooms out into the river. Hardly a Maginot Line, the ragtag chain nonetheless made its point. Vikings were one thing. But voters? Besides, whose jurisdiction was it anyway? Chirac backed down, and the boats headed off in convoy for a raucous party on the Ile d'Amour. Soon afterward, the boats that were only "tolerated" before finally had official standing.

No one could define *official standing*, of course. As one old-timer put it, with a textbook Gallic shrug: "This is the typical solution in France. Artistic vagueness." And that's what the crisis of the 1990s is about. Things may be getting less vague. Then again, don't count on it.

∞∞∞∞∞

Boat people are not wildly hospitable. Most see passersby as grizzly bears watch visitors to their zoo. They are on display, no doubt about it, but it is unhealthy to get too close. They imagine an expanse of water between themselves and shore, the way a garden fence, or at least an apartment wall, would shield them if they lived in more normal quarters. Too many people assume that if boat people are outdoors, they are fair game for conversation. This can engender violent defensive posture.

Those who are normally in the public eye can be especially edgy. Actor Pierre Richard, the tall blond with one black shoe, scurries furtively from scratched red Porsche or chopped Harley to Dutch barge. It is no time to ask for autographs.

Even we normal people are affected. I had no idea how fierce this phenomenon could get until I heard feet clomping on my deck one afternoon. Up top, I found a beefy-faced lout sitting at my table, grinning toward shore.

"What the fuck are you doing here?" I asked politely.

"I'm having my picture taken," he replied.

"Get off," I said. My gentler nature has often invited strangers aboard for photos, but this was not the way to do it. As his group of pals fumbled with the camera lens, he made no move to leave. By the time I found the sharpened gaff, he got up to go. In a voice thick with sarcasm, he said, "Thanks." I wondered how many years I'd get for puncturing a porkish passerby.

Some of us are a lot nicer. Eric Tempe, a real-estate appraiser whose boat is off the tourist track in Neuilly, is thrilled when people admire *Le Flâneur*. It is not your typical houseboat. Back during the last twitches of craziness after the Roaring Twenties, a loaded American couple fitted out a floating palace called *My Dream*. From ornate bow to teak-trimmed stern, it ran to 240 feet, too long for any locks but the Seine's. It was built about 1850, its hull in wood covered by thin metal, one of the first barges to use steam instead of horses on a towpath. Turbines turned a side-mounted paddle wheel. Converted to luxury, it had double spiral staircases leading to a grand piano. A vast galley and dining room gave onto a sort of ballroom, and rows of large guest cabins were equipped with fancy baths.

During World War II, Germans melted the engine into artillery shells. The boat was a mess. And the American couple, too old to start all over, didn't know what do with it. At the time, they were selling their building on the Ile Saint-Louis and had to evict a friendly French couple who had lived there for years. The couple received the boat as a present. With a rudimentary diesel engine, they got it to move. The new owners were Eric Tempe's parents, and he was born on board, the hard way.

Eric's Bohemian-hearted mother wanted to give birth on the Seine, beyond Paris, where nature starts. She did not count on trouble. Her son came out backward, choking on the placenta. He could not breathe, and fumes from the oil lamp did not help. The doctor, short of equipment, had nowhere to plug in what he had. He filled both brass basins of a guest bathroom, one with cold water and the other with hot. He dunked Eric repeatedly into the sinks, first one, then another, to shock his system. It worked.

Today, Eric is a large, friendly fellow given to tweeds, like a P. G. Wodehouse English gentleman who happens to be French. When I asked if being born on the water marked him as a *marinier*, he chuckled. "Actually," he said, "I get seasick." For years, the boat sat moldering on its moorings. In 1985, however, Eric was overcome by nostalgia and a draw toward the Seine. First he had a boat yard chop off a chunk toward the stern to bring the boat to the standard 126 feet. Then he poured his weekends, and his fortune, into restoring the thing.

One July evening Eric threw a coming-out party for *Le Flâneur*. Lights shined at the Temple of Love monument on the Ile de la Grande Jatte opposite his mooring at Neuilly.

Saddles of lamb browned on barbecues. Friends slaved in the galley over platters of delicacies. Several dozen people talked happily in the balmy air. Eric walked around pouring wine and smiling. Finishing the job would likely take the rest of his life. That night, he was in no hurry.

≈≈≈≈

If you establish communication, anyone who lives on the river has stories to tell. In *The Seine*, Julian More collected some recent quaiside classics. A *clochard* named Napoléon who loved to cook tumbled into the river and died of the cold when he leaned too far gathering water for stew. Jacques Rougerie and his friend Violaine returned to the *Saint-Paul* to find a giant in their bed, neither jolly nor green but stinking and drunk. Pierre Richard had succeeded in persuading a loony not to jump from the Pont de la Concorde until a neighbor shouted, "Idiot, you can't even kill yourself properly"; the guy tried, but, luckily, the neighbor was right.

My friend Paul kept me up half the night telling stories before selling me *La Vieille*. His least favorite is about the time he came home late one night and fell in the river.

To reach the boat, one leaps from the quai onto the barge to which it is tied. This is simple enough for a young goat with strong ankles. But it was icy, and the water was rushing fast. Paul leaped before he looked. He plunged currentward into the treacherous space between the barge's steel hull and the slippery stone quai. Someone might have helped, but he was too embarrassed to yell. Half in the Seine, he caught a tire hanging from the barge and hauled himself to safety.

≈≈≈≈

We've had no wet humans since, but there was the tragic and mysterious episode of Grabowski, a possible case of cat overboard. Grabowski, née Princess, showed up from California and went through eight lives within the first month. There was that night she dropped over the side and, somehow, extracted herself from the water. Other experiences followed. Long used to puny Marin mice, she emerged victorious against bodybuilder river rodents. Until she got her sea legs, she spent hours under her favorite car. Routinely, she squeezed out of the embrace of passing tourists. Yet again, she fell in and got out.

Late one night, Jeannette and I brought Grabowski in and went to bed in the aft cabin. It was full moon, and she was restless. Around 1 A.M., the cat made her usual escape. We can only assume that she leaped onto the bunk and, stepping on each of our heads for elevation, nosed open a porthole. That is how she always did it. But we were asleep at the time. At dawn, I woke up with an uneasy feeling. Grabowski was gone.

First, we looked around casually, confident that she was merely playing bullfighter with small animals on the quai. Then we got worried. Olivier reported that she had visited him on the bobbing red cork behind us, something she'd never done. He had called her, but she took off. Beyond that, there were no clues.

The search grew desperate. Jeannette taped posters to every vertical surface within a mile of the boat. We visited local vets, put ads in the paper and consulted the odd seer. For days, the phone rang. No, one lonely old woman said, she had not seen the cat. But she loved her own three dozen cats and wanted to recount the life story of each of them.

Unconfirmed sightings sent us prowling up distant back streets, calling the cat's name. For a week, we were embroiled in the Romanian underground, charging around Paris trying to find a mysterious young asylum seeker who had allegedly found the cat on the Champs-Elysées and taken her home in a sack. The guy's friend had seen a poster and called to report. The friend's description went beyond details we had given. He refused a reward. But nothing materialized except a request for us to sponsor his visa.

Boat owners tried to let us down gently. Everyone knew of catnappers who infested the quai, eager to pick up a low-cost gift for a girlfriend or a midnight snack. For weeks, at night, Jeannette haunted the local parks, calling the cat's name, a touching Madwoman of Chaillot. I lurked in the background, watching her back, anxious not to lose more than a cat.

Someone must know what happened to Grabowski, but we don't. Maybe the river took her. Maybe it was some piece of slime who has her still. Maybe she'll be back, after she gets tired of checking out the secret life of the Seine.

∽∾∽∾∾∽

Boat people like the idea of having no address—"Well, you go five boats down from the bridge, look for a big barge with man-eating geraniums, and cross the bow"—unless they want a pizza delivered. Several intrepid pizzerias deliver to the quai, in fact, but no one ever finds the right boat before the pepperoni congeals. It can get worse.

One Sunday, a woman flailed her arms at me and shouted in German. Her companion was curled into a ball near *La Vieille*, moaning something horrible. A crowd was gathering; no one knew what was wrong, but everyone agreed this was serious. The guy might not make it.

On my cordless phone, I pressed 18 for the *pompiers*. Paris firemen are swift and professional, as a rule. They've got to be with so much priceless old wood real estate at risk.

They save a lot of lives, and I was sure they'd save this anguished German.

A reassuring voice answered on the second ring. It asked the address.

"No address," I began. "It's on the quai just down the steps off the bridge . . ."

"There has to be an address," the voice said.

"But I'm calling from a boat. No address. If the driver comes down the quai, we'll show him . . ."

"One must have an address."

"Okay, okay," I said, beginning to panic for the guy. The moans had gotten louder but then subsided. He seemed to be losing consciousness. "It's on the river by the Cour de la Reine."

"What number?"

"Look, this man may be dying. There is no address. He is still very sick." By then my cool had gone completely, and I was talking louder in hopes he might pick up the urgency.

The voice began a haughty disquisition, outlining three points of Cartesian logic that would show beyond doubt that it was impossible to fall ill beyond range of a house number.

"Are you going to send an ambulance or give me a lecture?" I said, hard and angry.

"You do not have reason to speak to me in that way," the voice said, warming itself up for another peroration, this time on the respect due French firemen.

"Listen," I said, dropping down to his calm tone, "if this man dies while you are being a *con*, you are going to be the most famous fireman in France."

The ambulance was dispatched. Paramedics did something that helped, and I assume the guy lived. For a long time afterward, I tried to be sure I'd have my medical emergencies at the office.

This sort of river life is not for everyone. One morning, I had a visit from a friend on the quai, the Old Mariner. He was walking wounded, struck down by a party that lasted too long the night before. I poured coffee, and we sat back in the healing breeze off the water.

"This is the life," he said, or something similar in French. "The only problem with living on a boat is women, *les bonnes femmes*. The constant insecurity makes them crazy. Women need some stability in their lives, and there is nothing more unstable than a boat. In the end, they go."

His eyes glazed as he eased back in the canvas chair, flipping through the mental portraits of women in his life who had gotten crazy and moved on. A few women came to mind who did not fit that judgment. But the Old Mariner was in no mood to argue.

But it also suits some temperaments just fine. Olivier's, for instance. Once I happened to ask him he if had seen a Titian exhibit at the Grand Palais, a few steps away. "I don't go to museums anymore," replied Olivier, a painter. "I don't show at exhibitions. Art is not what's in a building. Life is art, nature is art, the river is art." Now I know how this sounds on paper. We've all met those guys, unfit to clip Titian's toenails, who denounce art for the effect of it. But this is Olivier. To him, life is art, nature is art, the river is art.

One night I poured him a drink, after he rolled out of bed to help me dislodge an errant telephone pole, and he recited his poems for half an hour. I did not know he wrote poems, and, in fact, he didn't. They were made up in his head and committed to memory. Paper, like extra socks, was encumbering overweight. Days later, he found me a poem he had written down. It was beautiful, a simple little allegory about a rat named Cismé who explained why rodents, or people, ought to dump their biases and get along.

On a summer morning, the red cork putted past. Olivier stood one-legged on the port gunwale, steering with his right foot. "I go to take my shower," he called. The port visitors' shower was only a two-minute walk from his mooring spot, but by quirk of whimsy Olivier was taking the river. Twenty minutes later, he passed by the other way, his bow squirming with three young women to whom he had not been previously introduced; he was gone for a day. God knows.

After a while, we got used to a class of people known as FOO—friends of Olivier. FOO-birds. Late one evening, I saw a young couple on the quai, obviously pondering directions. They were dwarfed by an enormous tuba. I didn't wait for the question. "Over there," I said, pointing to the red cork.

Another night, a tiny sailboat struggled past, pushed by a wheezing outboard and all but obscured by the nine people clutching its rails and stays. FOO-birds. Olivier's disciples often whiled away sunny afternoons learning his specialty: riding a moped while standing in the seat. Black-belt FOO-birds got to try a jump off the launch ramp. At night, they occasionally sang off-key until three in the morning. I was sad when he moved his boat, but I got more sleep.

∽∽∽∽∽

Whether the Seine manufactures characters or merely attracts them, the result is the same. My friend Charlie the Belgian boatmeister qualifies on both counts. His specialty is finding a hard way to do an easy job. For years, he worked on selling *péniches* in America, cutting them in two for easier handling and welding them together at the other end. Knowing Charlie, my guess is that he was stymied on discovering that U.S. mailboxes are too small for *péniche* halves. He finally found a way to box them up for a mere thirty thousand dollars in freight charges, not counting reassembly.

Charlie does some good work. He just likes a challenge. Once I needed a gangway for getting onto the barge we cross to reach *La Vieille*. Paul's story of falling in had stuck with me. Charlie designed a structure involving ramps, wheels, pulleys, flyovers, flaps and a few geegaws Rube Goldberg would have rejected as impractical. Instead, we stuck a short plank under a metal brace, and it works fine.

But there may be no more gentle or generous soul than ol' Charlie. Once I lamented that we had no time for firemen in wetsuits to clean the props before taking *La Vieille* for a cruise. We would just have to trust our luck. I went out and returned to find Charlie in his underpants, sopping wet, disinfecting himself with a bottle of Chivas Regal.

"I got them cleared," he reported, "but then the cops came by and made me get out of the river." He was indignant. "They told me I wasn't allowed to swim in the Seine, and I should know better at my age." That was what got him. "At my age," he muttered, a second time.

There are people of Charlie's age who would not be caught dead exploring the Seine's depths in scanty briefs, without so much as goggles. But barge people are a proud lot. Middle-aged bourgeois gentlemen start their day by flicking lint off a sleeve and stepping into an elevator. Charlie came ashore via *sauterelle*—a very long metal pole on a pivot to which one clings for dear life and launches oneself for a lift ashore, like swinging on a gate. It ain't dignified, but it beats dog-paddling.

〜〜〜〜〜

For years, I had been hearing about a front-rank character, ʾhe guy who owned the *bateaux-mouches*. He lived on a boat ʾs base of operations a few bridges down, and I wanted to ʾm.

The term *bateau-mouche* originated last century in Lyon, where little boats carried passengers on the Rhône and the Saône. They were built in a sector called Mouche, and the name stuck because the first engines whined like river flies, *mouches*. For a while, the company operated a concession in Paris.

This was a noble tradition. The first *bateaux-mouches* were small, with bird names like *Swallow* and *Sparrow*. They operated like the *métros*, carrying commuters from one end of Paris to the other. During 1900, a world's fair year, 39 million people rode the Seine. The service died out in 1934. Thirty years ago, Jean Bruel revived the old tradition in a new way, to carry tourists in a loop around the river. His tour boats have evolved into a fleet of giant, violently lighted cattle boats that make a lot of money. In 1992, 4.5 million passengers cruised the Seine, and much of that business is Bruel's.

The big boats' success was baffling. On the river, they're known widely as *bateaux-moches*, meaning ugly. Visitors can see the same sights on the Bateaux Parisiens, the Vedettes du Pont-Neuf, or others, including the Bat-O-Bus, which can cost half as much. Being far smaller, these others allow you to board without any mooing or baaing. Rather than a droning, witless recording that leaves you with a headache, live humans narrate the river.

Bateau-mouche dinner cruises offer questionable fare to a crowd, on a gaudy, glassed-in space vessel. For twenty francs less, a couple can dine amid crystal, linen, brass and varnished old wood, looked after by an accomplished chef, on the *Don Juan*.

You can't really see a lot of the postcard monuments from river level. Instead, you imagine your own magical city in its original setting. The Seine reveals her secrets on her own terms, a few at a time. For this, you may not want speakers blaring in French, English, German, Italian, Spanish, Pashto and Abkhazian, all describing what you can't see anyway. At night, when the charm is seeing people on quais and in boats, the big lights freeze life to a standstill. Stone is sharply outlined. The people, shielding their eyes, have no faces.

Yet I watched tourists flock to the monster boats, while the little ones went half empty. *Bateau-mouche* captains cruised the river like they owned it, blasting reflector lights into the homes of the rich and powerful along the Seine. The guy in charge had to swing a lot of weight. He took care of himself. In 1984, when *péniches* blocked the river to protest a contract given to a large company to haul wheat in convoys, Bruel could not persuade bargees to let his tour boats pass. To show solidarity with the striking independents, he handcuffed himself to one of their tugboats.

Bruel, I was told, did not like to see people. I asked a researcher to get me an appointment. After a week of unanswered calls, she barged into his office. He was about sixty, with dissolute eyes, she said, the sort of guy cast in old films as an Alabama farmer who took frequent refreshment after exposing his neck to the sun. "Why should I see some journalist when I can be interviewed by a pretty young thing like yourself?" he asked, leering. He urged her to stay. Finally, Bruel agreed to talk to me by phone the next morning at 9:30.

I walked over to call at close range in case he decided he also could actually see me. Considering the thousand times I had been importuned by people seeking directions to his obnoxious boats, I figured it was only fair. Besides, this guy owed me. My own boat was scarred by repairs after a *bateau-mouche* sideswiped it. Another time, a captain speeding well over the limit headed straight for *La Vieille* when Paul, the former owner, signaled for him to slow down.

Bruel's assistant said he had gone out, leaving no message. No problem, I said. Could he please tell me how many boats were in the fleet and how many passengers they carried? "I can't answer that," the man replied. But I could count boats and seats myself, I said. "Mr. Bruel does not want us to give out any information, even the most obvious." Could I make an appointment? "Mr. Bruel prefers to speak by telephone."

An employee who overheard the conversation tried to contain a laugh. She knew her boss. "Here," she said, handing me a brochure from a pile with pictures of Bruel's ten boats. "The eleventh one is not on there." Most can carry a thousand people, she said, but they almost never do. They are busiest about 9 P.M., but they run until 11 P.M. That was enough for basics.

Perseverance would have gotten me face-to-face with Bruel, but I lost my taste for it. These days, when someone asks how to find the *bateaux-mouches* I direct them to the Bateaux Parisiens, one bridge farther down.

∞∞∞∞∞

Before long on the Seine, I saw how the river could turn perfectly normal people into raving eccentrics. When a sleek hull slipped past at speed, guests on my deck gazed in admiration. I scurried below to catch the eggs that I knew would come flying out of the refrigerator in its wake. While they looked at the lights on the Pont Alexandre III, I puzzled over the *Richelieu* passing by, a floating engine with a steering wheel on top, and wondered where it had put those sand barges it had just pushed past.

I learned not to get too cocky. One minute I'd be sitting

up top smoking on a big cigar and exchanging smiles with people walking past. The next, I'd be crawling around among *La Vieille*'s privates, swearing, with grease in my hair. If the life is often privileged, boat dwellers pay for it, and few people brim with sympathy over their plight.

One crisp evening, a taxi driver brought Jeannette and me back home after a long trip. "You live here?" he asked, taking in the scene. "You're lucky." I checked out the ducks, the tower, and my neighbors rocking gently on their ropes. He's right, I thought. We are lucky. Then Jeannette yelled from inside, "Did you cut off the power?" It was one of those small lessons nature likes to teach about electricity and water. We spent Saturday night with candles. On Sunday, we ran an extension cord into Philippe's boat. We found the short on Monday.

That was nothing, but it gets worse. A nearby neighbor just hauled his *péniche* out of the water for a routine check. It will cost him one hundred thousand dollars in metalwork to stay afloat. I don't want to be around when his next visitor informs him of his good fortune.

On the river, I found, modern times are an illusion. My boat is equipped with the whole business: modem, fax, call-forwarding, VHF, VCR, PCP. Jeannette recently spent all morning trying to phone me but got an inexplicable busy signal. Finally, she called Jean-Jacques at the port office. He delivered the message in his dugout pirogue, the way Henry Morton Stanley's porters used to come tell him what the jungle drums just said.

In time, I picked up some secrets. Like France itself, the trick is not to look too closely at the river. You step back, let myth and romance blur reality into an impressionistic flight, and suddenly there is something exciting that exists nowhere else. When the sun starts to drop, or rise again, a good place to feel this is by the Eiffel Tower or Les Invalides, where there is plenty of open water to reflect the pinks and oranges. When it gets dark, head for the Pont Sully, where lights off the Quai d'Anjou melt into gold in the rippling channel.

Something else I learned: Water slaps against a plastic boat; against wood, it laps. For most of the year, I can drop off to sleep with the Seine gently gurgling in my ear. Not all the time, of course. Occasionally in winter, floating ice sounds like it is tearing off the planking, one board at a time. When the current races under the hull, you wonder if it is actually under.

But in those calm months, after midnight when the boats stop and the Seine is calm as a cup of soup, you listen for something else. A monster lives below. Honest. How else do you explain a sudden wave at dawn, powerful enough to clear the shelves of a thirty-ton boat? Every so often, *La Vieille* pitches before my alarm goes off. I hurry on deck to check the river. Nothing upriver. Nothing down. The locks are shut. It's the monster.

I have several theories. It could be Jean-Luc Ness, a distant cousin of Nessie over in Scotland. More likely, it is a freshwater sea snake that escaped from the Gauls' temple at the source and is now quite large after two thousand years of eating French garbage. I have yet to see Sequana's super serpent, I must admit. But every time I throw enchilada remains out the galley porthole, *La Vieille* pitches mysteriously the next morning.

9 *Good Neighbors*

THE GUY WHO MOORS next to Jillie Faraday is seldom home, given to long business trips. When she noticed a man skulking away from his door, she watched closely. In pelting-down rain, he pulled his hat over his eyes and fiddled with a large bulge under his raincoat. Then he glanced around and took off at a run. Jillie followed. The man scampered up the steps, gaining. She sprinted after him. On the Concorde bridge, she grabbed the suspect by his collar and whirled him around. "Hello, Jillie," her neighbor said, wondering what had gotten into her.

She would do it again, as would he for her. Paris is not known for neighborliness, but things are different on the Seine. Boat people are like frontier settlers who don't want a lot of neighbors but would not do without them. The art is finding the right balance between watching out for the commonweal and minding your own business.

Some loners want no part of village life. For years, the

retired English general next to Jillie showed almost no sign of life. But each night, exactly at eleven o'clock, she heard his door open. A bottle smashed and glass hit the river in splashes. A second followed, then a third. Finally, after a long *whisssh*, she heard a deep sigh. Then silence for another twenty-four hours. Nearby, an eighty-year-old count emerged only after his neglected hull corroded away, and firemen hurried up to refloat it.

Others are best kept at some distance. The river is a fine place to party, and boat people can be amusing hosts. Tourists might wander down the quai headed back to the hotel and reappear days later with a headache and a smile. This wears thin when guests come and go by stumbling across your bow.

But the river binds everyone into communities. This goes beyond borrowing a jar of Grey Poupon or a pipe wrench. On a large scale, people share the watch on sneaky authorities. When some official tries to cut back docking space or quintuple the fees, the alarm is spread in *L'Escargot Qui Flotte*, the floating snail, a newsletter put out by the Fédération des Associations de Défense de l'Habitat Fluvial. Closer to home, an extra set of eyes can deliver you from calamity.

One boatowner finished a nasty divorce and left on a six-week trip to Brazil. His ex-wife had been forced to hand over the keys to the *péniche* they had restored together. As soon as his cab pulled away, she slipped onto the boat and got in by breaking a window. She closed every drain and opened every water tap. By some miracle, the man's flight was put off until the next day. He came home to find the boat awash. Maybe someone would have seen it listing and called the *pompiers*. Maybe not.

∾∾∾∾∾

Jillie moved onto her Dutch *tjalk*, the *Waeckende Boey*, in 1969 when the quai was different. She bought it from my neighbor Philippe, who had found it in Holland. Back then, eleven boats moored permanently at the Port des Champs-Elysées, run by the Touring Club de France. Most were proper yachts. When a passing boat stopped, the port captain emerged in perfectly pressed white ducks and blue blazer with gold buttons stamped "TCF." He bent at the waist to kiss each lady's hand, including those that had handled the ropes at the last lock, and passed around flutes of champagne. It is not totally different today. When visitors arrive, the guy in charge is usually wearing a shirt.

In the 1970s, the speed limit was raised to four miles an hour, making waves in port. *Bateaux-mouches* made life miserable for small boats, and most moved on. Since *péniches* were not permitted to dock, the quai was nearly empty. Philippe fitted out a comfortable Freycinet, and spent years lurking under a nearby bridge. Finally, he painted his barge white, a *péniche* in yacht's clothing, and slipped into port. The ice broken, others settled in around him.

At the time, Jillie was married to a Canadian diplomat, who was transferred to Ottawa. Three years after moving in, they had only a few months to sell out and move. Only one person answered their ad, a wealthy antique dealer named Michel. River living was not done then in Paris.

"We asked 140,000 francs, only what we paid for it, but Michel knew we had no other offers," Jillie said. "Being an antique dealer, he insisted on bargaining. Every day, he worked on us. For three weeks, every day. Finally, he got the price down to 90,000. We were desperate, and he knew it. Out of the blue, we got a call from a couple in Belgium who saw the ad somewhere. They didn't dispute the price. When we told Michel it was sold, he called us every name he could think of—filthy foreigners, the lot. He offered us double, but it was too late. He had a fortune in antiques. One cabinet could have paid for the boat. But he had to bargain."

In Canada, Jillie and her husband pined for their *tjalk*. They pored over yachting magazines and finally located one in Cannes. As they were about to fly over to close the deal, the owner phoned. Michel had bought it. That was the *Suki*, which, once refitted and restored, was a showpiece of the Seine, among the world's most beautiful old wood yachts.

In the mid-1980s, Jillie heard that the people who had bought the *Waeckende Boey* were ready to sell again. It was in Toulouse, furnished in Swedish modern and painted an ugly brown. She went to see it. "You don't realize how attached you get to your boat, how much it is a part of you," she said. "After I saw it, I spent the whole afternoon vomiting."

She wanted to bring it back to Paris, but the quai was jammed. It was one of those French situations. Port officials liked Jillie and the boat and wanted to find room. But rules were rules; the limit had been reached. They could not say yes. The solution was simple enough: no one said anything at all. Jillie drove the boat up from Toulouse—it took six weeks—and tied up near her old mooring. She has been around since, den mother of the neighborhood.

∽∽∽∽∽

One morning, I dropped in on Jillie and found her free. She was talking on only one phone. As I waited, she punched hold several times to dispense with other calls. "I have the pope on the other line," she told someone, laughing. It is possible she wasn't kidding. Jillie scribbled "Do U want a coffee?" in Magic Marker on her marble table. I nodded, and she moved to the tidy little galley with the receiver on her shoulder. This gave me time to explore.

The *Waeckende Boey* is an advertisement for boat living, all funky wood and cozy cushions. A half dozen rooms climb up and down split levels. Books line every vertical surface, Virginia Woolf hard by *Narrow Boat Painting*. Aft, a deep blue enamel wood stove is set against Delft tiles. Up some steps, on a shelf, a goldfish in a bowl fights for space with a mountain of cassettes, from Mozart to Marley. Forward, there is room for Jillie's son to disappear for days.

The low-slung hull is forest green, white, and varnished wood. The deck is a garden. Altogether, it is as much a boat as a house. Once I ran into Jillie up the Seine. It is a kick to go somewhere and find a neighbor, front porch and all. Little persuasion is required to get her on the river.

One morning Olivier yelled across that some American person wanted to talk to me. It was a New York person, in fact, and he asked about renting my boat. I told him it was not for rent.

"Maybe when you see what it is . . ." he yelled from the quai. He looked as if he had no doubt. I met him on Philippe's boat. With a flourish, he handed me a card reading, "ABC News." He was a *20/20* producer. "Diane Sawyer will be interviewing Baryshnikov on the Seine, and we need a boat." There was something about the way he said it.

"Sawyer?" I said, scratching my head. "Kalashnikov? I'm sorry, I don't rent my boat. Try Jillie."

That evening as the sun dropped, I watched the *Wae-ckende Boey* drift by with Sawyer working over the supple Russian. It looked like a great party would follow. Ah well.

෪෪෪෪෪

"We don't see the bodies we used to," Jillie said when I asked her how things had changed over the years. "We used to see them all the time. Once, I was washing windows on a spring day. The sun was out, and it was beautiful. A friend yelled down, 'Jillie, there's a body,' and, hardly reacting, I said, 'What, another one?' "

A departed resident, a retired British marine, used to strut around the quai and make frequent reference to courage he displayed in one hairy situation or another. It got to be a joke but made his reputation as a local macho man. One night a body washed up against his bow, and he went green. Without a word, he went inside and would not come out.

Jillie's friend Max secured the cadaver with a boat hook and called the river cops. "They could be quite silly, the police," she said. "They asked for the victim's nationality, and Max said he didn't know, the man did not say."

Nowadays, even the live ones don't talk much. Faces change frequently. Colorful old-timers slip away, replaced by professional people with serious things on their mind. But you can still count on help. Not long ago, my power went out in the middle of the night. As I stood with flashlight, cursing by the big fuse box bolted to the quaiside wall, a stranger appeared with the fuse I lacked.

Such cooperation does not always come with a smile. At 6:30 one morning, my house and I dropped in on an Australian woman two boats away. We had lived near one another for seven years but had never met. This visit was not planned. As *La Vieille* was leaving on a cruise, I asked a crew member if the stern line was free. He said it was, but it wasn't. I jumped onto Philippe's *péniche* to untie us while the current moved the boat downstream. Jacques had to find a way to get me back on board.

La Vieille drifted backward toward the woman's boat. I crossed her bow to try a leap at my stern. She came up in a bathrobe and a foul mood. Someone threw her a line, which she secured. Snapping orders, she instructed me on how to proceed. There was a better way, but I was not about to argue. I hopped over my rail, rope in hand, and she pushed us off. As she went below, she made an unconscious hand gesture, like a *boules* player throwing a lead ball backward. Or like someone shaking filth off of fingers. Who could blame her? Later, we laughed it off together.

∞∞∞∞∞

On the first day of 1994, after biblical rains swelled the Seine and a dam gave way on the Yonne, all of us found ourselves in the same boat. The quai was awash in three feet of water, treacherous with an eddying current. A day's drive from Paris, I phoned Philippe. He had already pumped my bilges and adjusted my moorings. Neighbors had assembled a rag-tag little fleet of dinghies. The next afternoon, I hollered from shore. Philippe rowed over in a yellow tub and left for an appointment. I rowed back with the current, a piece of cake. Later, heading over to get Philippe, it wasn't so easy.

I stood in the bow and paddled, Cajun swamp style. Swirling water spun me sideways, and I rocked precariously. A crowd of louts on the upper quai above—land people— jeered derision. I reached shallow water where I should have hopped out. But the hip boots that had lain moldering in the forepeak were three sizes too small. To general merriment, Jacques and Bernard splashed out to help.

Only my self-esteem was in peril. Anyone would have helped. Jean-Luc of the *Banco*, for instance, showed up a moment later with fisherman's waders up to the armpits of his hand-stitched suit. Holding his briefcase high, he simply walked across the water, Jesus-style.

When I got my own waders, it was a snap. Back home, police would have sealed the area with Day-Glo tape to protect public servants from getting sued. Not here. We simply drove our cars onto the sidewalk, climbed into rubber-wear and walked into the Seine. That night, I dressed for a fancy reception at the nearby Crillon Hotel, and wondered if they had a wader checkroom. Probably not.

This went on for weeks. One Sunday I returned to *La Vieille* to find that rising water had worked loose a floating wood barrier that, in theory, deflected debris. It had taken my bow line with it. And, loose in the water, it was sawing through Philippe's lines. Had it gone unnoticed, our boats would have been swept downriver and over the Suresnes dam. But the neighborhood watch was out. A posse had been at work for three hours, chest deep in the freezing water, to tie down the barrier. My boat was saved not only by Philippe, Olivier, Jacques and Bernard but also by the guy on the next boat who had not smiled in three years.

∾∾∾∾∾

On those rare occasions when everyone gets together to play, the port is not your average Paris *quartier*.

On the longest day of the year, few motorists on the Pont Alexandre III noticed the pavement reverberating under their wheels. It was the summer solstice, and Seine people were celebrating La Fête de la Musique in their dank stone cavern under the bridge. The musty vault was done up like a Buenos Aires tango bar.

At the appointed hour, 9:30 P.M., a jazzish combo rumbled "A-Train" through the room as a few people stood around looking awkwardly French. Some old folks sat in silence. A few kids cavorted. Dockside politicians made the rounds. Mystery guests looked around nervously, wondering what they've gotten themselves into. By 10:30, they had figured it out.

A guy named Hugo was sparking fire from a Paraguayan

harp. His dark wife belted out a Chilean *cuenca*, and the place went nuts. Bernard, the quaikeeper, had ditched his greasy cap and polished his black hair to a glitter. He was wearing— I swear it—a tie. Not bothering with a partner, he struck flamenco poses and danced like Zorba the Cossack.

Just when things got going, the shift changed. New sounds whumped from a connecting hall, and someone speaking Frenglish evoked Shubby Shequer and bellowed: "Are you ready to rock and roll?" Everyone was. The moldy floor was a flash of blue Top-Siders, ostrich cowboy boots, sneakers and fruity Italian pumps. A Frenchman in a Harley-Davidson jacket, with gray hair tumbling from a broad-brimmed black hat, whirled a dazzling Dutch blonde, his wife. Little Bernard danced like an anaconda on amphetamines. He grabbed a tall woman and nearly decapitated her with jitterbug spins. No one was talking about gearboxes.

The pudgy lead singer, in red tam-o'-shanter and a double-breasted suit, slung his mike like an assault rifle. The bass man was deadpan in granny shades, sweat streaming down his neck. Moving from early Boss, they copied Beatles songs that no Beatle ever wrote. A dapper senior citizen in white shoes muttered pleasantly, *"Ça c'est de la merde."* An American lawyer in Levi's howled happily. It was not your average Paris party.

In the back, kids squealed over magic tricks. Outside, a young man mused in heavenly peace as he pissed into the Seine. I chatted with neighbors. The guy in the Harley jacket, just back from strange business in L.A., was setting up a bakery in Siberia. Bernard, out of dance partners, selected me. I felt a little awkward. The crowd didn't care, but I did not like the way Bernard's dog was looking at me.

It was, all in all, a wonderful day in the neighborhood.

Downstream

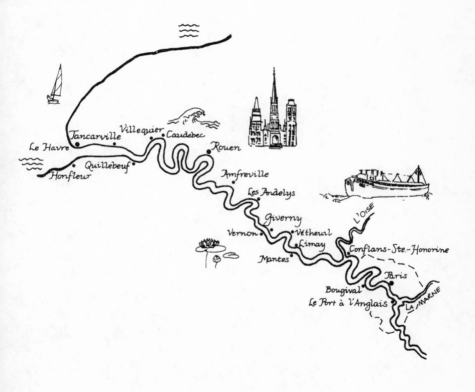

10 Conflans-Sainte-Honorine

On a Pentecost Sunday, Father Arthur baptized two babies, laying them on the velvet-draped altar under sunlight filtered through stained glass, against a backdrop of rich old paintings. His Saint Nicolas Chapel, scented with cedar and centuries, is like so many other French churches where traditions are timeless and foundations are set firmly in stone. Except that it floats.

Nicolas is the patron saint of river people, and the church is on a *péniche* named *Je Sers*. That means "I serve," and it does. Since 1932, the converted barge has brought solace to families who rarely venture onto dry land. In good times, people congregate aboard for marriages and christenings. During a pinch, they ask for help and pray for the odd miracle. These days, as bargees run ever shorter of blessings to count, Father Arthur and God are working overtime.

"These people's lives are getting to be impossible, and

nobody looks after them," Arthur Hervé told me, on a harried weekday morning. It was a routine day. He was up to his neck in papers in his cramped little office, with a bed in one corner and a washing machine in the other, in the forepeak of *Je Sers*. He was too busy for an unannounced visitor but too polite to throw me out. "The laws don't fit them. Politicians don't care about them. Maybe two thousand five hundred *péniches* are left in the country, ten thousand people at most. What's that to France? A little provincial village."

His metaphor was apt. The Seine is a long main street in a village with side roads that wind off in every direction. As in most French villages, its square is just outside the church. In Conflans-Sainte-Honorine, capital of the boat tribe, this is a patch of asphalt on the quai where people hang out to wait for a word with Father Arthur. More than their confessor, he is their Don Quixote. Some bargees, illiterate, cannot even read the fine print to find out what their troubles are.

"Every day, we have another case to fight," the priest said, seizing a paper from the mountain on his desk to make his point. "Someone gets a registered letter, but he's not here to pick up his mail. Legal actions, overdue bills, government stuff. After two or three tries, they figure he is not collecting it on purpose, and a judge rules against him." He flung the paper aside, in exasperation. "What can he do?"

Conflans is two towns. One is substantial, hilltop ramparts and medieval masonry on cobblestone lanes at the junction of the Seine and Oise rivers, forty miles downstream from Paris. The other is a community of floating clusters, *péniches* tied side-by-side, seven-deep, along a half-mile of quai. Neither of the two Conflans thinks much of the other.

Father Arthur understands boat people. They are what the French call "marginal," and he puts himself in that category. He is big and friendly, with silver hair and falling-off-the-nose reading glasses. When I asked his order, he laughed. "I don't believe in those kinds of reference. They make me nervous," he said. "I believe in God." He came to Saint Nicolas after four years as chaplain at the tough La Santé prison in Paris. "They threw me out," he said, with a touch of pride but no elaboration.

Patiently, he recited the litany every boat person knows, adding to what I'd heard in Saint-Mammès. After 1972, governments began turning their backs on the river. In the 1980s, a Communist transport minister named Charles Fiterman invested in the state railroads and expanded the highway system. Subsidies stacked freight rates against barges. If river transport was cheaper and less polluting, it was mostly a cottage industry in the hands of independents of mercurial temperament with no weight at the polls. What cargo there was seemed to end up with big operators who carry thousands of tons at a time. It has been an uneven battle.

"They have no lobby," Father Arthur said. "The *mariniers* thought they could survive on their own, that things would get better. But they need pressure groups to argue their case. In modern times, if you're not organized, you're finished."

During 1993, the twelve European Community members opened their borders, allowing freer movement of freight from one country to another. In principle, this should have been a shot in the arm for everyone. For French *péniches*, however, it was a shot in the head. Successive governments put off plans to lengthen and widen the locks on rivers that link France to the rest of Europe. Big boats headed up the Oise are stuck at Compiègne, a long way from Belgium. On the Marne, bastard-sized locks are longer than the Freycinet standard but too small for the next size.

"France has not seen its duty to expand its canals and make the commitment to revitalize the river system," Father Arthur said. He ticked off the steps needed to make French bargees competitive with Germans, Dutch and Belgians. "All of that has not been done," he said, with a grave shake of his head. "Who cares about the *mariniers*? People think that if they disappear, all the better. There is more room for pleasure boats."

The bargees' advocate-priest helps keep the village together. During 1988, when he came to *Je Sers*, 40 kids were baptized. In 1992, the total was 150. This is partly because families are now more sedentary. But even when working, they come home for baptisms. More likely it is as Father Arthur explains it: "I don't bother them with a lot of paperwork."

As if to illustrate his point, he scooped a handful of papers from his desk and handed them to me. They outlined someone's project to send several dozen idle *péniches* to Bangladesh to relieve flood victims. A noble thought, it would be a practical idea if anyone could get the barges halfway around the world. More than anything, it was an act of desperation.

Besides the church, *Je Sers* has a library and meeting hall in one large cabin. In another, mounds of donated old clothes await distribution to the desperate. Each Sunday, about three hundred people show up for mass, and thousands visit the boat during the course of a year. But no one knows the numbers.

Maybe a hundred of the *péniches* at Conflans-Sainte-Honorine are tied up for good, a floating retirement community of bargees who have given up the ghost. A rotating fleet of two to three hundred others base at Conflans between voyages, sometimes waiting two months for a new load. The last shipchandler shut down in 1991, and the repair shops are going fast, but there is still a boarding school for bargees' kids.

The life of this little community is logged on a bulletin board just off the gangway to *Je Sers*. It carries the usual notices from the Service de Navigation in Paris: obstructions, new rules on the water and administrative details. Lists of freight offers are posted regularly. Often, there are items for sale or functions about to happen. From time to time, hand-written items report on the river's secret life.

In July 1993, a single page entitled "Family News" singled out the *Léo-Mar*, owned by Léonard Willaert and his wife, Marianne. Then a few details: "Boat exploded in Lock #5, Canal du Nord. Léonard, 93 percent burned. Wife, half of body burned. Little daughter, Stéphanie, 5, escaped by miracle. Three other children under care in Douai."

Local charities had scraped together the equivalent of a thousand dollars for the family, it said, but a collection was being made by the Aumônerie Nationale de la Batellerie, the bargees' charity. The person to see, of course, was Father Arthur.

∞∞∞∞∞

Along the quai at Conflans, every captain knew what happened to the Willaerts and, even more, what was left unsaid by those few paragraphs of script. At lunchtime, I sat under the shade trees of L'Escale café waiting for an opening to talk with one of them. This is not easy. Barge people live their lives on public display, on the decks and corrugated cargo hatches of their slow-moving boats. But, when approached by *terriens*, land people, they tend to be as gregarious as hermits in a bad mood.

I fixed on a well-kept boat flying colorful banners from

its radio mast. A woman in a black dress was grilling meat on an open barbecue, its smoke curling among the laundry she had hung out to dry. The family gathered on the bridge to eat, and I could see only their feet under a blue plastic tarp lashed vertically for privacy. Finally, dog feet shuffled in a little canine dance. They had tossed him the leftovers and would be on the cheese. I waited for someone to come ashore.

When no one did, I approached the three men on the boat between the quai and my objective. "What is that flag?" I asked, pointing to the pennant of the Chambre de la Batellerie, the independent bargemen's professional association. One potbellied man in a black sleeveless undershirt just shrugged. "It's not because I'm standing here that I know everything in the world," he replied. Another, with Zapata mustache and grimy cap, cut fiercely into his sausage. He looked like he was auditioning for a film about Afghan madmen eviscerating a nosy tourist. I decided to wait some more.

Eventually, I called to the woman who was hanging more laundry. She yelled to her husband, and Marcel Rolland appeared, smiling. We talked for an hour.

"Léonard is dead," he said. "He was thirty-four. His wife will make it, but she was burned badly in the face, the feet—all over. The little girl happened to be fifteen meters toward the bow, or she would be gone, too. But she's in a terrible state of shock. Imagine, a five-year-old girl, to face this. And now what? The wife is in the street, with four kids and nothing. The church got together fifteen thousand francs [about three thousand dollars] for medical expenses, but how long will that last? The boat was her home, her life. Everything they had was on board."

These things happen, Rolland said. "Who knows the cause? It might have been a gas leak somewhere." *Péniches* use bottled propane for cooking and heating water. "More likely, it was something in the cargo. Wheat can ferment and give off fumes, which can ignite like that. You never know what can go wrong."

Rolland had his own problems. Like so many others, his family had worked on the river for more generations than he could remember. Compact and curly haired, with tattooed hearts and anchors climbing up his forearms, he was a picturebook bargee. But, at forty-one, after fourteen years of running his own boat, he was out of work with four growing kids to feed. At the end of 1992, he was forced into *déchirage*, that symbolic scuttling of a boat. He received two hundred thousand francs, or forty thousand dollars, in exchange for his permit to operate. "It's a little yellow piece of cardboard, this big," Rolland said. "Without it, I'm dead."

He and his wife can keep the boat to live on for the rest of their lives, if they can find a spot and afford the mooring fees, but it can't move. When they both die, it cannot be passed on to their kids. They can sell it, but to whom? *Terriens* who want a houseboat must first find a place to dock it. At best, it is worth the equivalent of three thousand dollars at a scrap yard.

"Scrap dealers have all the boats they can handle," Rolland said, "so who wants mine?" He nodded to his *Chemineau*, an immaculately painted *péniche* with a Cummins diesel in perfect condition. Living quarters were comfortable as a country cottage. "Right now, a junkman would give me eight hundred francs [$160]," he said. "That is the price of a truck tire."

The economics are simple and brutal. Independent bargees find work through a class of middlemen known as *courtiers*. River people have a rich lexicon of other names for them, including *gangster* and *mange-pain* (literally, "bread-eater," but closer to bloodsucker). *Courtiers* make deals with the people who need to have heavy cargos moved. They decide whether to use rail, road or river. Three times a week, in Paris, Conflans and Rouen, the government-run Freight Charter Office takes orders from *courtiers* and posts them. Bargees are eligible for the jobs according to their place in line, determined by the date of their last load.

It is the same system in Saint-Mammès, Saint-Jean-de-Losne and elsewhere. It works like an overloaded taxi stand at a corner without many passengers. At the end of each trip, the bargee gets a *boletin de tour* marked with the time and date that his *péniche* was unloaded. He then checks the posted lists until his next turn comes up. This can take three weeks to a month and, sometimes, up to three months. At one time, bargees had to shuttle between Paris and Conflans, which had separate lists. Now, at least, orders are coordinated.

Courtiers argue that they perform a vital function, putting together customers with transporters, and they are bound by the laws of supply and demand. Bargemen, and a lot of outsiders who understand the system, accuse these brokers of forcing down prices to the point where hardly anyone can survive. In 1993, boats carried dirt from near Paris to Poissy, taking much of the day to do it, for $1.50 a ton.

The luckier bargees can make yearlong contracts to haul sand or grain, but they are stuck with the going rate. Rolland went bust working on a contract.

"The minimum wage in France is five thousand four hundred francs [a thousand dollars], and I made three thousand," he said. "I'm supposed to break my ass for that? I made fifty-nine trips during 1992. For that? You can make a little more with export, going to Germany, Switzerland or Belgium, but then you never see your kids. If your boat breaks, you fix it yourself. No one can afford a mechanic. Insurance covers a broken propeller but not the time lost to fixing it."

Fuel once represented 10 percent of operating costs. It is now a third. A fifth of bargees' gross earnings go to what the French call social charges: even when idle, they contribute monthly to a compulsory government retirement fund, health coverage and social security. They have to pay unemployment insurance but can't make claims because they are self-employed.

Rolland said France's undersized locks limit the perspective of anyone who wants to get bigger. He knew one man who fitted out his eighty-meter barge for high seas and brought twenty-four hundred tons of cargo from the Rhine. After reconverting his boat, he is stranded in the Seine. He can't find enough local cargo to stay above water, but the barge is too big to go back to Germany by river. And he can't afford to rig it yet again for open water.

Fast going through his savings, Rolland was looking for work with limited skills in a country with an unemployment rate that was 10 percent and rising. He found an occasional gig on a tugboat but not much else. Big companies were letting people go, and several were closing down. "Someone has to sort this out, but no one will," he said, referring to the whole business of commercial life on the Seine. "This is a giant trash can that everyone shits in."

Ironically, Conflans's mayor, in office since 1979, is Michel Rocard, a former prime minister who wants to be president. He is pragmatic, a business-minded economist who worked hard to rebuild the Socialist party after a humiliating defeat in 1993. For years, he was also the National Assembly representative for the state of Yvelines, which straddles the Seine. I mentioned him to Rolland.

"Rocard has his qualities, but he does not give a damn about the river," he said. "Even when there is a big wedding, he sends his deputy. We are nothing to him. The town of Conflans-Sainte-Honorine hardly knows we exist. They do nothing for river people."

Others had said this about Rocard, but I wondered. I'd met him several times and came away impressed with his impassioned defense of working minorities in trouble. Here was one in his own backyard, and they were the last remnants of those boatmen-traders who plied the Seine two thousand years ago. In several books on boats and the river, Rocard wrote emotional prefaces about an endangered way of life. When I told Rocard's secretary that I wanted to ask about Conflans and the river, she barely concealed a snicker.

"He's much too busy," she said. "Call the mayor's office."

"But he's the mayor," I said, adding that city hall had referred me to her. I explained that I needed only a few minutes and could wait for months.

When I persisted, she said, "Listen, give me your number, and I will call you *quand c'est possible*," which is French for "when hell freezes over."

∽∾∽∾∽

When I asked at city hall who kept atop the boat situation for the municipal government, I was told to call Gaston Neyt, a retired captain who worked as a volunteer. He was generous, insisting on answering questions at length as his wife shuffled around, impatient to put his lunch on the table. But Neyt was no artisan bargee; he was from a rival tribe. He had been a salaried captain for Sanara, one of the biggest freight haulers on the Seine. He left the river to do an administrative job on land.

The big operators were caught in the middle, he told me.

Scarce river traffic meant they had to cut back, laying off people and trimming their overhead. At the same time, they were resented by small independents, who accused them of cornering the market. In 1984, this came to blows in the War of the Seine.

As Neyt explained it, Sanara had gotten a contract to haul ten thousand tons of wheat from Gennevilliers to Rouen. Bargees demanded the work. "We offered them four thousand tons, but they wanted it all," he said. They organized, for a change, and tried to block Sanara convoys. "It got nasty," Neyt said. "Some people broke up a barge and destroyed a tug engine. In a herd, it is easy to start a stampede."

Bargees' accounts differ. As most tell it, the company sought to cut them out of traffic that they had carried for a thousand years. When they got nowhere in negotiations, they blocked the Seine in the center of Paris. Some say the company purposely inflamed independents by sending empty barges to make it look as if hauling had already begun. The idea was to incite bargees to vandalism and discredit them, according to this version. "The company was insured against any losses," one *péniche* owner said. "It was like sending sheep among the wolves." The facts are not clear, and compromise settled the dispute. But, all agree, there was bad blood on the Seine.

Part of the problem, Neyt said, is social upheaval among a small group faced with changing times. "It's just not the same," he said. "People live differently. Before, suppliers bought a thousand tons of coal at a time, door-to-door. You couldn't order less than three hundred tons. Now they simply have it trucked in as they need it. A lot of boat people aren't ready to change with the times."

There are fewer boarding schools for bargees' kids, and most youngsters now stay in class long enough to take the *baccalauréat,* a standard exam that certifies them as ready for university. "An illiterate can run a boat," Neyt said. "Most of these kids don't want to go back after their *bac.*" Life on many *péniches* is still rudimentary, with space cramped and luxuries few. "Now people want a shower every day," he concluded with some regret. "They've gotten civilized."

His son, Lamont, had arrived for lunch. When I asked what he did, he pointed to the "Otis" patch on his shirt. He fixed elevators. For Lamont, running a boat had too many ups and downs.

〰〰〰〰

Down the quai, I found Claude Levaufre leaning on his elbows at Diesel Marine, one of the last businesses left in Conflans that have anything to do with boats. His showroom offered a Baudouin engine that would cost about one hundred thousand dollars, installed, and no one was lining up to buy it. Levaufre employs those mechanics Rolland cannot afford to consult.

"Things are bad. Bad. Bad," he said. When I stopped in to chat, his partner, Jeannine Magara, came from behind her desk to listen in. Just in case I misunderstood him, she added, "Things are bad."

The town's large boat-supply store closed when its owners got old and no one wanted to take it over. "Everything is closing," he said. "The chandler, the workshops . . . are going one after another. We have been here twenty-three years, but it is too hard now. People don't have money. They don't pay, and you try to track them down. You end up being a banker."

Even in good times, Levaufre said, most bargees count their centimes and invest as little as possible. "I know guys who have not changed an engine or a gearbox for thirty-five years," he said. "They just keep working on the old ones, keeping them in as good a shape as possible and living with their peculiarities. Now, what is their choice?"

He hoped for a business upturn in the mid-1990s when European unification allowed more boats from Germany, the Low Countries and England to carry freight on the Seine. But that would hardly help the devastated French fleet.

Madame Magara gestured to the far side of the river, where a dozen empty barges sat idle, waiting to be lashed together in a *pousseur* convoy, should the need arise. It did not look like any need was pressing. "You never saw that before, never," she said. "That is a lot of investment to be sitting there doing nothing. Those things could be carrying two thousand tons." Muttering, she left for the day.

Levaufre was just winding up. He waved an arm at the fancy modern brickwork along the quai outside, the sort of stuff a theme park might use by the main gate. It was clearly a substantial investment. "That's for the tourists. The town has decided it does not want any businesses along here to spoil the aspect." Here it was again, that senseless line of reasoning that grips the world: a town with a unique and irreplaceable resource was blotting it out and coating the remains in plastic to please tourists who were supposed to come to see what was obliterated.

A jolly mechanic sidled up to join in. He nodded in vigorous agreement each time his boss made a point. Soon, he was adding his own bleak colors to the picture. As I walked to the door, Levaufre followed: "Soon Conflans-Sainte-Honorine will be a dead town. There is no other industry here, but they do nothing to benefit the boat people. It will die." The mechanic nodded, harder than ever.

Their picture came to life a few doors down at Le Chaland, a sort of cheerless Cheers, where the regulars' complaints all involve the same woman, Sequana. Raucous jokes enliven the atmosphere, but no one seems all that happy. It is a few steps from the *péniche* graveyard, the kind of place where grounded bargees come to drink up the last of their years, and their savings. After a while, one conversation is like the next, the pattern of the river. It got too hard to make a living. The kids went to school on shore and learned another way; how you gonna keep 'em down on the boat after they've seen Paree?

The hole-in-the-wall bar is named for those large economy-sized barges, *chalands*, which run twice the length of *péniches*. Most carry five times the 250-ton payload of the smaller barges, with no more crew than the old mom-and-pop *marinier* combo. That leaves a lot of people with extra drinking time at Le Chaland. As the afternoon wanes on, the regulars filter in. Without a word, the bartender reaches for a different bottle and glass. A geezer in a beret gets something out of a long green decanter. A younger man with a beer belly drinks red wine from a carafe. They talk about better days to come, but no one seems to believe it.

Lambert Rivert, grizzled and lumpy-jawed, spoke in a low growl. "Progress is killing us," he said. "The big tugs can push four barges at once. That's 1,400 tons. They're driving little guys out of business." At seventy, he'd retired after half a century on the river. "European unity," he added, with a snort. "You wait. Soon all you'll see will be German flags, Dutch flags. Only the French government does not care about barge traffic."

He had seen the Seine profaned not only by foreign haulers but also by "*les yachts*." Bargees pronounce the "cht" part with great throat-scratching and projections of moisture. The word means any boat which is not earning someone an honest living, hauling. When I told him I lived aboard a boat myself, his lip curled. "Ah, yes," he said, scowling again. "A houseboat."

At the end of the bar, I saw two old duffers who would have stories to tell. Both were nearly seventy, with bowling-ball bellies. One wore a black T-shirt with Day-Glo wolves on it. The other had on khaki shorts and a crapped-out Caribbean straw hat. Before I could approach them, they headed out the door. Passing me, wolf man stopped to shake hands and smile warmly.

I followed them outside and watched them pick their way across a half dozen bows and along the side of a handsome barge in the middle of the pack. This was a disappearing gold mine. Desperate, I cast aside all norms of etiquette and set out after them. If anyone climbed onto my boat uninvited, I'd spear him with a boat hook. But the wolf guy had seemed friendly enough.

I moved slowly and got within calling distance. The two were around a table on the bridge, with plates in front of them and food steaming in a pot. Oh shit, I thought. Besides being bargees, they were Frenchmen about to eat. Wolf man glared at me. I stammered, "I'm sorry, I'll come back later." The other guy called, with a derisive snicker, "Yeah. Leave."

∽∽∽∽∽

The welcome was much friendlier up the hill at Le Musée de la Batellerie, in a gorgeous old mansion of whimsical neomedieval style. It is run by François Beaudouin, the high priest of the Seine. A former merchant-marine officer and ethnologist, Beaudouin decided to devote himself to the river, his consuming passion. His fat coffee-table book, *Paris/Seine*, is in its second printing, and a shelf of other volumes carry his name. The museum has some books on the river, but his personal collection is vast. The problem is finding him.

Beaudouin, his indulgent employees explain, keeps erratic hours. He goes off on short notice to fascinating places. Two days away might mean four. If you call him on Friday, you have to remember to do it before noon. His aides do their best. Once I went to Conflans for an appointment with him that he didn't know about and didn't keep. After three trips to the museum, I decided to settle for his books, which are helpful enough. If I still needed a high priest after digesting them, I'd try someone easier, like the pope.

The museum has bits of hull from the earlier horse-drawn barges, along with crudely forged hardware and enormous gears cut from wood. It traces the use of the Seine from long before Christ to today's electronic navigation.

On the second floor, a weathered document says it all about what the river, and the barges, meant to Paris. It has a cargo manifest from a voyage upriver of the *Mantes*, in April 1682: "Forty bales of pepper, 55 barrels of [spices], 111 drums of olive oil, 77 casks of whale oil, 38 barrels and cases of sugar, 4 bales of cloth, 42 bales of tobacco and 260 large smoking pipes, 240 baskets of glasses, 2 trunks, an armoire, 11 tables, 567 reams of paper, bottles, licorice, tar barrels, torches and candles, cheese . . ." And so on.

But on one visit, I chanced upon a former captain who was eager to bring that up-to-date. He had sold his *péniche* in the 1970s, when the getting was still good. "I knew that if I stayed," he told me, "I would sink with the rest of them." The truth, he said, taking care that I would not invite wrath on his head by naming him, is that authorities do not want small artisan barge traffic, which is hard to fit into tidy systems of administration.

"If you have an animal you don't want, you say it has

rabies, and you kill it," he said. "That is what is happening with the *batellerie*, pure and simple."

∽∽∽∽∽

Back in Paris, I decided to visit the Bureau d'Affrètement to see the *bourse* and *courtiers* in action. It is in the drab Maison de la Batellerie on the Quai d'Austerlitz near a floating commune of retired bargees. I scanned the large hall and settled on Lucien Blancpain, a large, friendly-looking man who sat on a wooden bench with his crew: his wife, Joseline, and his mother-in-law. Blancpain's Freycinet barge is called *Revanche*; that means "revenge," but these days he is not sure where the irony points.

Blancpain was looking for his next job. On June 28 (this was 1993), he had picked up 250 tons of wheat in Vernon, a lovely river port below Conflans. He delivered it near Dordrecht, Holland, on July 3, which is flying for a *péniche*. Having spared the highways from twelve trucks, he pocketed his *boletin de tour* and returned empty to Compiègne. On July 12, he took an hour's train ride to Paris to see if he might luck out with another load. We both watched to see what fate would deliver.

At 2:45 P.M., the action started. I didn't understand a thing. A woman drew the microphone up to her lips and screeched words and numbers, which tumbled from tinny speakers and bounced around the empty room. Two men in seedy suits shouted briefly. Someone made chalk marks on a board with room for one hundred entries. Then it was over. In that orgasmic flurry, Blancpain was screwed, as was almost everyone else. Five boats were hired to carry 1,650 tons. A hundred were still waiting. Blancpain would be back, three times a week, probably for a month.

"You've got to be here," he said. "If not, someone else gets your load."

Blancpain introduced me to a friend, a *marinier* since the age of thirteen, who had retired in 1989 at sixty-five but still came out of habit. He liked to reminisce with his pals about the days before paltry pickings, when bargees turned up their noses at all but the good jobs. When I asked when the charter system began, he yelled to a small man in a suit, who scuttled over.

The man was Roger Van Reeth, a *courtier* for forty years. He pronounced: "The first *bourse* was in 1936 on the Pont-Neuf, outdoors around the statue of Henri IV, next to a bar called Madame la Blonde." Then he wheeled away, Joe Pesci playing a lightning-lipped dealmaker with no time to spare. "Can't talk now, busy, gotta go, I'm here every session at two o'clock." What about August? I asked; Frenchmen habitually knock off in summer. "Every session," he said. "Never miss. Forty years."

Blancpain did not mind dealing with middlemen. *Courtiers* found what little freight there was. Some played off rail and road rates to force bargees to cut their price, he allowed. "All's fair in war," he said, shrugging. "We've got to compete."

Nor was he worried that big foreign boats would crowd out *péniches* if France enlarged its locks to European standards. There was nothing for them to take over. "I knew the Moselle when it was a little river, with little boats," he said. "Five boats waited at every lock, and a trip to Germany took a month. Now there are big locks, but no traffic. What's the point of investing money in something that's no longer needed?"

The problem, he said, was that no one important cared about small-time bargees. In the old days, they always found a way to work out the numbers. For his five-day run, Blanc-pain was paid eight thousand francs. Half went to expenses and charges. His profit, worth less than eight hundred dollars, would feed his family during an idle month as long as nothing broke and no emergencies arose.

"Everything is harder for us," he said. "A trucker can declare bankruptcy three times in a year. If we do it once, we're finished."

His wife, Joseline, remains enthusiastic. "As long as the children aren't sick, it's all right," she said. Both sons are in boarding school at Conflans. Unlike the Rollands, the Blanc-pains look for lucrative faraway jobs, figuring it is more important to feed their kids than to spend each weekend with them.

Blancpain's three brothers had left the water for well-paid jobs on land, but he had no such plans. "I have the most beautiful profession in the world," he said. He suspects that his sons will also leave the river tribe when they finish school. "You can't really blame them," he concluded, shaking his head at the numbers he had just reviewed for me. "I guess you've really got to be a fanatic."

∽∽∽∽∽

What struck me was how quickly this era was ending. One classic river film is Jean Epstein's *La Belle Nivernaise*, of 1924. A good-hearted *marinier* named Louviau finds a war orphan in Paris. He raises him on his barge until the boy's real father recognizes him and takes him away. Day by day, the boy wastes away, pining for the river. Together, the two fathers set him up on his own *péniche*. He marries the beautiful Clara, a bargee's daughter, and yet another river dynasty begins.

Much later, but only a generation ago, Anthony Glyn

took a ride down the Seine with a *péniche* hauling sand. "There is something exhilarating about a growing prosperous industry," he wrote. "The water traffic on the Seine was expanding all the time; over the past three years it had grown by about a quarter each year, I was told. There was plenty of work for everyone; six to eight hundred boats, including the *Sacolève*, were carrying sand from Montereau to Paris for the rebuilding and refacing now going on in and round the capital." Now hardly twice that many boats are working all over France.

The crisis has mellowed some of the more philosophical bargees, like Blancpain. But others, gruff and grumpy to start with, are now fit to be committed.

"A lot of these guys brought this problem on themselves, and now they are making it worse," observed my friend Charlie Godefroid. "When there was lots of traffic in the sixties, they were kings, and they acted like it. If there was a Communion in the family somewhere, off they went. If they didn't like a contract, they had to visit a sick sister in Strasbourg. Finally shippers got fed up with all those sick sisters in Strasbourg."

Few French bargees thought of the present, let alone the future. Most Belgian boats were motorized by 1925. The last French *péniche* hauled by horse, or by man or wife when the animal got too tired, was retired in 1963. When the government decided large barges should replace *péniches*, Charlie said, it had to move cautiously. "You can't tell someone who has been doing something since the Middle Ages to stop overnight," he said. "Instead, they just let canals and small locks deteriorate. Many of these guys don't even know it's happening."

It is not so clear-cut. Barge families might be perfectly

aware of how they ought to modernize. But who can afford it? And who is about to lend money with a *péniche* as collateral?

If the sudden wave of waterways tourism has forced French officials to think again, offering hope for the *péniche* trade, it has yet to impress the bargee tribe. A lot of fanatics blame their troubles on any convenient scapegoat. Among the handiest are pleasure boats on the Seine. *La Vieille*, for instance.

One season, as she headed back from drydock, the old boat was sparkling. Sun flared off the varnished offsides and the blinding white hull. It had taken a month's time and a summer's salary, but every seam was recaulked. Carpenters had fitted new planks where hurtling logs and river ice had chewed up the bow. Hardware was replaced and repaired. At Andrésy, near Conflans, we worked our way into the crowded lock, feeling like that powdered cartoon skunk, Pepe La Pew, among the alley cats.

As it happens, Charlie was driving; I was still learning the Seine and had deferred to a practiced hand. Charlie is particularly good at eating enormous lunches with multiple bottles of wine. Unfortunately, this was after lunch. He handled the boat all right but definitely looked like he was having too much fun. We had room at the back, but Charlie wanted to leave space for any *péniche* that might show up while the gate was still open. He threaded us between the two rows of barges tied up to either side of the lock. This was a noble gesture but a difficult maneuver.

Normally, Charlie looks at locks the way bullfighters look at horns. The easy way—and it's not that easy—is to hug the wall and run lines over bollards, fore and aft. When the gates open, water spills out, and the boat drops. Then you haul in your lines and go. He prefers to work the props, staying in the center, which is like balancing yourself in a subway without holding on.

In the Andrésy lock, we could do neither. Having left that spot by the wall at the back, we could only tie up to a barge and drop along with it. As we inched forward, one bargee yelled, *"Yachts* go last." He pronounced *yacht* as though trying to clear some hideous substance from the back of his throat.

Finally, Charlie selected a *péniche* toward the front. He maneuvered slowly as a dozen captains watched with impatience. As we threw lines over the barge's bollards, the master scowled. Then I saw an evil gleam light his face. He goosed his starboard prop, and the wash shot our stern sideways. The bow, of course, headed into his steel hull. A friend up front, holding a tire on a rope to cushion shocks, screamed, "What do I do?" By the time anyone could tell her, we had struck the barge with a sickening crunch.

We shoved with boat hooks, but the brand-new bow beam pressed against steel, bending at a frightening angle. Finally, we backed away. The rest of the way, we took turns hanging over the rail to watch for cracks that might open and ignobly cut short *La Vieille*'s first century.

∽∽∽∽∽

Farther down from Conflans-Sainte-Honorine, the yachts strike back. By the nondescript town of Les Mureaux, the Cercle Voilier de Paris unites 350 members, a happy family of people who take their sailing seriously. One Sunday, I sat on the terrace of *le cloob'owse* as yachtsmen howled derision at pretentious window dressing—portholes decorated with something resembling ox yokes—on a passing *péniche*. Few resent the bargees, who keep the river alive. But many are pleased to see their number dropping fast.

"Twenty years ago during a regatta, you couldn't go twenty meters without having to worry about altering course because of a *péniche*," said Boy Desouches. "Now it's what, 2:30? Maybe three have passed since ten o'clock. It has changed around here."

Boy would know. His father joined the club in 1900, and he followed in 1931, at the age of twenty. That was when women were banned from the rambling wooden clubhouse. His mother ate sandwiches on the dock with the kids—the rest were older sisters, which is why he is Boy—while his father luxuriated inside with his cronies. The revolution came in 1932.

In that year, Jacques Lebrun, the club hero, won a gold medal at the Los Angeles Olympics. So did Virginie Hériot, a French teammate who was not a member. The CVP threw them both a cocktail party. Inside. The women on hand, some sailors and some wives, peered through the windows at Mademoiselle Hériot alone among the males. They pushed open the forbidden door and stayed.

For the Cercle Voilier de Paris, that is recent history. The club was founded in 1858 at Argenteuil. Those little white sailboats the impressionists loved all flew the CVP's pennant. Back then, it was a green, flowered suburb just downstream from Paris, a short voyage from La Fournaise restaurant near Chatou, where Renoir painted the customers and Maupassant composed on the walls. In 1893, however, the railroad put a bridge across the wide stretch of water, cutting the yachtsmen's playground in two.

The club moved to Les Mureaux, twenty-five miles north, settling into a rambling wooden clubhouse. In 1994, the CVP celebrated the first century of its quarters, now shabbily elegant and stuffed with souvenirs. Priceless wooden models line the walls, original builders' mock-ups of hulls that would be famous. Among them, from 1901, was the *Sequana*. A fortune in silver is shaped into cups, trophies and plates, all symbols of victory. But the eight Monets in the dining room are now only reproductions.

Monet was a member. Whenever his bar tab got out of hand, he painted some lovely boats and settled his account with a canvas. Until World War II, they hung on the walls along with sepia-toned photos of fast bottoms. Germans occupied a nearby air base, however, and the club fell onto hard times. All week long, German officers lounged around the place, sleeping in the eighty little cabins and guest rooms and eating on the terrace. Only on Sundays did members show up, and they enforced a rigid rule: no Germans. Amid postwar penury, the club sold its Monets to survive.

Today, the place bustles with life. The president is Jean-Robert Villepigue, a Sunday sailor who otherwise designs product packaging. He was the friend who took me around Marcilly. Jean-Robert loves the club and delights in showing it off. Although he also keeps a boat off Brittany, he does not think people should sneer at sailing on the Seine.

"Down there," he said, pointing to an aging man in shorts, sanding a keel, "is a two-time world champion. A lot of Olympic medal winners have trained here." He gestured to a patch of water perhaps five hundred yards wide, where prevailing east-west winds could whip you along for about three miles until a bridge snapped your mast. His sweep took in a few Belugas, sleek little boats that were once made of wood.

"Those were born here," Jean-Robert said. "During the war, when Jacques Lebrun couldn't go to sea, he sailed the Seine in open hulls with no cabins. He put up tents, makeshift shelters. So he told Jacques Herbulot [the club's marine architect, an Old Master], 'Look, you've got to make something I can sail and live in that will do for the ocean when the war is over.' Herbulot designed the Beluga. France has made a thousand of them."

When I first met Jean-Robert in Paris, and he asked me to lunch at the CVP, he wore a blazer with a fancy patch on his breast pocket. This being a French yacht club, I came ready for anything, a cravat hidden away just in case. I knew it would be all right when he pointed to a blue plastic bucket on the bar and invited me to fish out my own ice cubes with my fingers.

Only Boy looked the part, in blue jacket with pink striped shirt, club tie, and polished black loafers. His bushy waxed mustache bristled skyward, but his sunburned nose aimed down at a friendly angle. "When the club moved here, this was the end of the world, and people didn't want to come," he recalled, "so the railroad laid on a special car every Sunday. It brought up members in the morning, and took them back at night. . . ."

I knew this story. The car was dropped off at Saint-Germain-en-Laye, near a brothel of high repute. Members often took their time getting home. This custom went on until after the war when a prudish cabinet minister shut down the whorehouses. Others, who knew the story better than I did, broke in: "What about the brothel?"

But French yachtsmen take much of their vocabulary from the English, and the first term they learn is *gentleman*. Boy looked around at a lady of his generation, coughed hard, and replied: "Never heard of it. An ugly rumor."

He recounted the brutal cold war, since settled, with the Yacht Club de l'Ile-de-France, just next door. Now the smaller rival is down to a hundred members and faced with money troubles. No one wants it to disappear and leave its installations available to something else. Boy grimaced at the idea.

Jean-Robert guffawed. "Right," he said. "The last thing we need is a free, open Republican club with motors and"— he paused to sniff dramatically—"pedal boats."

After lunch, we left on a boating party in the grand style of the canopied launches that took elegant couples on the Seine a hundred and some years ago. Our party fell slightly short of the gathering Renoir depicted in his *Déjeuner des Canotiers*. We had no ditzy black poodle, only an overweight golden retriever that barked at swans. None of the four women wore bonnets or bustles. Six of us weighed down a little flat skiff with a wheezing nine-horse Johnson.

We putted toward the regatta, twenty boats in a line, all billowing spinnakers in crimson and fuchsia, yellow and black, French blue and bordeaux. Villepigue steered us into a side channel, almost overgrown with thick trees. Stone towers were half masked by foliage. Old men fished from their piers. Deep greens were broken by hedges of brilliant red roses. I was on the river, almost in it, with bilge water lapping at my ankles and spray cooling my face.

Back in the main channel, Jean-Robert laid on the lore. He pointed out where Jacqueline Auriol, daughter-in-law of a French president and the first woman to break the sound barrier, crashed to her death while she was testing a sea-plane. He nodded toward a big rust-flecked hangar masked by trees. "That was where Germans made patrol boats during the war," he said. "A Frenchman at the plant sabotaged them all. Not one of them worked."

This was yacht country, but it was the Seine nonetheless. Whatever international rules say, working *péniches* have right of way over boats at play. And, head-on, who wants to argue? I watched that familiar old tug the *Richelieu* push eight barges through the little fleet of sailboats like they were gnats around an elephant's trunk. On the way back, life's order of things made itself crystal clear.

We passed Aérospatiale's huge factory at the airfield the Germans once occupied. It is where the European Space Agency makes the Ariane missiles that carry satellites into orbit from Kourou, French Guiana. The most prominent feature is a massive corrugated steel wall that drops vertically from a wharf by the main building. On top is a row of bollards, for mooring barges tightly to the dock. Naturally. Each Ariane missile, just about the most advanced piece of technology the world can produce, starts its voyage into space with a piggyback ride on a Seine *péniche*.

11 Plastic Man's Magic Hammer

JEAN-PIERRE ARDOUIN'S caulking hammer looks like the Flintstones' nutcracker, a thin chunk of metal on a homemade handle carved from a tree branch. His grandfather used it, and so did his father. Ardouin calls himself Plastic Man because of his other pursuits, such as making thirty-foot-high Perrier bottles and theme-park monsters out of high-tech fiber, but his real love is his boat yard. He may be the last craftsman left on the Seine capable of hauling *La Vieille* safely out of the water.

You do not take a boat to a *chantier naval* like you take a car to the shop. At least not to Jean-Pierre's. First, there is foreplay. Picking the date depends on the currents and the calendar. If the Seine is fast and high, forget it. When it's too cold outside, the paint won't properly set. But if it's too hot, planks dry out and shrink. In summer, everyone is on holiday. Other boats occupy the huge hangar for weeks on end.

Getting there is an adventure. In fresh water, a solid wooden hull can go three or four years between drydocks. By then, however, it is usually a mess. The plastic pellets that plague the Seine have stuffed up its sea cocks. Paint is cracked and peeling. Most likely, something significant is not working, or is loose. When I first took *La Vieille* to the yard, we left at dawn and chugged unevenly past the leafy jungle that flanks the river below Paris. We were for all the world like an old scow slinking out of a tropical backwater with a load of desperate refugees.

But then there is the coming home. This is a scene from a different film, more Fitzgerald than *Fitzcarraldo*. We are gleaming white, with fresh varnish on the offsides, blue and red panels at the waterline, and rich brown paint on the striker rail. New ropes are coiled, and woven jute fenders dangle at the sides. Brass glints in the sun, and the well-oiled hardware all works. The captain, a Jewish reporter reared in the Arizona desert, is trying hard to look like he knows what he is doing. Only in the locks, when an enthusiastic but inexperienced crew lets the virgin hull bounce off a sand barge, is he prone to scream.

Performing such miracles of transformation is the daily business of Ardouin's yard. It is something to see. The process starts with the *maître* waving energetically as we approach his dock. A friend, he is happy that we have made it; he is also relishing yet another challenge to old skills and wondering how he is going to spend the sizable windfall.

La Vieille is hauled onto a wheeled chassis on railroad tracks that run into the water. Then comes an hour or two of high anxiety: with chocks and ropes and howls of pain from fingers caught in the wrong place, Jean-Pierre secures the boat and rolls her up into the hangar. The old girl, awkwardly in the air, sits there like a dignified matron enduring a physical.

The next step is dinner at the big table next to Jean-Pierre's barbecue. It is good, seldom with anything less noble than a decent Gevrey-Chambertin, but it is hard for me to enjoy it. As we eat, I know, Stéphane the carpenter is crawling around with a screwdriver, poking at *La Vieille*'s most private places in search of rot. Before the *tarte tatin*, he will appear with the diagnosis. There will be a major transfer of resources.

Once we dined with Ardouin for social purposes, with the boat comfortably back in Paris. I brought my friend Dev Kernan, a master artisan from Colorado, and they were talking wood.

"See what you can do with this," Jean-Pierre said, producing a primeval Rubik's cube, a wooden block of double dovetails. His grandfather had made it as a young man, and two generations of kids had played with it, gnawing at its corners and banging it on rocks. It was worn smooth from fondling. But the pieces still fix snugly, nearly impossible to separate.

"Marine carpentry is a vanishing art," Ardouin said, "and everyone is looking for boat builders. The skills were passed on from hand to hand, and for forty years they were dying out. Now apprenticeship is coming back. The only school in France turns out maybe fifty marine carpenters a year, and the demand is ten times that."

It is not that so many people want boats, he explained. More and more, aerospace engineers and architects design complex shapes that require molded plastics. That means someone has to make the molds. And marine carpenters do it best. Just as Ariane missiles start out on the Seine, their first requirement is wood.

Ardouin, short and dynamic, with a self-assured air, looks like he might be the sort who boasts. He is what the French call an *homme à femme*, a lady-collector, with warm brown eyes meant for elsewhere than a paint hangar. He is not hamstrung by that frowning French adjective *sérieux*. One time, on the deck of *La Vieille*, I heard a gleeful voice yelling my name from the river. There was J.-P. on a *péniche*, dwarfed by his latest creation: a Perrier bottle lashed to the deck on its way to advertise bubbly water at the traffic circle by Orly Airport.

When he discusses his craft, however, he states the facts with reverence, as though he is talking about someone else's abilities. If prompted, he describes each variation of plane, adze, drill and hammer, speaking their traditional names as if he were reading poetry. The *rabat* planes slices of wood as fine as peach skin. The *varloppe* is huge; the *riflard*, much more narrow, cuts deep. Marine carpenters often make their own tools for a special bias and hollow.

Jean-Pierre was building a drakkar with the same type of tools the Vikings used. Their power drill was a large bare-chested man leaning on a long awl, rapidly turning two crosspieces with both arms. The only difference is that Ardouin's would probably wear a Seiko watch.

"It is not the same as ordinary woodworking," he said. He searched for words but said it better with his hands, absently running his fingers down the grain of the old puzzle. "You feel the wood, understand it, respect it. Wood is alive, always working. You must think like it. When it has to stand up in water, year after year, it must be right. There is a challenge—a sense of honor in your work—that is something unusual."

Dev leaned forward to listen, elbows nearly in his *haricots verts*, and his habitual beatific smile beamed a new intensity. We outsiders appreciated Jean-Pierre's words, but Dev had locked onto them like a Freemason recognizing the secret salute.

"I made that same puzzle as my first exercise in woodshop, and I took it home to my mother," he said. Dev, a genius at anything fashioned with tools, is impassioned by wood. He started with furniture and moved on to fancy buildings. Once, I asked him to fix a leaking deck on *La Vieille*, and he said he'd try. After a day on board, I couldn't blast him off with dynamite. Dev had discovered that most of all he was a marine carpenter, but he did not realize it until Jean-Pierre's disquisition.

When you build a table, you can always try something else if the customer finds that it came out wrong. With a boat, it is different. A customer who has to swim to a telephone to make his complaint is likely to be hopping mad. Fancy cabinets do not have to slip along at speed against strong currents. But for marine carpenters, seaworthy is only part of it. There is a right way to do each step, and everyone knows what it is. No shortcut is honorable. Materials improve with time, but tradition determines the procedures. Beautiful counts, even on a work boat.

The last time *La Vieille* went to the yard, Stéphane found dry rot in the cross beams under the aft deck. It went far beyond anyone's reach, spreading behind the fuel tank. He could not tell how much of the decking itself had been weakened. I had hoped to get by with a simple paint job. Instead, he would have to rip out a teak deck that had been there for most of a century. And then he would have to put it back.

The job took six weeks. Half of the planks were new, sawed from fresh teak timber. Joints were sealed in the traditional way, with new materials. Cushioning strips of treated fiber were fit under flexible black caulk. Planks were pegged; if there was any metal, you couldn't see it. Original fittings went back in place. After a little teak oil, the deck was as good as old.

Ardouin keeps a book on every boat that comes back to him for drydock. *La Vieille*'s is a fat red one, tattered, with detailed sketches of replaced planks, worn joints and ice gashes on the bow. Most of the detail stays in the master's head. For example, it takes eight days of running the pumps before the dried hull swells up again to watertight. If it still leaks on the ninth day, some sleep is lost to worry.

∽∽∽∽∽

Being a purist, Jean-Pierre does not do machinery. When we last hauled *La Vieille* out of the water, I found worrisome play in the port propeller. The bearings were shot. Like everything else, this would be a big job, and I didn't have the first clue about how to do it. Neither did Jean-Pierre. As fate would have it, I had come downriver with a low-country European named Edy. An old bargee of towering self-confidence, he volunteered.

In fact, the procedure is simple if you have the right tools and know what you're doing. With a propeller puller, you yank off the heavy brass blades. Then you mess around with the collars and packing and whatnot, replace what is worn, and shove the prop back in place. Of course, some problems arise. Where do you get a puller for a prop that was cast in the early Iron Age? Or bearings? Or all the other little pieces? Edy would do it.

As weeks went on, alarming reports filtered down from Limay. Lacking a puller, Edy used a hammer. Failing to detach the propeller, he used a blowtorch and nearly set the boat on fire. Still unable to get the thing loose, he detached the propeller shaft by separating the flanges that held it to the drive shaft from the gearbox, under the main cabin floor. In doing so, he broke a flange, yet another unfindable piece of marine history. He also fractured the collar that held the prop assembly in place.

Edy was reassuring, and certainly enthusiastic. A metal shop made a new flange that sort of fit. The bearings were located at a supply house in England. The collar was made of wood; that was a snap for Ardouin.

From time to time, I visited the yard. Boat people being who they are, I was swept into a family of fellow sufferers, each with a problem to solve and all with varying degrees of knowledge. A Dutch marine engineer who was laying a new deck on his antique boat took a particular interest in Edy's labors. He greeted me each time with a look of profound pity.

In the end, Edy came through. The propeller play was gone. No extra pieces lay on the floor. When everything else was finished, we headed back to Paris. Over 1,000 rpms, which is not many, the port gear lever had a palsied shake. The shaft, under the cabin floor, sounded like a washing machine with rocks in it.

"Perfectly normal," Edy said.

"Shut off the engine," I said.

We limped home. The vibrations had paralyzed the port gearbox, and I was nearly suicidal. I had just gotten that gearbox back from England. The shop that made it originally had taken four months to rebuild it. A mechanic friend had driven it back to Paris. Getting it in took most of a day, all the skin off two sets of knuckles and more swear words than I had heard in several decades of hanging out with foul-mouthed people.

But Sequana smiled. A friend happened to have an Irish mechanic on board his boat who unstuck the gearbox for a minimal fortune. He also looked at the shaft. The two sections were out of line, and they had been joined back together only by a set screw in a groove rather than a heat-sealed sleeve. "A few more revolutions in reverse, and you'd have lost the whole thing," the mechanic reported. That, of course, would have left a two-inch hole in the bottom of the boat.

I learned the epilogue of this story only four years later, when *La Vieille* came out of the water again. By then, wiser, I'd brought an engineer from England to inspect the running gear. He did not need a prop puller. With two fingers, he yanked out the rusty remains of wire Edy had used instead of stainless steel pins to lock the nuts. Just as easily, he spun the nuts off the shafts and lifted the blades free. At any moment, either prop could have done that without anyone's help.

∞∞∞∞∞

I inherited Jean-Pierre along with a crew family scattered across Europe and headed by a spiritual leader named Val Gardner. Hardly settled in Paris, Paul and Jill ran into him, quite literally, minutes after casting off for a trip up the Marne.

"A friend and I had taken a year off and were wandering around French canals in an extremely rotten converted lifeboat called the *Diddlywot*," Val recalls. "They had just taken the boat out and got it turned sideways across the river. The gearbox packed up." I would be hearing more about this gearbox and its equally cantankerous twin. "We were sleeping off tremendous hangovers when they rammed us. We eventually all went up the Marne together on the *Diddlywot*. A friend of theirs fixed the gearbox and brought their boat later. It all ended up in an extremely drunken weekend at Château Thierry."

This was May 1968, during the student uprising in Paris. "I remember the date," Val said, "because when we weren't on board, people were pitching paving stones at us." This was a fortuitous mishap. Val happened to tune racing-car engines for a living and could wire twelve-volt circuits while taking a nap. More, he was one of those rare good guys of whom the modern world produces steadily fewer numbers. He adopted *La Vieille* and looked after her as if she were an enfeebled aunt.

Val comes in a small package: a slight frame, a handbag full of personal gear and nothing to prove. He shifts frequently among temporary quarters, visiting friends scattered across four countries who are always happy to see him. In Paris, he shows up when least expected and most needed. Meantime, I can usually track him down within five phone calls.

"Um, Val," a typical conversation begins, after niceties, "is it normal for river water to be gushing up from the condemned pasta cock aft of the fazool?"

"No."

"Um, what should I do?"

"Let me think."

He always has an answer. If not, he drops the various threads of his life and finds someone with an answer. Before pasta water floods the fazool, I'm back in business.

Val does not condescend. Soon after acquiring the boat, I announced that I planned to degrease the engines and paint them. He knew my skills. This was like an unsteady art illiterate planning to reproduce the Mona Lisa with a spray can. He said only, "Try not to paint over the injector ports."

When I decided to make *La Vieille* riverworthy, he rallied nobly. We (he) rewired the running lights and fixed up lamps in every cabin. Val tracked down a reasonably priced diesel heater and made it work. Instruments were repaired or replaced. If we couldn't find parts in France, Val combed the yards in Britain. When we fired her up and headed out, without smacking any *Diddlywots* on the other bank, he beamed as though his race cars had set a lap record.

Jim Ravenscroft, another bantam Brit of a similarly gentle nature, was the diesel-engine specialist. He had a job he couldn't leave but found time anyway. I took possession of the boat minus that balky gearbox. It was in England being rebuilt by two elderly gentlemen who would soon retire and vanish with their skills from the face of the earth. Months later, he drove it over to install it.

The gearbox weighed more than a small car and a great deal more than Jim. Somehow, the two of us got it off the quai, across the neighboring barge and into my wheelhouse. We rigged up a chain pulley, suspended from a beam across the floor. The monster box descended precariously. "Try not to drop it," Jim observed. "It will go straight through the bottom." For a moment, I thought he was joking. In fact, that stuff happens.

It is difficult to explain the value of a good crew, however many solar systems they might have to travel to reach you. Ordinary repair skills aren't enough on a boat, at least not on the Seine; too many corollaries alter the laws of physics. For example, there is porthole magnetism. Once Dev and I were in the galley inspecting a brass oil lamp that had ceased to work. It was nothing. The barrel that held fuel and wick had corroded to the base and needed cleaning. Dev tugged on it. The barrel came out with a pop, spiraled once in the tight space and sailed in a perfect arc out the porthole, without even banking off the rim.

On a house, workmen fix the roof, and, barring earthquake damage or gunshot holes, water rolls off it into rain gutters. When water drops land on a wooden deck, however, a curious homing system directs them to a pinhole in the rubber coating made by the edge of a high-heeled shoe. They then form into cohorts and sneak three feet down a hidden seam to the crack in the wood through which they can drop and short out a computer.

It is amazing how much wind and cold a simple uninsulated wooden plank can keep out if it is fitted snugly to planks on either side. More amazing still is how wind and cold get through a scarcely visible chink in the planking. Any desperate klutz can fix this himself with caulking cement, but his walls will look as if a three-year-old had smeared them with peanut butter. Instead, someone competent must scrape out the seams without cutting into the wood tongues and grooves, fill cracks, and sand and paint, inside and out. If you are lucky, this is done only once a year.

One season when Val was feeling too poorly to crawl around in *La Vieille*'s entrails, he asked if he might be elevated to the role of technical adviser. This seemed fair enough. Since he never wanted money, I had begun to feel guilty. Dev, another sucker who has never read Tom Sawyer, was eager to try his hand.

The system works perfectly. Let's say the gearbox slips out of adjustment, which does not take much hypothesizing. Dev pores over the water-stained, moldy manuals that were printed before the Germans bombed London. He finds a feeler gauge that measures .23 somethings on the Whitworth standard. After much bloodletting and explosions of Dev's foulest oath—"Shoot!"—we find the Val page in my tattered red book. After five calls, we get him.

"Wiggle it around until it feels right," Val says.

Dev nods sagely and disappears for several moments. *La Vieille*, yet again, can reverse on the starboard side. Then Dev goes to Siberia to build a hotel, Val drives off to see friends in a phoneless corner of the moors, and the old girl accommodates me by breaking down only in the simpler ways I can handle on my own.

∽∽∽∽∽

I always hate to call *La Vieille* a houseboat, but when she is laid up at Ardouin's, the term has a true ring to it. My house is in the shop. This can take some getting used to. For example, how do you lock it up? That's like putting a coat and tie on a guy headed for surgery. No one working on the boat takes things. But last time my binoculars vanished, and I counted myself lucky. A yard is like an open ward in a busy hospital where nurses leave patients asleep and take their break. Visitors wander around. It is no place to leave a Rolex on the night table. You have to gather up things you don't want to lose along with stuff you'll need and put it all somewhere. Right. Where?

Ideally, this is a great excuse to go lie on the beach. Hey, my house is at the doctor's. The problem is that you want to hang around to wiggle your drive shafts and drive the boatyard people crazy. It is time to call in the brothers from Amsterdam and South Greenwich and Silver Plume, Colorado, and assemble them at the abbey. This means everybody has to have a place to live.

Boat people get used to this situation, and each has some solution. My neighbor Philippe repaints his steel-hulled barge only once in ten years, and he gets it all done in four days. That includes time for a high-pressure water spray to clean off the algae; judicious sandblasting in rough spots; a coat of primer and then several of color; and a quick trip back to his spot on the quai. No one dawdles when Philippe is around.

You can't do that with wooden boats. First they have to dry. It takes time to replace damaged planks. Painting comes only after caulking and filling. There are the inevitable surprises. The good part is, you get to know exotic products like Sikaflex and Rubson and compounds the French call *antifooling*, as in anti-fouling. The bad part is, you don't want to. Most boat people on the Seine are smart enough to have metal hulls.

Péniche owners can choose from five yards near Paris, massive *chantiers* with cranes that can lift a hundred tons. For barge builders, the tool of choice is a welding torch. With little more than a hot flame, workmen can cut through a hull and put it together again, adding a dozen meters or reducing the length by half. Weak spots are fixed by welding plates over them. That is the basic principle at least. If you want to get tricky, your imagination is the limit.

Purists work around *les écoutilles*, the ribbed and curved metal sheets that cover the cargo hold. These leave only the *plat-bords*, narrow walkways at either edge of the *péniche*, and the wheelhouse deck as outdoor play space. The more whimsical gut their hulls and start from scratch. Although ruinously expensive, this allows for picture windows and bowling alleys. Jacques Rougerie, a marine architect, has an underwater aquarium that extends to the bottom of his boat and an *orangerie* of such magnitude that he needs television cameras off the bow to see where he is going. Another boat is mostly swimming pool.

Interiors are a separate art form. Antique shops in big ports offer brass compasses, old stoves and hardware. Tropical woods and spar varnish, in the hands of a fanciful marine carpenter, can produce great beauty. Some allowance must be made. One journalist, I am told, left it to movers to unpack his mountain of books in a newly refitted *péniche*.

Unpracticed in the art, they stacked them all against one wall. That tipped the boat enough for water to seep into a drainpipe, adding to the off-center weight. Soon after, my informant reports, the boat sunk.

For people who take *batellerie* seriously, what counts is the cut of the hull. Since the first Parisii boatmen, shapes and sizes have evolved according to need. The early boats did not last long. When the time came, they were torn up. Craftsmen recuperated every nail. Sound beams went back on the river in another vessel. The rest was sold to fuel someone's stove.

During the mid-1880s, boat yards began plating wooden hulls with thin layers of metal. Thus reinforced, these could handle the heavy motors that were slowly coming into use.

Size depended on where the boat would travel. For the Canal de Berry, with its long distances and little locks, bargees used three different shapes, including the stubby *berrichons*. After Freycinet set his standard, sizes stayed the same for generations. These days the good old snub-nosed *péniche* is by far the most common craft on the Seine. But exotics abound.

The shorter Dutch *tjalk*, a sailing barge, looks like a miniature Spanish galleon squashed flatter to fit under low bridges. Racy wooden scallops called leeboards are lashed to either side. Though only decorative in the Seine, they are meant to cut into the water, like off-center centerboards, to prevent the boat from rolling over in choppy Zeeland seas.

Dutch barges come in assorted other shapes, often mixed. One friend's boat has an *aark* stern; the word means "horse's ass," and a glance at the hull explains it. The *klipper* bow is low-slung and rounded. *Luxemotors* are about thirty feet long, with pointed bows and a wheelhouse far to the aft. Hazel Young and Jean-Luc Brouic of the *Occitaine*, both devotees, run a workshop at Saint-Jean-de-Losne called the Luxemotor Club.

To people of other interests, the fine points can get tedious. Subtleties are as numerous as the tools in Jean-Pierre Ardouin's cabinets. Boat people can get passionate about them; they are basic elements of a different sort of life. What surprised me when I first began to notice the river was how easy it was to slip from one category to the other. If it's lurking within you, a day or two will bring it out.

∽∽∽∽∽

When you feel the call to live on the river, be sure it is not temporary insanity. Shortly after I acquired *La Vieille*, a friend observed with a nasty cackle: "Owning a boat here is like standing under a cold shower and tearing up five-hundred-franc notes." He'd have been closer to it if they made one-thousand-franc notes. But money is only part of it.

The river takes you over. Weather is no longer a subject of idle curiosity, easily mastered with an umbrella or an electric radiator. Sandpaper, you will find, comes in more varieties than fine, medium and coarse. If you dozed in physics on the day they explained capillary action, expect a refresher course the first time water finds a pinhole on your deck. A whole new world awaits you in the Yellow Pages under *"Accastillage"*—shipchandlery.

When you cruise, some pleasant surprises await you at the day's end. That perfect mooring may appear, with a power hookup and water. Often, however, you'll be as welcome as a gypsy wagon in the outskirts of Hitler's Berlin. You need to find a safe spot, especially on the Seine below Paris, where monster convoys can squash small craft like an elephant tromping on a gerbil. But bargees don't seek company, and tidy little villages offer limited parking space.

"It's murder for people to find a comfortable overnight dock," Ardouin told me. "They [authorities, collectively] should be setting up stopping places, with water, power, trash cans—even a supermarket on a boat that passes at certain times. But nothing." He is indulgent with people who squat at his boat yard and leave without so much as saying hello. "They expect a public facility and think I'm it," he said. "I pick up their trash in the morning."

Ardouin is doubtful about a Seine revival, with more boats in the water and places to take advantage of them. "Fifty years ago, there weren't many cars, and everyone came to the river," he said. "People swam, ate on the banks, danced at *guinguettes*. They were happy. Now they sit fuming in their cars, waiting in line to pay tolls on the *autoroute*. Boat people are a tiny minority. It makes no sense."

This is the downside. If the river gets hold of you, all of it is a small price to pay.

When people ask my advice on moving onto a boat, I suggest that they cruise awhile with someone who has figured it out. For this, a hotel barge is not enough; you will learn more about your fellow passengers than about boat living. My Belgian friend Charlie loved taking some groups on week-long charters but gave up the business because of those who wore down even his Jobian patience.

"It was a nightmare sometimes, with my Americans," he said. "Once an unexpected current swelled the Saône just as we were starting a cruise. The passengers demanded that we go anyway. 'We didn't cross the Atlantic to sit here,' one of them said. I told him, 'We can either wait until the water gets higher and we can go over the bridge or wait until it drops and go under, but we can't go through it.' They insisted." Charlie found a competitor on the other side of the bridge who was willing to subcontract. The passengers refused to ride a French bus, which was not air-conditioned. He hired a Mercedes. But they would not go with the North African driver; they wanted a real Frenchman.

∞∞∞∞∞

To sample the river, find a couple who take only a few people at a time in order to offset the cost of their own addiction. I have the perfect barge in mind, but the people who own it have asked me not to identify them. They're overbooked, and anonymity is part of their freedom. We'll call them Irving and Griselda, aboard the *Pimpernel*.

Working in Northern California real estate, they wanted something different. Irving was a sailor, handy with tools. Griselda did everything well, cooking included. They made a plan and had monthly meetings. On the second of March, six years hence, they would be on the plane to Europe to buy a boat.

They made the plane. After finding the perfect barge, refitting it and running it for three successful seasons, they sold it for double the investment. The *Pimpernel*, their second boat, is a jewel. For fourteen weeks a year, they take along people who book through their friends back home, two or four at a time. They clear a lot of money, and they are free. Once a week, Irving calls his answering service to talk to the outside world.

"It's scary sometimes," Griselda said with a cheery laugh. "We might not turn on the radio for days, and who ever sees a newspaper? Once we had some guests who went into town and brought back an old paper. It said Gorbachev had been overthrown in a coup. We listened to the BBC and found out it was all over before we even knew about it." This was deep into 1993, and she talked as if she thought Gorbachev were again running the Soviet Union.

She knew about the lockkeepers' children, however, and where you could pick mushrooms on the Canal de Briare. And, though tiny, she could stop a seventy-five-ton barge dead in the water by throwing a line over a bollard and whipping out a fast figure eight. Well-thumbed charts in the *Pimpernel's* wheelhouse show which locks sell unknown but excellent wine and home-packed honey. A few, getting into the tourist spirit, even offer been-there T-shirts.

"What amazes me is that we never get bored," she said, as we cruised a stretch of river she knew well. Irving was not amazed. "It's always different," he said. About then we passed a very well shaped woman sunning herself atop a boat headed in the other direction, and Irving recalled a happy variation.

"Last time we came this way, we passed a boat with three incredible women, topless and just strings for bottoms," he said. "A guest with me in the wheelhouse pointed them out, and we both stared. Their timing was perfect. When we drew even with them, all three stood up and started putting on suntan lotion." Griselda did a bump and several grinds to demonstrate. She had also seen the sunbathers and had come up to mention to Irving that he was headed straight for rocks on the bank.

One night we stopped in the wildest, loneliest place we could find, up the end of a canal. Irving rocked his lumbering barge back and forth like he was parallel parking a Plymouth. A few machete whacks cleared enough brush to lay down a gangplank. Stakes hammered into the ground served as mooring points. We could have bicycled into town for food but did not need to. The gas refrigerator was stuffed, the twenty-four-volt lights glowed, and there was a generator in case anyone wanted a hair dryer. We were home.

The next night we pulled into a port to a chorus of hellos and *salut*s on every side. I was steering and nearly ran down two people in a dinghy. They waved; it was a Dutch welder and her English boyfriend, old friends of the *Pimpernel*. Later, at an exquisite dinner, the innkeeper's daughter recounted her adventures on a recent trip to America.

This happened to be the Saône, but next it would be my turn to be host on the Seine. Just as soon as Jean-Pierre stopped banging on *La Vieille*'s sides with his funny-looking hammer.

12 Monet to the Monks

CÉZANNE SETTLED IN AIX-EN-PROVENCE by his beloved mountain, but Monet never left the Seine. A short cruise past Mantes takes you by his lily ponds at Giverny, where most people remember him. But on the way is an ochre bungalow at Vétheuil where an old woman turns away the odd curious passerby with a curt "There's nothing to see inside." She is right. When an art critic visited Monet there in 1880, he asked to see the studio. "My studio?" the bearded painter echoed, from the depths of his barrel chest. He swept an arm toward his river outside. "That is my studio."

Early on a fresh August morning, I went where he'd pointed. A few steps down a flowered lane, a grassy slope drops off to the water, which reflects light in a paletteful of hues. Monet might not have run into that guy in the orange helmet with the vrooming weed whacker, but otherwise it was pretty much as he left it. A silvery willow leaned at a sharp angle, its trunk a good five feet in diameter. Hip-high weeds spilled fuchsia blossoms along the bank. Clover scented the air, and dandelions speckled emerald grass. For a while, my pen scratched feebly at my notepad. Then I stuck both in my pocket and sat. This was out of my league.

If the Seine has a biographer, it is Monet, who depicted the river from the estuary to the edge of Paris. Writers never came close to getting it down on paper. Flaubert lived by the Seine all his life; Hugo and Zola each spent years along different parts of it. None gave it more than walk-on parts in their novels.

Maupassant did his best. The title of *Mouche* refers to a mistress at Chatou he shared with his painter friends. In it, he wrote of true love: "For ten years, my great, my only, my absorbing passion was the Seine. Oh, the lovely calm, varied, and stinking river, filled with mirage and uncleanliness! I loved it so much because it gave me, I think, a sense of life. Oh, the strolls along the flowery banks, my friends the frogs dreaming on a water-lily leaf, their stomachs in the cool, and the frail, dainty water lilies in the middle of tall, fine grasses that all at once, behind a willow, opened to my eyes a page from a Japanese album as a kingfisher darted off before me like a blue flame. I loved it all, with an instinctive love that spread through my body in a deep natural joy."

He described the misty mornings and tender nights. "And all that, symbol of the eternal illusion, was born, for me, from the foul water that drifted all the sewage of Paris down to the sea." In the straight shaft of the Seine that runs by Vétheuil and Giverny, Parisian pollution appears only if you look for it in a test tube, or a water glass. Instead, there is only the "rosy light that ravished the heart, memories of a moon that silvered the quivering, running water with a glimmering radiance where all dreams come to life."

Yet, in a journal, Maupassant describes how he backed away in awe as he watched Monet capture the Seine on canvas. "I have seen him seize a glittering shower of light and fix it in a flood of yellow fires," he wrote. And the full effect is "an unseizable, dazzling brilliance."

For all the beauty and drama of details that might be put to words, the power of the river is the spell it casts. Those who love it feel a part of something indescribable, a secret source for the soul. Monet and the impressionists did not define the Seine, or get beneath its surface. They simply helped us feel it for ourselves.

Exploring the Seine meant understanding something about Monet. With an art education rooted in baseball cards, I had some learning to do. When I explained my predicament to Claudette Lindsey, a lovely woman of French-Uruguayan blood who married an American, her face lit up like an Argenteuil sunrise. She has helped run Monet's place at Giverny since it opened to the public in 1980, after Gerard Van der Kemp brought it back from ruin.

Monet's wife died at Vétheuil, and in 1883 he moved to his funky two-story farmhouse, where he stayed for his last forty-three years. After seven years, he bought the property and created a small universe. First, he worked in an upstairs room. Then he built a detached studio. When he began to paint enormous panels of water lilies, he put up a soaring atelier with skylight. His gardens spread to the coach road way out back. Beyond, he dug his lily ponds and spanned them with delicate Japanese bridges.

When Monet died, his mildly estranged second son lived elsewhere and kept Giverny as a place to leave the old man's paintings. At his own death in 1966, he left the collection to the Institut de France, which hung them in the Marmottan Museum in Paris. No one did much with the moldering buildings, fetid pools and gardens gone to seed. Unheated, the house decayed. Worms ate the wood and a staircase collapsed.

In 1977, the Académie des Beaux-Arts asked Van der Kemp to be curator. After thirty years of restoring Versailles, he wanted a challenge. And rebuilding a two-and-a-half-acre universe with no money qualified as a challenge. With the help of American friends, he got the Internal Revenue Service to list the Monet Foundation as tax deductible. A flood of donations followed.

The first year, eighty thousand visitors came to Giverny. Now the figure is stable at about four hundred thousand per seven-month season. This means a lot of people bumping into your reverie, back among the irises. I spent ten minutes waiting to pay for a book at the museum shop and then gave up, with the crowd ahead of me hardly diminished. All in all, that is a pretty impressive total considering there is not a Monet in the joint.

"No, not any," Madame Lindsey said, with a dignified chortle. "Monsieur Van der Kemp decided not to try to bring the paintings back from the Marmottan. People can find his work in a lot of places. This is really a museum about Monet the man."

Monet the man is a broad enough subject. From memory, she rattled off a basic bibliography: five volumes of Monet's letters to people; scattered collections of people's replies to him; art criticism; social commentary; monographs; the Monet cookbook. Then she unlocked a monster cabinet full of everything that had slipped her mind, shelf upon shelf on the general subject. Separate stacks got into specifics.

His biographers tend to hang their theses around a re-
mark by his pal Cézanne: "Monet is only an eye, but, my
God, what an eye." He knew what he liked. Before Giverny,
he lived in Poissy, but he hated it; uninspired, he packed fast
and left. Madame Lindsey offered: "I think the problem was
that Poissy is on the left bank of the Seine. Monet always
preferred the right bank, the way the river looked from that
side. Giverny, Vétheuil, his house at Gennevilliers, were all
on the right."

And so is Le Havre, where Monet started out happily
enough sketching satirical caricatures. His father sold bulk
groceries to ships heading across the ocean, and he was
doing something different. One stormy afternoon, Eugène
Boudin took him outside. No one had a name for it in the
1850s, but Boudin had a new style. He painted the brooding,
often violent skies over the Seine estuary. Corot called him
the King of the Heavens.

"Everything that is painted on the spot has always a
strength, a power, a vividness of touch that cannot be found
again in the studio," Boudin told young Monet.

Another time, Boudin talked of the shifting, shining
light that changed everything before his eyes. "I simply can't
put that across with my grubby palette," he said. "It must be
twenty times now that I have started all over again to try to
capture that delightful quality of light which plays on everything around. What freshness there is about it. At once
fugitive, a shade pink. Objects become dissolved so that there
are only variations in density everywhere."

That was enough for Monet. He looked down at the
water, not the sky. Until he died, that was his subject. He
hauled his easel to Honfleur, across the estuary from Le
Havre. Soon, he wrote to a friend: "Every day I discover
more and more beautiful things, enough to drive one mad. I

have such a desire to do everything, my head is bursting with it."

Breaking rules was not good for business. When his little pack of outcasts squatted around La Grenouillère at Bougival, he wrote to his friend Frédéric Bazille: "Renoir is bringing us crusts from his house so that we don't starve. For eight days now, we've had no bread, wine, fire to cook on, or light. It's horrible."

Much later at Giverny, he figured it out, walking each dawn among the red poppies and leafy poplars along his favorite waters. By then, other tendencies were getting popular—the pointillists, the Fauvists, the Nabis, the early cubists—but Monet was making a decent living following his own lead. "The subject is secondary to me," he wrote. "What I want to reproduce is what exists between the subject and me."

This was that magic spell. Over the decades, his depictions of it amounted to the most convincing portrait of Sequana since the Gauls carved a goddess floating on a duck with a pomegranate in its mouth. As Olivier would say in Paris, we shouldn't be letting other people define art for us. But Monet is an open-and-shut case. The most minor segment of his mosaic is worth a whole stack of mint-condition Gil Hodges and Peewee Reeces.

〰〰〰〰

Giverny is not exactly on the Seine. You dock at Vernon, one of those eternal villages that grew into towns of lovely homes and cobbled streets, one shaped stone at a time. The Seine suddenly runs straight for miles here, 250 yards across and peppered with islands of woods and wildflowers. When medieval Paris oppressed him, the beloved king Saint Louis came to Vernon to unwind.

Half-timbered houses with exposed beams set at jaunty angles signal that the river has reached Normandy. Rollo the sedentary Viking picked the site when he struck his deal with Paris. He wanted a town on the French border, and he built towers and walls at either side of the Seine in case peace soured. Back then, Vernon was pivotal. Richard the Lion-Hearted, king of England and also duke of Normandy, ceded the town to Philippe Auguste in 1196. In the wars that followed, it was a fortified foot in the door.

Now Vernon is only a pleasant backwater at the tail end of impressionist country. A cluster of pointy stone towers by the old bridge offer a sense of what it was like from the river. Some rocks and ruins suggest the style. For the rest, you get to explore your impressions. What counts is not the subject itself but what happens between you and the subject.

From the west end of Paris and on past Vernon, islets and inlets fire the imagination. "Between the islands scattered along the stream," Zola wrote in *L'Oeuvre*, "there was a shifting and mysterious city, a network of passages along which, with the lower branches of the trees brushing them in a caress, they swiftly glided along . . . with the ringdoves and the kingfishers."

A lot of the magic remains. Herblay, just above Conflans, was a favorite spot for the painters. Now, walking down the Sente de Bellevue, you need only aim away from the purification plant and power lines across the river. It is all honeysuckle and hollyhocks, clover and conifers, ivy and irises. At La Frette, nearby, you can lunch at riverside tables among sprays of flowers and watch blue barges drift past. The young woman on skates, with radio antennae sprouting from her crash helmet, blends right in.

A right turn at Conflans takes you up the Oise, past Compiègne to the rest of Europe. Not far along you pass Van

Gogh's last home at Auvers, a well-preserved old riverside town where many of the impressionists stayed for a while. The Oise is the last turn off the Seine. A few tributaries join in farther along, but the Eure and the Risle are not navigable, and the others are so small you might miss them.

In places, the imagination needs a turbocharge. Jeannette and I dined one night on an island off Chatou now known as the Ile aux Impressionistes. The stark metal bridge leads you head-on into a seedy Italian circus, and you turn past some forgotten construction. Another turn takes you to La Fournaise and the wrought-iron canopied balcony where Renoir painted *The Luncheon of the Boating Party*.

The balcony seems as it was, if you ignore the plastic flowers. The view is concrete UCLA dormitories gone wild, the back end of a power plant and an industrial-strength bridge. The clientele runs to unmodulated young American professionals who take pains, while in Europe, to call their suspenders "braces." Service and food can range into that you-geeks-and-gawkers-don't-deserve-better category. Diners are reminded far too often, in too many ways, of where they are. But somehow, for that down-deep thrill of what is still there, it is worth the visit.

Toward the Giverny end, the thrill is plain as a jolt of electricity. Here it is not the official sites that count, but rather places you've never heard of until you tie up the boat, or slam on the brakes. La Roche-Guyon, for instance. A sign at the entrance says it was judged by somebody to be among the most beautiful villages in France. It is certainly in the running. But the charm is in its lack of pretense.

La Roche-Guyon is dominated by the remains of twelfth-century satellite surveillance. If you were, say, king of France and wanted to watch your neighbors in Normandy, you found the highest rock near the border and got some underpaid suckers to pile up a tower of squared stone. And if your tower happened also to be on the one thoroughfare into the kingdom, you built sturdy walls to defend it. What is left is the tower and a fine château of later vintage being restored by the Rochefoucaulds, a family of philosophers, merchants and money.

As anyone would have guessed, in the shadow of the stone keep, or *donjon*, is the Auberge du Donjon. A pleasant lady who has owned it for a long time serves excellent coffee and brioches on the terrace. When I asked more than the approximate date, she spread her hands in mock horror: "Ah, that's the ten-franc question." The eight-hundred-year-old ruins were simply what was out front, like an old oak tree.

History comes out in bits, just part of normal conversation. Some bizarre troglodytes dug homes into the face of limestone cliffs against which the town is built. Later nobles built splendid mansions, which the government is restoring. Cézanne and Renoir painted here. Oh, and Rommel made his headquarters in the castle; the plot to assassinate Hitler was hatched there, and phases of it were directed from La Roche-Guyon.

There is not much else in town to hang a Michelin star on except the place itself. The stone-colonnaded market is no Acropolis, but you can imagine Middle Age mamas selling cider from a hand-hewn barrel. Down a cobblestone lane to the river, I saw a wisteria trunk, big as an old oak stump, in an arm-wrestle death lock with the thick iron bars of an ancient fence.

On the main street, I cursed at my forgotten camera. Two gray-haired citizens talked in great animation, their antique noses a foot apart, against a towering backdrop of fat red roses. But then again, what was the picture? It was the light and the setting and the feeling. Mostly, it was what was happening between the subject and me. And I ain't no Monet.

∽∽∽∽∽

Driving along the Seine to Vétheuil, I stopped short at the Auberge du Lapin Savant. This means, sort of, Wise Rabbit Inn. The place looked like the cover of a Beatrix Potter book—cozy, tidy, and afire with red flowers.

At the end of last century, the inn was a one-room dump where workers at a local cement plant stopped for the lunchtime *plat du jour*. When the plant closed, La Mère Hoebeke turned L'Espérance into a very small hotel. Several of her employees were animals. Each morning, one goose hiked nearly two miles to town to bring back the paper in its bill. Another one, the watchgoose, chased off undesirables. I don't know what the goat did, but Mother Hoebeke's stars were the three rabbits.

One rabbit set the table. A second shined guests' shoes. A third scrubbed laundry in a small tub. In the evening, all three relaxed to smoke their pipes. Occasionally, they played music on a small piano and cymbals. Sunday was show time. Two rabbits in tux and wedding gown climbed into a little cart, which a flock of doves pulled up to an altar. Mother Hoebeke read out a Christian service. The bachelor of the trio, on his hind legs, carried a cup among the assembled crowd for a collection.

In photos, the old lady looks like one of those obese South Pacific matriarchs with a sweet smile who fling victims into a smoking volcano. Apparently she wasn't that bad. When she didn't like a guest, she merely flashed a discreet signal to the killer rabbit. He'd jerk the guy's napkin with his teeth, spilling plate and silverware onto the floor, and then hop his ass to safety.

Edouard Marx bought the inn early in the 1950s, moving from Strasbourg. "Les Marx Bruzzehrs also came from Strasbourg," he assured me. "Well, not them, but their family," His passion was cooking rabbits, not nattering with them. Also, flowers and the Seine. Marx built a sprawling Normandy-style hotel, in stone, timbers and tiles. He terraced a lovely willow-shaded picnic spot on the island just out front, reached by romantic little skiffs. With a postcard reading, "E. Marx, *Diplôme Cuisinier de France*," he was in business.

Each winter, someone digs up all of his 650 canna bulbs and brings them inside; by the time they come in from the cold, the red flowering stalks are seven feet high. Each spring, he replaces the 600 geraniums and 1,200 impatiens.

"We get a lot of people because of Giverny, but mostly they come for the Seine Valley," Marx said. "It does something to people." We were talking about painters, and he went to his guest book to jog his memory. Among hasty sketches by American artists who had passed through, I noted a few familiar French signatures: a filmmaker, a politician, some entertainers.

A lot of serious tourists visit the valley in chunks. The Auberge du Lapin Savant is at the center of the first section, the painters' Seine. It begins at Bougival and reaches to the splendid Rouen Cathedral, a favorite subject of Monet's. After that, the abbeys start. From Rouen to the English Channel, it is the monks' Seine.

Marx sent me off with directions to Monet's old studio, the riverbank at Vétheuil. "You can't miss it," he told me. "Anywhere you turn, it is beautiful."

It was beautiful, all right, but I realized I was missing a crucial angle of view. Like most bankside towns, Vétheuil and Vernon were built with the river in mind. They rise from stone pilings up to hilltop towers in layers of angled roofs and terraced gardens. Proportions were meant to beguile visitors with wealth to leave behind, or dampen the ardor of those who planned to plunder. Trying to appreciate them from the shore was like a subject in a painting trying to lean out in order to see the whole canvas. It was time to fire up *La Vieille*.

∾∾∾∾∾

How might you picture starting off with your loved one on a romantic river trip aboard your floating home deep into these magical Seinescapes? In my case, I began on my knees at the tail end of my car sucking gas. Jeannette and I took what we called in advance the Trepidation Tour to Giverny; before it was over three days later, we had worse names for it. It was great.

The old boat had not seen Ardouin's yard in four years. Her gears were hardly capable of grating Parmesan, their reverse cogs linking desultorily only when the mood struck. Both engines needed tuning, and none of the technical staff was closer than two countries away. I would be taking her up to Limay for drydock in less than a month; it was folly to tempt fate by working her hard downriver, locks away from help. Besides, I had notes scattered from aft to forepeak, all of which would need shifting if she got stuck somewhere. Screw it, we figured. We'd go.

Departure was fixed for 6 A.M. Jacques showed up on time, with the generator he'd promised to bring but I thought would forget. We needed gas. I tried to siphon from the car to a jerrycan; my tank was empty. By the time I found an open gas station and got back, it was 7:30. We'd have to run the motors hard to make our first port by dark. But the weather was good. For most of the day, we acted like people of leisure and ate like pigs, and I managed not to scare Jacques even once.

From Paris to Limay was our milk run, past some humdrum, but it always thrills. Unlike along the highway, patches of blight by the Seine do not jar. Moving slowly, there is time to notice the nuggets. In Neuilly, amid the modern sprawl, is the Temple of Love, a stone gazebo on the Ile de la Grande Jatte where King Louis-Philippe threw his fanciful Venetian parties.

When not much is interesting on shore, you watch the water. Once, flanked by industrial slurry, we followed a stiletto-thin scull, varnished to a gleam, streaking along so fast it seemed to be planing over the surface. A young woman in bicycle tights, dramatic platinum hair floating on the wind, was doing her version of a morning jog. Over the past year, I've seen the Seine produce a Venetian gondola, an African pirogue, a Viking drakkar, a million-dollar yacht and a blue whale so big it barely cleared the Paris bridges. This last was of papier-mâché.

Just beyond Neuilly, we passed the Ile aux Ravageurs, once the hangout of an outcast band of bums whom Paris paid to fish corpses from the Seine. Its new name is the Ile aux Chiens because it is a dog cemetery, a canine Père-Lachaise. Gravestones honor, among others, a French German shepherd named Rintintin, trained to warn soldiers of gas attacks in World War I. Also, there is Barry, a Saint Bernard that, according his epitaph, "saved forty people and was killed by the forty-first."

Even near Paris, it is amazing how much is left of what inspired the impressionists. If industry has overrun Gennevilliers and Argenteuil, Bougival is an unspoiled line of storybook houses fringed with tall trees through which light plays on the water. Only a minor effort blots out a Holiday Inn–type motel, the Forest Hills (pronounced *For-ehst Ills*). We settled into deck chairs and watched a world I'd passed twenty times in a car and never knew existed.

By Bougival, the moored converted *péniches* are no longer houseboats in a city but rather country homes afloat. On one of them, I knew, William Wharton was beavering away. After his novel *Birdy* made a smash, reporters and fans scurried to find him. They knew he lived on a boat and his name was not really Wharton. He laid low along the Seine, just another eccentric outsider who had come to taste good bread. Later, he blew his cover. I'd thought about stopping but decided he was either writing or stripping varnish. Both took a lot of private concentration.

We'd sailed through the huge Suresnes lock with little company. By then, I gave good radio. When I announced our approach to Bougival, a helpful voice came back: "I'll prepare *la petite*." By the time we reached the locks, the woman on the radio had filled the smallest basin and opened the gates. We slipped in, tied up and dropped a couple of stories. I had stayed up top to handle the ropes. This is cake, I thought, looking for the usual slimy ladder to get back to the boat. There was none.

I peered over the side at slippery green scum. No footholds or handholds. *La Vieille* was a toy boat far below. Finally, I grabbed the sodden stern line, figuring I'd shinny down the way those goofy cadets did in *Police Academy*. The lockkeeper emerged from her glass tower, lips pursed, and pointed to rungs cut into the stone wall, which I had overlooked. It was one of the few times I've ever heard a French person go, "*Oh, la la.*"

Past Poissy, the bridges are vast utilitarian spans, spaced far apart. In more than a dozen places before Honfleur, ferries shuttle cars across the Seine the old way. At Herblay, the painters' paradise near Conflans, we watched a rusty little boat tie up and take aboard the waiting throng: a small Peugeot, its driver and a handful of schoolkids on bikes.

Halfway to Limay, we gave up trying to reverse the port propeller. We simply approached hairy places slowly and hoped for the best. Then we lost forward on the starboard side. The lever would not move. This is like running a car on half its cylinders with no brakes; it is possible, but not such a hot idea. We made it to Limay and bumped to a stop. A few beers later, we forgot all contretemps. This, I had to acknowledge, was living.

Here we were, feet up and at home, sixty miles away from the *bateaux-mouches* wake. The generator chilled our Bandol rosé. I'd filched someone's hose and, with a cigarette lighter to soften the plastic and a strategic clamp, hooked up water for hot showers. It was a fine night for musing.

I had enough serious adventure at work. This was something else, an adventurelet with pleasure you had to earn. When the river tossed up its challenges, I could be Bogart on the *African Queen*. But I knew the Seine's leeches had small appetites.

The river offered escape. On land, someone was always trying to keep order. Land people at the navigation office had just imposed a river tax, and I was supposed to have a sticker. At one lock, a stern woman demanded, "Do you have your *vignette*?" I mumbled an excuse. She laughed, hard. By coincidence, I'd just heard someone on the BBC reading a few lines from "Mandalay." The Seine may not be the Wild East, but, approaching the twenty-first century, it is where there ain't no Ten Commandments and a man can raise a thirst.

I cut the power and lighted oil lamps, and it got better. We drifted back into the continuum of the Seine. This might have been 1360, when the king's engineers built the bridge we'd just passed. Or five hundred years later, when Corot painted a Limay he'd be hard put to recognize today. In another half a millenium, who knows what might be on shore? But the river, most likely, will be the same.

In a time when so much of reality is vicarious, filtered by the tube, when food is artificial, and unseen systems shield us from surprise, I felt very much alive. Bobbing gently on our river, we roasted a chicken, watched several billion stars, sniffed fresh breezes and slept in spite of all the fish doing noisy back flips just out the portholes.

The next day we had to make a choice. We were having a great time at turtle camping—taking the whole mess along without bothering to pack. I was constantly saying things like "Damn, I forgot to bring the zoom lens," and then realizing that I was wrong. Once I started my usual paranoia, wondering if anyone was messing with the boat back home. Then I stopped; no one would break in this time. I only had to worry about pirates.

But there was the other side. If our house threw a rod in some reed swamp, we couldn't call a tow truck and go home for a restorative rum. Assuming we found help to a safe mooring, someone would have to keep watch on board until repairs were completed. This would be fine if we had nothing to do for, say, seven weeks. But the lights go after the third night, and then the propane runs out. And there is always the dreaded S-word, "sink," which means a lot of soggy shirts. One can take only so much voluntary reality.

Weighing the extremes, we pushed our luck and headed on downstream. At 7 A.M., it was moist and nippy—hot-coffee weather. Swans left rippled wakes on the still river,

veiled in thick morning mists. Early light dappled the surface, reflecting trees on the banks. *La Vieille* was doing fine.
We had unstuck the gears. The Méricourt lock was a snap,
and the Seine began to get decidedly beautiful.

Along with the odd *péniche* piloted by a bargee in baggy
trousers, we crossed twenty-two English motorboats on a
rally, each bearing earnest couples in crisp new orange life
vests. I raised ten fingers to one skipper, and we chatted on
the VHF, channel ten. He was formal and nautical, a boatman from waters with Ten Commandments. As the polished
hulls bounced past *La Vieille*, with her cracked paint and dull
brightwork, a great deal of tsk-tsking echoed over the water.
Then we saw the other extreme. At a silo dock, a Turkish ship
and an indeterminate vessel carrying West Africans waited
to exchange scrap metal for wheat. It was unclear where
scrap stopped and ship started.

Jeannette and I were getting into this river business.
Standing in the stern, we began to spin out fantasies. How
many charters would we need to do this full-time? I glanced
at Jacques and saw the angle of his eyebrows. Sure enough,
a clutch was slipping. But it was only on one side. I decided
to concentrate on watching the river.

La Roche-Guyon, nice enough from the road, was stunning from the river. Sycamores trimmed like a privet hedge
lined the quai at the edge of a lush park. Although steel
uprights made a perfect mooring, large markers warned that
the water was too shallow. Dredging would have fixed that,
but the last thing the village wanted was boat tourists who
brought their own food and lodging.

Vernon, also more thrilling from the water, had a different attitude. A well-equipped marina by a cluster of medieval turrets offered visitor space. *La Vieille*, needing deeper
water and more space, hauled up to the center of town, next

to a handy row of bollards and a Welcome sign in two languages.

Jeannette and I did Giverny slowly, checking out the flower beds in front of people's houses—blazing bouquets, waist high but delicately bordered with little succulents. We saw the paintings I missed before, by American impressionists who sniffed around Monet. They are hung in something called the American Museum, a modernistic structure liberally marked with the name of its Republican benefactor. "It is an unfortunate name," a hostess allowed. "People expect to find medals and war graves."

We bought a tablecloth, ate *un hot dog*, and went home. A cabbie took us back to the boat and dreamed out loud about what it must be like to go rolling on the river. Oh-oh, I thought. Such thoughts invariably piss off the gods.

We left at 2 P.M. and headed back, hoping to make Limay by 5:30. Pretty soon we reached a patch of river that was a half mile wide and far too shallow. An upstream tug pushing four thousand tons of sand took the main channel, to the left, and I began passing him, far to the right. About then, a *péniche* approached us, with plenty of room between us. When the captain drew even, I waved. He shouted obscenities and circled his finger at his temple to signify loose screws. In translation, that meant: "God damn it, I'm commercial and you're a yachkch(spit)cht. You're supposed to tear out your bottom to prove that I'm king of the river." Sigh.

When I radioed the Méricourt locks, the news was bad. Gates had jammed on the main basin; the other one, a lot smaller, worked erratically. It was just filling up with downstream traffic. We would have to wait along with that giant barge convoy and everyone else who had automatic priority. It was the day's end, when Rouen-Paris traffic was hurrying to get through the lock. Jacques cut the engines to idle and threw both levers into reverse so we could wait in place.

"Gone," he announced, churning the levers. I asked him to repeat that, but I speak Jacques, and my heart had already dropped to the wheelhouse floor. The gears had gotten unfixed, all of them, in both directions. Soon we were drifting helplessly into a 360-degree circle, and high wind was pushing us swiftly toward stakes that warned of jagged, shallow rocks.

I glanced at Jacques, hoping that he might know something comforting that I did not. He had the look he normally reserves for a nerve-gas attack. Quickly, I calculated our options. We had a hundred feet of strong, thin rope on the bow, enough for an emergency line. But there was nothing to tie it to. We had two anchors, but our fragments would be washing around the English Channel by the time I got them shackled and into the water. That left death and desolation and wet socks.

With a mighty shove, Jacques got us into gear. By the time we straightened out on one engine, the lock gates were opening. We squeezed in, and, with an awkwardness that had two dozen people rolling about in laughter, we tied up. Then another *péniche* appeared, and we had to move forward and do it again, a few feet from the monster tug's prop wash. *La Vieille* is hard to secure in locks. The bow cleats are far forward, causing her to roll along her curve and send the stern sideways. Wind makes it much worse. You can correct for this with reverse thrust, if you have any. A stern line helps, if you have an extra hand. But Jeannette was busy shoving tires between the hull and the killer stone wall. We looked very silly.

The lock nightmare took an hour, and we limped into Limay at 7 P.M. We discovered that the gearbox had sprung an oil leak. It was easy enough to fill, and the levers moved again. I found a yellow pad, already black with writing, and added: "Port gearbox leak. Why?" Then we dressed for a Viking-style assault on Ardouin's wine cellar. We ate merrily, under the stars.

Mellow with Charolais in shallots and cigar smoke, I cornered Jacques. We'd survived a harrowing day, and it was time for my rites of passages. The master was at ease, unsuspecting. But I was determined. Before leaving Paris, I'd had this silly obsession. Though a practicing boat owner, I had yet to learn the ropes. My two half hitches usually slipped, dumping expensive fenders into the water. I tied bowlines by trying to remember the kid's crutch about the snake crawling around the tree, but my snake always slithered down the wrong hole. Iron Jacques the sailor would teach me.

"Okay," I said, looping a length of rope around my waist. "Show me a bowline." He looked away and muttered. "What?" I asked. "I can't," he said, sheepish. "We always used steel cable." Jacques could lock ropes to a bollard in a sound sleep and also tie his shoelaces. Beyond that, he was knot illiterate. Somehow, that made it all seem a whole lot easier.

The next morning, we headed back to Paris, treading carefully in the Limay channel, under an ancient stone bridge with an arch chopped away to let boats pass. Things went smoothly in the first lock until Jacques observed, in a voice he might have used to ask for the cigarette lighter, "We've lost an engine." With more mirth among the bargees, we left the lock sideways.

La Vieille cruises at seven miles an hour on two engines. On one, she can still do five. After that, it drops off rapidly. Also, we were hardly certain of having working gears on the same side as a working motor. This was a crisis. Jacques stripped down and dived into the engines, Crocodile Dundee with a wrench in his teeth. He reemerged. "Nothing to be done," he said.

I decided to fix the engine. Those who know me realize this is a hilarious statement. Let's just say I'm no mechanic. But diesels are simple enough. It could not be the ignition because there is none. The motor turned over, so nothing had seized or blown. That left fuel. I crawled into the smoking, thundering engine space and disassembled the two fuel filters.

I knew the filter elements would be dirty. Val had looked for three months in England to find the last two that would fit my old BMC engines. We hoarded them, hoping to avoid a bothersome retrofit. We had overdone it. The old elements looked like someone had melted caramel in them. Sludge clogged them solid. I replaced them, pumped the lines and bled the injectors. It worked.

Jeannette could not talk from the shock. I tried to act humble but preened like a show cock. This miracle occurred just before the next lock, and we entered it under full power. Feeling like Thor Heyerdahl, I nonchalantly threw a loop over a bollard and wrapped a deft figure eight over the cleat. A sudden pain brought to my notice that all four writing fingers of my left hand were caught between the rope and the steel.

"Back, go back," I yelled at Jacques. He shifted to reverse but—guess what? Thirty tons of forward momentum crushed my fingers while I watched in fascination. They went purple and misshapen. "How," I managed to wonder, "can anyone be such a dumb fuck? Do they make elbow-operated computers?" Pain increased, and so did fear. A yachtsman's jackknife hung around my neck, an affectation that sometimes proved handy. It would have saved my fingers if I'd had two hands to open it.

Jeannette was straining at the stern, unaware of my private drama. Jacques knew something was wrong but had his hands full. I thought I could hear bones making noise. Then a wave raised the bow slightly. With my free hand, I was able to yank a loop of rope off one side of the cleat. My liberated hand looked like the coyote's in a Roadrunner cartoon, after an anvil landed on it. Though slightly mangled, all fingers worked.

For three hours, we frolicked and lazed on deck. We kicked on the generator to make ice for my hand. What else could happen? Right. We pulled up to the last lock, cut the engines to idle, and Jacques delivered yet another deadpan line: "The engine is out again." I must have left an injector sleeve loose enough to suck in an air bubble.

Approaching the lock, I had made the usual radio call: "*Plaisancier, montant.*" That meant a "pleasure boat" was arriving. It seemed like a pretty amusing misnomer. No problem, however. By then, Jacques was used to flying on one wing. We made it through the last lock, with only an hour to go.

Coming into Paris, I took the wheel, anxious for more experience at dodging *bateaux-mouches* and sand convoys with a single engine. Cops and firemen streaked by, leaving wakes that flung food out of the freezer. Wind and waves edited our course. At the port, Jacques drifted the boat into its tight mooring space. I leaped onto Philippe's barge and looped us fast. We were back home on our little piece of the Seine. The Trepidation Tour was over, and I couldn't wait for the next one.

13 Ronald Reagan
Ate Here

BEYOND VERNON, it keeps getting better. In Paris, with so much present and future, the past seems optional. Down this far, where the Seine resumes its placid meanders, you cannot help but reflect on what went on over the last thousand years. Among the new summer homes, mossy old stone suggests a richness to anyone who takes the trouble to investigate. When hills above Les Andelys appear, this sense of history rises to flood.

High atop a cliff, Château Gaillard commands the valley from every direction. The sturdiest stronghold on the river, among the most famed castles in France, it was built for the same reason that Philippe Auguste walled Paris and put up the Louvre. Blood would spill over the Seine Valley.

Philippe and Richard the Lion-Hearted went off together on the Third Crusade, uneasy allies who knew one another too well. Philippe returned early to lay plans for seizing Normandy. Richard followed but spent years in an Austrian prison, the victim of other intrigue. Back home, he marshaled three thousand workers to build Château Gaillard. Its walls were fifteen feet thick above a dry moat that plunged forty-five feet.

"If the walls were of iron, I'd take them nonetheless," the French king said. The English king replied, "By God's throat, if the walls were of butter, I would hold them." Richard died in battle before any test came. His brother, John, was less interested in Normandy. When a delegation from Rouen sought an audience, he dismissed them to return to a game of chess. In 1203, Philippe besieged Château Gaillard.

Half the residents of Les Andelys fled to the castle ahead of French forces. After a few weeks, the defenders assessed their food stocks. Unnecessary mouths were dispatched to their homes. When the townsfolk tried to return, the French barred their way. The general wanted them back in the castle, eating and drinking the dwindling provisions. Neither side budged, and families spent the winter in the moat. The weakest died quickly of exposure. The strongest ate the flesh of neighbors who could not hold out. In the end, at least six hundred people died.

The castle had a double moat, with bridges in two sections. An attacking army might seize one side, but they still had to take the inner keep, where the governor and a guard of twenty could wait forever for reinforcements from England.

After eight months, Philippe got sneaky. He sent sappers slithering up the plumbing. Latrine pipes ran down the Seine side of the castle, a sheer drop, and no one expected such a dirty trick. The commando let down the bridge, and troops stormed the castle. French armies hurried down the Seine, welcomed by Normans who knew what was good for them.

They seized Rouen and then secured the whole course of the river. Normandy was folded into France.

Less than two centuries later, Britain and France were at it again for a Hundred Years' War that went on longer than its name suggests. Henry V of Britain led the next siege of Château Gaillard, in 1418, and it lasted twice as long. After sixteen months, the water ran out. French troops, inflamed by Joan of Arc, took it back the following year and lost it again within six months. In 1449, Charles VII defeated the English, at the castle and soon in the war. Henri IV worried about who else might take the place, however, and he had most of it demolished.

Townspeople have since stolen a lot of stone to build down below. Only ruins suggest what Château Gaillard was. But enough is left. There is the prison, which had perhaps the best view in the history of incarceration. Higher up, window seats in the governor's keep look down on the meandering river, set among white limestone palisades, hills, rich meadows and wooded banks. It is a very lovely panorama.

Settlements like Les Andelys amounted to convenience stores for plundering armies that ranged the Seine. After a quick smash and grab, commanders moved on to the big stores in Rouen or Paris. In normal times, however, Les Andelys made up for it by gouging travelers of lighter armament. A chain across the channel to an island *en face* stopped all traffic for a sizable toll. With no affection, boatmen called it the Golden Chain. I stopped for lunch at a fancy old inn on the spot, La Chaîne d'Or.

"It has a lovely view on the river," Madame Lindsey had said, accurately. But I immediately realized what she had also seemed to be communicating in her tactful, well-bred manner: the place was a mortuary. Outside, glittering warm sunlight played on vivid colors. From the picture windows, you could see windsurfers and picnickers in full summer frolic. Inside, the waitresses wore severe black suits, black bow ties and black hose, each looking as if the Vikings had just disemboweled her trained rabbit.

The restaurant was full, and I strained to see the Seine across tables of other diners. Nearly all were what the French call people of a certain age—powdered ladies with hair teased to the edge of violence and men in drab ties who moved their lips when they weren't talking. They ate with deliberate slowness, shaping each piece of bread torn from the roll and looking around from time to time as if to see when the corpse would be rolled in.

The maître d' appeared, lugubrious in a double-breasted gray flannel suit. He fussed with the silver on a tablecloth in deep pink, the sort of hue that levels out all social differences. Eventually, lunch appeared. The food was wonderful, served with skill. Everyone seemed to be enjoying themselves. Afterward, I chatted with the maître-owner, who turned out to be a nice guy and fairly relaxed at that. He wore, after all, a heliotrope shirt. Apparently, the place had its measure of fame. Ronald Reagan and Nancy ate a presidential lunch there.

What had I expected? With so much lore and history around you, it is easy enough to forget the present. Everything else aside, the Seine is a fat strip of water that winds through the thick of deepest France. My fellow diners weren't floaters like me; they were comfortable locals, an emeritus rank of a blessed bourgeoisie. These days, Teutonic and Anglo-Saxon visitors paid well for their plunder, and life was worth savoring.

La Chaîne d'Or was not a morgue but rather a temple. Its congregants had no place else they had to be until the next social-security check. Sea trout *à la nage* needed its trappings. Their grandparents had raised them to believe it is preferable to dine out among cuff links and stiff collars, as opposed to grubby white Levi's, and this had a certain logic to it. I suppose I was lucky to sit at their table. The other option was just upriver, a McDonald's with a drive-through window and have-a-*bon-jour* smiles.

～～～～～

From Vernon on down to Honfleur, the river's power and beauty add up to far more than the sum of its separate sites. The Michelin green guide bestows three stars on the whole Seine Valley and spends seven pages explaining why, not counting long entries for Rouen, Jumièges Abbey and everything else along the way. It touches only briefly on how the river made it like that.

Over millenia, as water coursed down, it skidded around the corners. At each bend, swift currents undercut the inside curve, digging into the bed and bank. Silt eddied off at the far edge, creating shallows. Eventually, the river shifted its path, leaving rich alluvial soil at one side and carving sharp banks in the chalky rock on the other.

By the time the Gauls and Romans found it, the Seine was wide but seldom deep. Their shallow-draft boats got by in most seasons. Sometimes they sat in the mud and waited. Past Poses, on the upstream side of Rouen, tidal currents began to deepen the river but also made navigation hairy in the best of times, with channels a tricky proposition.

The Vikings needed all their skill to maneuver drakkars upstream, especially when also dodging slings and arrows from the banks. Their boats were up to seventy-five feet long, with seagoing keels that needed six feet of water. The closer they got to Paris and then the wine country beyond, the harder it got to advance. Except in the wettest of seasons, you could hardly get a decent boatload of booty back to Denmark.

Once the Norsemen were housebroken under Rollo, they put their energies into engineering on the river. First they dredged a deeper channel among the maze of islands, using the mud they recovered to fill narrow passages between islets and sandbanks. By consolidating archipelagos, building up banks and directing the flow, they raised the river to a reliable level from the mouth as far as Vernon. With less risk of floods, people built fancy and solid all along the river. Trade was brisk with a Nordic commonwealth that took in much of the Western world. Normandy thrived as perhaps the first independent medieval state.

Six centuries later, Louis XIV's master minder, Colbert, ordered work on the Seine. The Sun King needed better access to the sea. Where the river lost its purpose in wide marshy flats, banks were drained and diked. Colbert hired Dutch engineers to reclaim wide patches of swamp. By the time steam-powered world trade grew intense in the 1800s, the Seine was still hit-and-miss for deep-water bottoms. Ships were seldom more than a hundred feet along, carrying a few hundred tons, with sturdy steel hulls. They headed up the estuary and moved only at high tide. After hours of progress, they found a safe spot for a *posée*; they sat high and dry until the water came back. A trip up to Rouen, a short day of steady steaming, could take two weeks.

The first steamer appeared on the Seine in 1816, the *Elise*, scaring the hell out of people on shore. Sparks and flames shot from the stacks, and the noise was ungodly. Soon, such vessels were common. Later in the century, regular passenger service linked Paris and Rouen. A train took people up to the little port of Le Pecq, beyond Chatou. From there, they cruised all night in relatively uncomfortable circumstances. When the river fell in summer, these *coches d'eau* called a halt.

It was Napoléon III, after 1860, who wrestled the Seine into submission. A series of locks and canals reached Paris and beyond, but the key was Amfreville. The emperor's massive dam held back the river until it covered rapids and shallows with at least ten feet of water. Since then, new locks and a more flexible dam have replaced the original installations. They are worth a visit.

From an overhead walkway, you can watch fifteen *péniches* jam into a single chamber, built for monster convoys and oceangoing ships on their way to Paris. Or rather, you could if fifteen *péniches* ever got there at once. "We don't see that many anymore," explained a helpful woman who kept track of business at the Amfreville locks. I was happy to have run into her.

Far up the canals, I'd met lockkeepers who might have dropped out of a Balzac manuscript. On a cut along the Saône, Madame Bernier had a lot of time to garden. At the approach of a boat, she turned off the *boeuf bourguignon*, shooed aside the cloud of children, and shuffled to the lockhouse in slippers and housecoat. If you weren't in a hurry, neither was she. At this gigantic lock on the Seine, I thought, it would be different.

In fact, the lockkeepers work in a glassed control tower with VHF radio and a dashboard of fancy electronics. Crises come up. But here was a coiffured incarnation of Madame Bernier. This was the river. People joked. When someone said, "How're you doing?" they waited for an answer.

At the time, France was going through a police-state phase, the result of too many people without the right papers, and not enough income from levies and fines. For more than a year, the authorities had directed all private boats to display their *vignette*, evidence that they had paid a healthy toll. A crackdown had begun. When I asked about it, the woman chuckled, as the lockkeeper had done on my trip to Vernon. "Oh, I don't know how seriously anyone takes that," she said. "Maybe *La Fluviale* [the river police]. We certainly don't check."

This was that other world, with fewer commandments and more to see. Now you can barrel from Paris to Rouen on the A13 *autoroute* in an hour and change. Only the sign reading "*Vous êtes en Normandie*" tells you when you cross the old border. Trees are trees. The fields of Ile-de-France blend seamlessly into those of its neighbors. At a distance, you can make out the stone spires of Mantes-la-Jolie. But you get a clear view of the Porcheville power plant; a highway panel boasts that the steel cathedral puts out twenty-four hundred megawatts. Another marker says, "La Seine," and its arrow points downward. If not too busy staying in lane, you catch a glimpse of water. You see a fine range of factory outlets and *hypermarchés*. The *autoroute* is fast, but you pay for it.

A boat is good way to see the other side of things, but so is a car. Stick to road numbers that start with D, for *départementaux*, and keep the river in sight. On land you can stop to eat, often the best part of traveling in France. And you can look into unsettled mysteries, such as the incident at Two Lovers' Hill—the Côte des Deux Amants—near Amfreville-sous-les-Monts.

Back in the misty pasts, a jerky king of Pîtres had a gorgeous daughter he was eager to keep. To win her hand, a suitor had to carry her at a nonstop sprint to the top of the hill. It is a big hill. One day, a handsome youth named Raoul started up with Caliste in his arms. He made it to the top, gazed into her eyes and dropped dead in a heap. She also died, her heart not burst but broken, and they were buried on the spot.

Another version says Caliste pined away in a nunnery or battered her father about the temples with an artichoke or moved to Akron. Whatever the answer, it is a drop-dead panorama. You can see over the whole valley, where the little Andelle empties into the Seine and boats drift in and out of the Amfreville locks.

As the river approaches Rouen, guidebooks are a good idea. If impressionist country needs little explanation, the rest of the river is rich in a past full of significant details. When Clovis embraced God and Paris, he set to work on a string of abbeys along the lovely loops of the Seine. His wife, Clotilde, was cloistered in one. Like the missions in California, a series of *châteaux de dieu* stretched from the magnificent Abbaye Saint-Ouen in Rouen to an outpost by the now-landlocked port of Harfleur. In most of them, the monks are still there.

〜〜〜〜

The tide is first felt at Poses, near Amfreville, ninety miles from the estuary. Twice daily, waves wash in fast and hard from the English Channel, pushing the fresh water back up the Seine. During big tides, water collects at wide points and then thunders up in a single roll against the current with a force that can tear ships loose from moorings in the port of Rouen.

"When it comes in hard, in three waves, one after another, all you can do is stay in the middle of the channel until it passes," Jacques explained to me once. "You face it head-on, like ocean waves." Once, in Rouen, he was on a tug pushing barges loaded with oil, and a tidal roll snapped the mooring. "We started drifting fast toward a passenger ship. The engine was churning full speed—four hundred, five hundred horses—and it was out of control. We were all running around, ready with life vests." The tug captain managed to steer clear. By then, the roll had passed, and he regained control.

Hydrologists have wrestled with these ebbs and flows for centuries, trying to tame them. They say the freak waves are merely the result of a tidal bore, a function of the shape of the Seine's banks and bottom. Paging through the old books, I found an alternate explanation for this twice-daily backwash and periodic surge. Bernardin de Saint-Pierre, who wrote *Paul et Virginie* two centuries ago, offered details from the old legends.

Seine was once a beautiful young nymphette, the daughter of Bacchus, god of wine. She served as handmaiden to Ceres, goddess of wheat, who was roaming the world in search of her own daughter, Proserpine. Hades, god of the netherworld, had snatched Proserpine in a foul ruse. Ceres wanted her back.

After combing the corners of what is now France, Ceres gave up the search and discharged her faithful servant. As severance pay, Seine asked for the valleys she now waters. Ceres complied and added a bonus: the power to grow rich wheat wherever she walked. For safety, Ceres left Seine with a guardian nymphette of her own, Heva. She was afraid some sea god would carry her off as Hades had grabbed Proserpine.

Sure enough, one day Seine was at the beach, collecting shells and frolicking in the waves, when Heva screamed. Under the surface, she saw the flowing white hair, purplish face and blue robes of Neptune. Seine fled to her familiar inland meadows. But the sea god was smitten. He mounted up with his marine horsemen and galloped after her. Just as the slimy old creep reached out an arm to sweep her away to the ocean, Seine beamed a message to her father and her friend. In god circles, both were big guns.

Seine turned to water and slipped through Neptune's fingers. She melted into a long, lovely river. Her green gown, which had billowed in the wind as she ran for her life, settled onto her as a rich emerald tint. Neptune was undaunted. Twice a day since, with great heaving and grunting, he thrusts himself after his lost love object. Each time, the Seine recoils, reversing the natural flow of a river, to keep her gentler green waters separate from his salty waves of blue.

Who knows? River people reject nothing out of hand.

<u>14</u> *Bovary Country*

AT ROUEN, the Seine goes big time. It is no romantic ribbon laced around the heart of a city. The bridges' names evoke a rich past—Joan of Arc, William the Conqueror— but they are raw concrete spans across a wide waterway meant for business. The port of Rouen handles three thousand ships a year, freighters of up to 160,000 tons. Eight million tons of grain a year goes out, to Russia and beyond, and every manner of cargo comes in. But like almost everywhere else along it, Rouen people love the Seine.

At the height of cherry-blossom season, I took the train to Rouen to catch the *Normandie* and finish the river in style. My cabbie, Lucien Salaün, brightened when he heard my purpose. Unlike Garry Droissart in Moret, he was not a grounded *marinier*. He was just interested. Salaün offered a tidbit: Did I know about *les boules de moulin*? I didn't.

"Ah," he said, happy to be of service. "In the old days

invaders besieged Paris and blockaded the Seine. People inside tried to send carrier pigeons, but they were shot. So they used hollowed-out wooden balls to send messages. They floated them downstream, and their allies behind the siege lines fished them out." He didn't explain how answers were delivered—or much else, for that matter. It was, however, a great Seine story.

"Come back for the tall ships," Salaün said, as I left his taxi. He got out to pump my hand with both of his. "Don't forget."

Like Paris, Rouen celebrated the bicentennial of the revolution with festivities on the Seine. The City of Light fired spectacular pyrotechnics over the Eiffel Tower. Rouen invited wooden three-masters from the ends of the earth: Argentina's *Libertad*, Chile's *Esmeralda* and the others. Even the *Amerigo Vespucci* from Italy squeaked under the Tancarville bridge by removing a top chunk of its mast. It was such a success that Rouen decided to do it again, a massive regatta for July 14, 1994—the Armada of Liberty.

Ships from thirty nations accepted, including the thrilling Spanish four-master I'd once seen materialize off a Tahitian reef, the *Juan Sebastian de Elcano*. After three days in Rouen, the ships would parade down the Seine to the sea.

The old Norman capital grew strong because of the river, and only the unwanted urban renewal of Allied bombers caused the city to draw back from it. Rouen, first a Celtic village, became Rotomagus, the last point downstream where the Romans could span a bridge. Like Paris, the site was a sprinkling of islands at the start of a bend in the Seine, protected by hills. In the eighth century, Vikings found it a handy base for upstream depredations. When Rollo got the keys to Normandy, he made Rouen his capital.

Rollo's calmed-down Vikings began to tame their part of

the Seine a thousand years ago. While they held Normandy, traffic to Paris passed at their pleasure. Off and on during wars with England, nothing got past Rouen. Even later, boats moved slowly, and a lot of the riches moving upriver to Paris stayed behind in Rouen. It was the crossroads into Brittany and the marketplace for fertile Normandy fields.

With the Renaissance, Rouen bloomed with rich mansions, a new façade on its immense French Gothic cathedral, and law courts of elaborate wood and stone scrollwork. The Saint-Ouen abbey, among other retreats, made Rouen a religious capital. Teamed with navigators on the coast, merchants sold textiles halfway around the world. The clothiers' guild seal, with three ships masted in gold, read, "O Sun, we follow you to the ends of the earth."

Culture flowered in every period. Rouen produced a pioneer of French Romanticism, Théodore Géricault. The wreck of the *Medusa*, however, was not on the Seine.

Rouen was beaten up badly during France's persistent wars with Britain. That was nothing next to World War II. Bombs smashed the place, toppling towers and walls into a medieval mess. Old neighbors between the Seine and the cathedral were flattened. The left-bank industrial zone collapsed to smoking rubble. All the bridges and quaiside charm crumbled into the water. When it came time to rebuild, the banks were cut off by express lanes, and port activities all shifted to the far side of the city.

Thanks to loving restoration and a lot of lucky misses, much is left to see. Cobbled streets closed to traffic wind among the remaining spires and under overhangs, past intricate façades of stone and stained glass. Houses are framed on exposed oak beams set at odd angles, many still roofed in thatch.

The Archbishop's Palace looks like it did when Joan of

Arc was sentenced to death as a witch there in 1431. The vast abbey nearby has changed little since prelates within cleared her name, fifteen years too late, and made her a saint. But a modern-art chapel of soaring glass stands in the obliterated marketplace where Joan was drowned at the stake. History claims she was burned, but locals know that Rouen is never dry enough for that.

Rain was pounding when Christine Guyot took me around town. She was cruise director of the *Normandie*, a free-lance fireball who roamed the travel industry in search of interesting things to do. Her English was flawless, but so were her German, Dutch, Italian, Spanish and God's knows what else. She had been everywhere, from sailing cruises in the South Seas to treks up American mountains. Christine loved the Seine.

On every street, she showed me the history of France stamped on city walls. Traces remain of the Vikings, who tore up Rouen before settling in as the Norman bourgeoisie. Christine was more interested in the wars of religion, the centuries of vicious bloodshed between the English and French to determine who better exhibited Christian virtues.

The French Revolution left a lasting mark on Rouen. Bullet holes from two centuries back crater the Palais de Justice like a biblical pox. Aroused *citoyens* lopped the heads off statues outside churches; unadorned necks are still in place. By far, the most widespread damage occurred during the lifetime of anyone over fifty. For all the pomp and smiles over a united new Europe, a lot of people still quietly scowl at the sound of German spoken harshly.

No sign remains of Rouen's first reported tragedy. In the seventh century, it was eaten by a Seine dragon named Gargouille. Saint Romanus, the archbishop, slew him.

In every period of upheaval, the Seine made its impact,

not the least during the last one. Before dropping me off, Salaün had laughed hard at the thought of occupation forces scrambling to get home, ahead of liberating troops, confounded by all the river's hairpin curves in the way. Road markers had disappeared, leaving panicky Germans to figure things out for themselves. "Every time they got across the river, they went, 'Oouuuff,' thinking they were home free," he said. "Then they got to the Seine again."

Christine pushed on. "Are you getting too wet?" she asked. It was not a necessary question. Rain came down as if spilled from fifty-gallon oil drums. Rivulets streamed down our necks and noses. Neither of us had an umbrella or rain gear, and our clothes hung like sodden dishrags. She meant: Was I ready to stop? I wasn't. She beamed happily and splashed on down the cobblestones. "I hope this is open," she said, picking up the pace. "It's my favorite place in Rouen."

We turned abruptly into a narrow lane, wide enough for a carriage, and ducked under an oak-beamed overhang. Two wide doors opened into a vast inner courtyard. Suddenly, we left the city for a remote country monastery. Rows of sturdy carved doors faced onto a rambling verandah, which circumscribed an open park. A stone fountain burbled at the center, watering lush growth. This had to be what they meant by island of peace.

I stopped to look at the wood panels around the stone walls of the verandah. They were carved death's-heads set among shovels and picks. One window was open slightly, and I peered inside. A pile of skulls grinned back at me. Originally Saint Macloud Abbey, this was the morgue when bubonic plague nearly wiped out Rouen. The friezes commemorate that, and the skeletons are relics found on the property. Now it is a fine-arts academy.

The rain had slowed to a drizzle. I sat by the fountain

and tried to conjure up the past. In such surroundings, it was a cinch. The students in baggy Levi's changed to brown cassocks, aged a bit, and buried their noses in fat leather volumes. It was perfectly still except for the occasional clatter of hooves beyond the wide wooden doors. Presently, one of the monks looked up and gazed pensively. Wasn't it about time for a fresh load of Châteauneuf-du-Pape to come floating down the Seine?

∞∞∞∞∞

Another attraction, four wide blocks up from the river by Hôtel-Dieu Hospital, is a white stone domed mansion around a courtyard where Gustave Flaubert spent all of his early years. He was born on the second floor of his family's apartments in the building. His father was chief surgeon, and the Flauberts' garden overlooked a ward where bodies were dissected for autopsy. Now the rooms are a museum, with Flaubert's books and letters.

Young Gustave was not on the Rouen tourist board. At nineteen, he wrote to a friend, "Confined in this oyster of Rouen . . . I believe that I have been transported by the winds to this land of mud, and that I was born somewhere else, because I have always had memories, or instincts, of balmy shores, of blue seas. I was born to be emperor of Cochin China." Rather than his due of six thousand women and pipes of pleasures, he said, "I have nothing but immense and insatiable desires, an atrocious boredom, unending yawns."

Three years later, Flaubert excoriated his native city. "It has beautiful churches and stupid people," he wrote. "I hate it. . . . Oh, Attila, when will you return, great humanitarian, with four hundred thousand horsemen, to burn this beautiful France, this nation of doormats and suspenders? And start, I beg you, with Paris first and with Rouen at the same time."

Flaubert might have enjoyed the Allied bombing. He died sixty-two years too early, eaten with syphilis at the age of fifty-eight, never having spent much time beyond an easy stroll from the Seine. Where his villa stood at Croisset, just downstream from Rouen, is an ugly red-brick paper factory, with corroding iron gates. The Seinescape out front is a back end of the Rouen port, nothing to write George Sand about.

A tiny museum squats in the corner of the villa's gardens, a room where Flaubert and his last few pals sat and sipped. There are some photocopies of manuscript pages; a few of the goose-quill pens he insisted on using when fountain pens got to be the rage; the unremarkable Amazon parrot that Julian Barnes made famous; Flaubert's favorite kind of small varnished clay pipe with a tobacco jar; and busts, photos and assorted whatnot. The writer would not have been pleased to know entrance was only two francs.

A helpful curator answered questions without a lot of false cheerleading. When I asked whether disputes continued among nearby villages over which was the real Yonville-l'Abbaye, Bovary's hometown, she shrugged. "Normans," she said, "are rather indifferent on the subject of Flaubert."

Not in Ry. In that little village on the way to nowhere, a mute Flaubert makes up the better part of the gross municipal product. If it is not the place, no one can make a better case for anyplace else, and the author is not talking. Late in the afternoon, I rolled into Ry, past La Bovary restaurant and Le Flaubert bar, and headed toward something called the Madame Bovary Automat Museum. It promised five hundred animated puppets depicting three hundred scenes from the novel. But it was closed.

I found the doctors' offices, in the old red schoolhouse. Emma's husband was the local physician, and that seemed like a good place to start. The waiting room was filled with sick people whose minds were not on literature. At Le Flaubert, none of the beefy-armed workmen staring at their beer looked like readers. The bar lady said, yes, Bovary attracted a lot of saps such as myself and was great for business; what would I have?

The Bovary house is reputed to have been what is now a drugstore, clean, well lighted, and computerized. The alleged textile shop where a conniving old lech played on Emma's vanities to draw her into ruinous debt now sells toy airplanes and spools of thread. And so on. I went back to the museum, where it looked like some other crafty citizen had found a way to profit from the woman's torment. Then someone directed me to Michel Burgaud, the jeweler—the crafty citizen in question.

"All right," he said, with some reluctance. "But just for a minute. I have an appointment and then I've got to be somewhere else." We returned to the museum, a converted cider mill, which he opened with a foot-long iron key. With a flipped switch, he lit up Bovaryland. Hundreds of stiffly moving little characters brought Emma back to life.

We saw a dullard medical student helped through school by connections. We watched his first wife die, old and ugly, without leaving him a franc of the fortune he thought he'd inherit. A seventeen-year-old, not bad looking but for her chipmunk cheeks, married the widower; all of the forty-three guests Flaubert put at the wedding dinner were around Burgaud's table. Then there was the splendid ball where Emma fell in love. Doc Bovary snored as Emma primped despondently at her vanity mirror. The tax man popped out of a barrel (can't help you here). It's all there.

In one scene, a little lace-cuffed white hand shoots in and out of a closed coach window. This is Emma, being ravaged inside and tossing away a billet-doux she decided not to deliver. In another, at the Hôtel de la Croix Rouge with Léon, she pops her corset ties, exposing crimson nipples. She buys more fripperies she can't afford, and the cops close in. Finally, she raids the chemist's poison cabinet.

"I've done these over twenty years," explained Burgaud, a man of genuine passion. "I had trained in *beaux-arts*, I was a jeweler, and I repaired television sets. All the skills were there. I thought, why not this?" It was original, all right. He acquired the old chemist's paraphernalia and reproduced the shop down to its door half covered with the owner's pretentious titles, ending in *etc*. A separate room displayed Flaubert memorabilia and item after item that showed Ry was the place.

First, there was circumstantial evidence. Flaubert mentioned a town with a single street as long as a rifle shot, a church and market set off to the side and a fair complement of loutish people. So far, so good. But there was much more.

Just before Flaubert started the book, a Doctor Delamare died in Ry. He had studied under Flaubert's father. His wife, Delphine Couturier, led an Emma-like life. Delamare borrowed money from the Flauberts that he could not pay back. Old files showed that the doctor sued his former mother-in-law for lack of inheritance, as Bovary did in the book. A letter to the author from a friend asked how he was doing on the Delamare saga.

The clincher was the wordplay. *Boeuf* means "steer" or, if you want it to, "cuckold." "*Boeuf à Ry*, Bovary, get it?" Burgaud said. "There are so many more connections, I could go on until tomorrow morning." He tried his best to do just that. Our few minutes had gone to well over an hour, and I was grateful. Less of an opportunist, he was a man with a mission. At least someone in Normandy remembered Flaubert warmly.

Heading back to Rouen, I took the double-lane highway. Had *Bovary* been set in more modern times, Emma could have hopped in her Renault Clio and made it home for supper. I liked it the old way. Each time she caught the coach to town and, the next morning, slinked home to her stick-in-the-mud doctor, the horses trotted her slowly across the Seine.

∽∽∽∽∽

The *Normandie* left at dawn, when most passengers were sleeping off bingo from the night before. It had been moored with its bow into the current, facing the wrong direction. On the bridge, Philippe Veillard peered down the quai and spoke orders into a radio. With deft short strokes, he operated the bow thrusters, and ninety-one meters of fancy river liner moved sideways and then backward into the main channel. At a slightly wider spot in the water, the ship turned in place and headed for Honfleur.

Driving the *Normandie*, I found, is like running *La Vieille* or a rowboat except that its ropes are thicker. You aim it and goose up the throttle and try not to hit anything. But the ship is like a floating skyscraper, complete with conditioned air, television in the cabins, tables groaning with food in rich sauces and a shop. With sleeping room for just over a hundred passengers, it is not much next to the *QE2*. But the Seine has never seen anything like it.

Though born to the river tribe, Philippe was an unlikely Seine boatman. His black mustache, perfectly tended, swept to a jaunty angle. He wore a starched shirt, no visible tattoos, and he slurred no words. When I met him on shore, he seemed like a lot of Frenchmen in their thirties: easygoing, mildly cocky but polite to elders, a boisterous joker among his old buddies, possibly good at his work but deeply interested in more basic issues like the sports page and *gigot*

d'agneau. At the wheel, which was really a complex set of
levers, buttons and controls, he was Captain Picard of the
starship *Enterprise*.

Philippe needs a pilot like he needs water wings, but
rules are rules. Passenger ships, like all freighters, must carry
an official minder between Rouen and the roads. Ours was
Bertrand Queré, son of a Brittany shoemaker, who had covered every part of the world in the merchant marine. He
seemed a little dour as first, so I approached cautiously. By
the time he warmed up, I was just another curious passenger
who had not announced a particular purpose.

Queré spewed out facts and lore like a set of head-
phones at a museum. Rouen's huge port was in danger. City
planners were eager for another way to cross the wide water.
Tunnels were expensive, and bridges high enough to clear
big freighters were not a lot cheaper. That would mean
closing the port to most ships. I looked over at a 130,000-ton
behemoth loading wheat for Poland. Wouldn't that be a little
silly? I asked.

Queré launched into the river catechism I had gotten to
know well. But I hadn't realized its implications for shipping.
From the commanding view of the *Normandie* wheelhouse,
he pointed to forty trucks waiting in line for a crane to lift off
their bagged wheat. Each truckload was prewrapped so that
a single swing of the hook could unload all twenty tons.
Whether the trucks unloaded at Rouen or farther down at Le
Havre did not make a lot of difference.

We saw a second facility, for *péniches*. High-speed hoses
could suck up their loads of grain, like elephants snorting
soup. Each barge carries as much as twelve trucks; a full
convoy can replace a hundred. But not a single barge was
tied up at the quai. This was not strict survival of the fittest.
Trucks offer more flexibility provided one is willing to over-

look their greater fuel cost, pollution and impact on traffic. Most politicians are.

"You take a truck," Queré said. "How many voters does that represent? Between manufacturing it, servicing it, supplying it with spare parts, fueling it, replacing it every two years, that's a lot of people. What is a *péniche*? One family who has no money and doesn't bother with elections." If the transport system is geared to roads, he said, it is easy enough to eliminate a middle step and load in Le Havre. "With all the money and organization the truck lobbies have, what is the future?"

Also, he went on, railroads practice *le dumping*; this is a French term meaning they cut their rates to below cost in order to corner the market. Tracks ran to Le Havre as well as Rouen. An inland port made sense mainly if *péniches* had a major part in hauling grain to the docks. But in the face of all this, Queré said, as had Hazel and the Conflans bargees and everyone else, the river tribe was in disarray. People fought among themselves.

Finally, there was the character of shipping. Movements are fewer because the ships are much larger. Not long ago, one-thousand-ton boats came to Rouen to load grain. Now even a ten-thousand-ton ship is a banana boat. The big ones run over one hundred thousand tons.

Some years back, unions would have howled down any plan to cut back at the port. Each big ship needed 120 to 130 dockers working for up to four days to load sacks of grain. Now two or three people at the controls can do the job in hours. Many former dockers, with other jobs they have to drive to in a hurry, would not mind a handier new crossing.

Already the last bridges are none too high. For the tall-ships regatta, the Russians' tall ship had to drop out or chop a yard off the top of its mast. When the river rises and

empty freighters loom ten stories above the waterline, an-
tennas can scrape the overhead span. Only two bridges cross
the Seine after downtown Rouen; a third is under construction. Elsewhere, cars shuttle across the old way, on red and
white ferries from village landings.

But there was the other side. The Rouen tourist office
had given me two pounds of glossy handouts on the port. It
was the world's biggest in wheat exports, and France's biggest in grain. It was the fifth busiest seaport in France and the
tenth in Europe. If you took away crude petroleum, Le
Havre was only a little bigger, some public-relations hypester
had calculated.

According to the handouts, the twenty-four thousand
jobs related to the port, in one way or another, amounted to
a tenth of all employment in greater Rouen. Activities on the
Seine pumped $1.5 billion a year into the economy. Besides,
one report added, foreign cruise ships were coming up the
Seine. In 1993, Rouen counted fifteen passenger boats. With
splendid irony, one major company had added the old Norman capital to its itinerary: the Royal Viking Line.

〰〰〰〰〰

Just out of Rouen, the river exhibits a marked change in
character. The radio language is often English; nearing the
roads off Le Havre, almost no French is heard. *Péniche* traffic
drops off, leaving the extremes: small English pleasure craft
and towering freighters. Still, stone villages on forested and
flowered banks are hardly different from the scenery along
the river's gentler stretches south of Paris. The contrasts are
startling.

"You can imagine what it is like to be bicycling along a
country lane and look up to see masts and a ship's bridge
towering over your head," Queré said. "It is even stranger for

sailors who come from weeks of staring at cold, high waves to look down and see all this green and pretty thatched roofs just under their noses. Crews fight to take this run."

Russian ships are the most frequent visitors, taking away 4 million tons of grain a year. You can recognize them from the used-car lots balanced precariously on the cargo hatches.

"The first thing a Russian captain asks is the number of a good wrecking yard," the pilot said, with a guffaw. "They buy up all the Ladas and Mercedes they can carry and smuggle them in back home to sell for parts. The profit is at least ten times, probably a lot more." Smuggle? Fifteen cars strapped down in plain sight? "Well, they just pay something to the customs guy. You know how it works."

As we cruised downstream, Queré kept up his patter. "Over there is where the flasher hides," he said. Philippe laughed; this was a recurring nuisance. The *Normandie*'s aging lady passengers had mixed feelings about a lunatic who periodically sprung from the bushes wearing only tennis shoes.

It went on and on. I learned that the Seine ran eleven meters deep at Rouen, just enough for the heavy traffic, but farther down it might drop below ten meters at low tide in the dry season. Queré told me about cool English captains and crazed Poles. He pointed out a famous singer's home and relayed some shocking gossip about what allegedly went on inside. At the stately château of Louis XV's minister of money, I learned the history of minting in France.

At one point, I asked about Napoléon's ashes, which a Rouen chauvinist had claimed where buried nearby; I'd always thought they were behind Les Invalides, near *La Vieille*. For the next two miles, I heard the details. A black-painted frigate, with crew dressed for mourning, brought the ashes

up the Seine. When it passed Quillebeuf, veterans of imperial wars flung themselves into the cold water. At a spot now
marked with a white pillar and an eagle, a crew of rowers in
a galley took the cenotaph ashore. It was transferred to a
golden carriage flanked by footmen for the ride to Paris.
Queré was about to describe their costumes when something even more fascinating hove into view.

Soon we switched to artichokes. The pilot drew my
attention to a hamlet of centuries-old *chaumières*, the
thatched-roof houses so evocative of Normandy. Each had
foot-thick artfully shaped roofing of bunched swamp reeds
that hung low in front and back. Why, I asked, did *chaumières*
always have a line of artichokes growing along the peak, like
a row of raised fists? Because, he replied, they pump out the
dampness.

This brought us back to the water. Thatched roofs were
rare now, and few people cut reeds in the marshes of the
estuary. As a result, the ecological and hydrological balance
was changing. I made a note to explore that later. Meanwhile, I asked about fish.

Had I heard about the three or four dolphins that got
disoriented and swam up to Rouen? Dolphins in the Seine
sounded like a fish story, but I had clipped a paragraph on
them from *Libération*. They all died, either from propeller
wounds, lack of salt water or too little food. Or Seine-water
shock.

Queré was now into fish. "Over there," he said, "by the
dock." I looked. "About three or four years ago, a fat lady
caught a three-foot salmon. It was in the papers." What did
she do with it? "Ate it." I shuddered, remembering the outlet
pipes at Achères.

Next I discovered that Napoléon III tried to cut one of his
ambitious canals across the loops of the Seine. Engineers

warned that this would change the currents, seriously affect-ing the flow. Queré had a fresh story with every turn of the props, but I was musing about my gratitude to the imperial engineers. We were swinging into yet another tight turn, the Landin curve, and getting into loveliness the likes of which I had not seen before.

Gnarled old cherry trees bloomed by the hundreds, crowding the banks. Beyond the river's bend, soft light fell on hills of spring colors that stretched to the horizon. Scattered buildings were mossy and massive, from the days when ar-chitects knew their proportions. Poplars and willows broke the shafts of sunbeams that played on rippling water. The tail end of Queré's narrative caught my ear: ". . . and they let you pick as many cherries as you can carry away."

Philippe had been drifting in and out of the conversa-tion since Rouen. This time, three of us were watching the banks together. "People who don't know any better think you get bored going up and down the same river," he said. "What a thought! It is always different. Those hills change colors every time I see them. The cherries flower, or the leaves are rich green, or they are bare against the sky. Differ-ent boats pass. Life on the banks changes, the people on board. The same river? Hah." Queré, who had made the same short run back and forth for a decade, nodded in grave agreement.

The captain and the pilot also agreed on the river's treachery. Muddy water rounding bends leaves silt banks behind. Depths and currents change. You have to read the river, if you know how, and give yourself plenty of room. This is not simple in a narrow channel when you are likely to encounter an enormous freighter that is also giving itself plenty of room. Among themselves, river people have a saying: "I escaped the Landin."

For a while, Queré chatted with Philippe. It turned out that he lived across the street from the house in Rouen where Philippe's parents had retired when they left the river. "They have a Nissan sedan," Philippe said, to situate the house. "Ah, yes, and they keep it in very good shape," Queré added. Even on land, these people are a tribe.

Soon we passed a converted aircraft factory, and Queré was talking about four French aviators who left Caudebec and died at the North Pole, taking Roald Amundsen on a rescue mission to find a lost Italian dirigible. And there was something about Abbé Pierre, the kindhearted Paris priest who fed the homeless and whose order is based in an ancient monastery off the Seine.

For a brief moment, Queré paused for breath, and I quickly exercised my fingers, cramped from trying to capture in a notebook the facts and lore he had poured out nonstop since Rouen. To contribute something to the conversation, I mentioned why I was so interested in the Seine. He looked wounded. "But you should have said so before," he said. "I could have told you some interesting things."

We docked at Caudebec, and Queré got off to drive back to Rouen. Our trip took all morning, but he'd be home in forty-five minutes. Clearly, he was reluctant to go. "I love this job," he told me, in parting. "I used to like the merchant marine, but it is different now. Everything is automated and there's nothing to do. Crews were larger back then, and everyone had something specific to do. Now your shipmates are Filipinos and Indonesians and whatnot; there is nothing in common, and no social life aboard. Then when you get to port, what can you do? Ports in Brazil, Asia, were a lot of fun. Now with crime, AIDS, craziness, it isn't worth it. I like the Seine."

15 Surfing on the Seine

CAUDEBEC-EN-CAUX is where people used to go surfing on the Seine, whether they wanted to or not. Maybe ten times a year, a freak killer wave rolled backward up the river and crashed up to nine feet high onto the quai. This is what sent Jacques's oil barges askew in Rouen port. As happens in Calcutta and along the Amazon, a tidal bore forces a mass of water into a restricted channel and up the sides of sloping banks. The French call it *le mascaret*.

At a richly stuffed Museum of the Seine by the town quai, I watched news film of *mascarets* in the 1950s. They were a soggier version of running with the bulls in Pamplona. Crowds scampered just ahead of the white geyser rising behind them. Some participants seemed to be involuntary: bearded men in Victor Hugo top hats and overcoats hung ten on the cobblestones of Caudebec like the Beach Boys at Malibu.

Depending on lunar circumstances, some tidal bores were bigger than others. The monster equinox waves, announced ahead of time in the papers, drew up to ten thousand people. Merchants lost some to the floods, but tourists made up for it in spades. The occasional regretted casualty was usually an out-of-towner.

The wall of water came down at the speed of a horse's gallop, visible on the horizon ten minutes before it struck. Crashing on the Caudebec quai, it splashed thirty feet in the air.

Recreational purposes aside, *le mascaret* was seldom welcome. The rolling backwash was at its most dramatic in Caudebec, but it rode the river from the estuary all the way up past Rouen. Ship captains found it awkward when a loaded freighter suddenly started acting like a Frisbee. Rouen port was paralyzed when a bore was expected. Even with precautions, havoc was wreaked. What with the tide and other hazards, worldwide insurance policies usually excluded the Seine.

A map in the Caudebec museum shows only a few of the more spectacular shipwrecks on the lower part of the Seine. It is a pox of red dots. Between 1789 and 1829, sixty-six ships sank. Another one hundred five went down in the thirty years that followed. With the coming of steamships, the toll fell dramatically. Pilots could follow narrow channels, cheating the winds and currents. But navigation was treacherous.

In the late 1800s, engineers dredged sandbanks in the estuary and moderated the *mascaret*. Later, a breakwater was built off Le Havre to deflect the tidal roll. The waves kept coming. Finally, scientists at a lab in Grenoble created a model of the river, replicating its mouth and the English Channel beyond. By tracking the water and calculating slopes of the riverbed, they determined where and how a dike should be built. In 1961, the seawall was finished, spoiling all the fun.

Now *le mascaret* is a low rumble on the surface of the river. It is seldom more than a foot high, but it still rips into Rouen. When it is about to arrive, all oil tankers disconnect. The sudden current lifts up bows and drops them again, putting such a strain on stern lines that they can snap.

"It's gone from the surface now, but don't think it has disappeared," Claude Michel had once warned me. He is a public-works engineer who runs the Abbaye Saint-Georges museum on the river north of Rouen. "If you're standing on the quai and it catches your legs, you may get swept into the current. Every year, someone drowns."

∞∞∞∞∞

Even without surfing, Caudebec draws crowds. It is at the heart of old Normandy, near thatched-roof villages and fruit orchards, and two of the oldest Seine abbeys are a short ride away. The lesser known, Saint-Wandrille, does not overpower. It is interesting not so much for it architecture as for what goes on today. After twelve centuries, it is still functioning.

The monastery goes back to Wandrille, a muscular, pious count in King Dagobert's court who was known as God's True Athlete. On his wedding day, he went to live with hermits and his bride got herself to a nunnery. He started the abbey in 649. The Vikings, naturally, demolished it.

In the tenth century, Benedictines rebuilt Saint-Wandrille. It was a thriving center for their new order, which spread quickly in Normandy. Eight centuries later, the French Revolution scattered the monks. The place collapsed in ruins. For a while, it was owned by a textile-mill magnate.

Then an English lord took it over, and, later still, an author moved in. Benedictines came back in 1894 but dispersed again. In 1931, they returned to stay.

I visited Saint-Wandrille because of Abbé Pierre. The elderly monk was famous in Paris for his help to the homeless. He organized a string of shelters and kitchens, rallying Parisians not known for excessive charity. His careworn, bearded face was a fixture on television talk programs, a strident voice for legions of forgotten people on the streets.

These days, someone told me, Abbé Pierre and the Saint-Wandrille brothers were doing secret high-tech business for the French Defense Ministry. They had branched into microfilm and computer data processing. Monks wore beepers under their cassocks. The back rooms are off limits, however, and curious visitors are directed to their souvenir shop. Judging from that, the ancient monastery sustains itself by selling furniture wax and perfumed bubble bath.

Jumièges is in no shape to harbor monks. Before I got there, I had read about its overwhelming power and beauty. Don't miss it, friends insisted. Thus primed, my anticipation rose as I got close, in the back of the bus with passengers from the *Normandie*. Just beyond the Bar de l'Eglise, I craned my neck and saw it. Mostly, it was empty spaces where the abbey had been.

Advance billing had let me down. So much was there, in one of France's most spectacular structures, that I wanted more than I got. But months later, I was speeding down a back road to somewhere, not paying much attention to my location on the map. The abbey's two façade towers hove into view, and I nearly ran off the road. As advertised, they were overpowering and beautiful.

Whatever your first impression, Jumièges is magnificent. Seeing it as it was requires some imagination, but much is still standing. With a briefing, you can picture the vast sweeps of stone, the heavy timbered roof of the nave and the sculpted choir and galleries. From the outbuildings and immense grounds, you can sense how much of a big business faith was in the early years.

Saint Philibert built Jumièges in the seventh century just in time for the Vikings to tear it down. After the peace treaty signed at Saint-Clair-sur-Epte, a better class of Viking put it back together again. A year after seizing the English crown, William the Conqueror came to Jumièges for the consecration.

Over the centuries, back when the distance was slight between secular and spiritual, the abbey shaped Norman culture. Its vast fields amounted to experimental agricultural farms. Its thinkers defined early literature. Nobles dropped in for advice and inspiration. And its driveway was the Seine.

Like Saint-Wandrille, Benedictine monks ran Jumièges with only minor contretemps until the French Revolution sent them fleeing for the hills. For a very short time, caretakers sought to preserve the magnificent church and its surrounding cloisters. But in 1793, it was sold in public auction to a greedhead timber merchant who dynamited the nave and transept to sell rock by the ton. Delicately carved stone exploded into powder. Vast chunks were wrestled onto boats and sent down the Seine to Britain.

A half century later, someone else bought what remained of Jumièges Abbey, and he set about saving the fragile ruins with his own dwindling fortune.

∽∽∽∽∽

I had walked around Jumièges with Tom Kongsgaard, a graying and bespectacled judge from Napa with an adven-

turesome spirit. "Have gavel, will travel," he'd chirped. He
and his wife were old cruisers, but mostly they went by sea.
At each new sight and experience, they enthused like kids. I
had not talked to many tourists about their impressions of
the Seine Valley, and I asked for his. The judge labored nobly,
fishing for words: Calm. Peaceful. Beautiful. Changing. He
grinned and shrugged, knowing he had fallen short.

Facing the same problem—getting spirit and splendor
into words on a notebook page—I went back to the *Normandie*'s bridge to settle for facts. At Caudebec, we took a new
pilot aboard. Jacques Mevel wore a clipped black beard,
rumpled corduroy pants, a clean, stylish sweater and a half-
amused look of inner peace. Mevel had published papers on
the river and its history, and he wanted people to know
about it. Like all Seine pilots, he had spent years at sea as a
senior merchant-marine officer. Now he devoured anything
written about his new waters.

"Everyone who knows this river learns to love it,"
Mevel said. "And they also learn to respect what it is capable
of doing."

As it happened, just off to starboard was Villequier, a
pretty town strung out along the river. Before silt added
miles to the course of the Seine, Villequier was where estuary and upstream pilots traded places. By the 1840s, it was a
peaceful, protected spot, and Victor Hugo settled in to write.
Léopoldine, one of his daughters, went punting one Sunday
with Charles Vacquerie, her husband of six months. Their
boat capsized. It was not *le mascaret*, just an inept maneuver.
Dressed in the flowing finery of the day, Léopoldine sank
below the surface and drowned.

Hugo's other daughter had gone mad when her husband died. He took this accident as God's punishment,
and he plunged into such depression that he published

nothing for a decade. His next works were thick with re-
morse and memory. "Victor Hugo looks ten years older,"
Balzac wrote.

The Hugo house is now a museum, last on the list of
what French tourism people call the Historic Route of
Writers' Houses. Like the string of abbeys, it follows the
Seine. There are ten, from François René de Chateaubriand's
sumptuous manor near Paris to the tragic site at Villequier.
Alexandre Dumas lived by Port-Marly. Zola was a little farther down at Médan. Casimir Delavigne's house was close to
Les Andelys, and Jules Michelet's was not far from the Bovary village of Ry.

Pierre Corneille lived outside of Rouen, not far from
Flaubert's place at Croisset; they were separated by a mere
two centuries. A ninth house is off the track somewhat, but
I'd never heard of the guy anyway. The tenth was a pleasant
surprise.

Once I spent a weekend visiting Ivan Turgenev's dacha
far south of Moscow, a rambling hunting lodge where he
could closet himself in a little studio with a potbellied stove
while his friends raised hell in the main room. As it turns
out, he also had a gardened dacha at Bougival, near his great
flame, Pauline Viardot. One of his regulars was Saint-Saëns,
the composer, yet another lover of the Seine.

Past Villequier, the river commanded Mevel's attention.
We had come to the tricky part, where big water washing in
from the estuary made navigation more than pointing in the
right direction. The same feats of engineering that tamed the
mascaret have solved some of the old problems. Mostly.

"There used to be violent currents at Quillebeuf," he
said. "The big ships had to wait until the tide came in and
then go like hell toward Rouen. If not, they might run
aground until the tide came back. When it came, a stranded

ship had one chance in two of getting rolled over in the rushing water."

Until recent times, Quillebeuf was the gate house for France. Beyond was rough open water. The Vikings used it as their base camp. Later, nothing substantial got up the Seine without help from the town's pilots and haulers. A royal charter gave Quillebeuf boatmen a monopoly on handling river traffic. The town grew fat and wealthy.

Quillebeuf pilots were such folk heros that women from surrounding towns sometimes tried to have their babies within the town limits so that, if male, they would qualify under the king's patent. These days, Quillebeuf is quiet, a handsome town laid out in a line along the Seine. It feels like a seaport, but even the river passes it by. Gazing out from a quaiside café table, you look across at a circle of hell.

At Port-Jérôme on the far bank, giant stacks spit an eternal flame. From foreground to horizon, the view is tanks painted "Esso" and "Mobil." Port-Jérôme might be Corpus Christi or Vladivostok, a generic oil port choked with vessels doing vital dirty work. No one who uses gas and plastics can disparage such activity with a clear conscience. Crude oil has to be unloaded and refined someplace. But here near the mouth of the Seine, it had an apocalyptic quality I decided to leave unexplored. I turned my attention back to my friends at the ship's controls.

Subtly, Philippe and Mevel had shifted to another gear. Though no less cool, they were checking instruments and clocks, and paying more attention to the background drone of the radio. As I was absorbed in scribbling notes, we had gotten into deep water.

16 *The Big One-Hearted River*

HIGH UP ON THE *NORMANDIE*'S no-nonsense bridge, passing under the sweeping arc of the Tancarville Bridge, and looking out at nothing but weather and chop, Paul Lamarche's pristine trickle in a mystical glade seemed a pretty faint memory.

Here is where captains make their choice. Bargees, driving their half-submerged bathtubs filled to the brim, headed to starboard up a straight cut off the Seine, one of the canals Napoléon III did finish. That leads to the tame side of Le Havre. Freighters nose into the open-water roads toward the right bank of the estuary and the raw-boned and thriving Le Havre seaport. The *Normandie* could handle the big water, if authorities weren't watching. But anyone sensible heads for Honfleur. This lovely port, in a spiritual and practical sense, is the river's end.

Honfleur is on my short list for the best little town in

France. Its ancient boat basin is flanked on three sides by pastel buildings, some medieval, some seventeenth century, all blended in thrilling harmony. Ships that conquered half the world and colonized Canada set sail from here. The first marine propeller, invented at Honfleur, was tried out in the harbor.

Up winding cobbled streets, you get a sense of every epoch. Middle Age splendor fades to modern. Downtown, a rickety wooden seamen's church leans askew. On a hill nearby, ship models dangle from rafters of a chapel to remind God to keep an eye out; it was built in the fifteenth century to thank the Lord for clearing out the English. Peeling paint from a forgotten time announces the old drugstore: *"Pharmacie Passocéan. Remède pour Mal de Mer."*

The food is good, strong on seafood, which fishermen from colorful trawlers dump still squirming at the restaurants' front doors. Late at night, laughter rolls out of the cafés amid sailor talk in a half-dozen tongues. It is peaceable yet still what the French call *le Far West*. One night, I watched a young man lurch from bar stool to dockside, puke placidly into someone's cockpit and go back for more. In winter, it is beautifully bleak. In summer, flowers spill from the balconies. And the entrance to Honfleur is Sequana's last bad joke.

The harbor is, in effect, a giant lock. Gates open an hour before the tidal peak and close an hour after. Water trapped inside keeps hundreds of boats afloat, from rowboats to the great white *Normandie*. The entrance is narrow, just beyond a stone watchtower on a spit of land. You have to turn sharply into the passage and dodge the stubby trawlers that ignore one-way rules.

Philippe slipped his liner through the gate with less fuss than an average driver pulling into an empty two-car garage. He weaved through the tight channel to a second passage so narrow it seemed likely to scrape paint from both sides at once. Then, to get to his habitual mooring spot, he did it again backward. When I congratulated him, he looked at me funny, as I might look at him if he had been surprised that I could tell a verb from a noun. It was what he did. But, he allowed, Honfleur could be a bit tricky.

On the way in, I had peppered Mevel with questions.

"What happens if you get to the gate a little late?" I asked, having seen no alternative accommodation for people with slow watches or bad luck.

"You don't get there late."

It was that simple. Like a lot of waterways, and more so than many, the Seine leaves little room for screwing up. I had seen this repeatedly since the first hand-cranked lock by Marcilly. If you are lucky, a dumb or careless move might leave you hung up until someone comes along to help. Or you might learn another word of river talk, *immatriculer*, which means to hit another boat.

Mevel went home, and then I said good-bye to Philippe. We talked about the future traffic on the Seine and the fate of the river tribe. He offered some leads that I might pursue. Mainly, he said, I had to find his friend Alain Bridiers, captain of a *chaland* called the *Exelmans*, who personified the challenges in almost every way. I'd try hard.

Then I had a look at Honfleur. People in the little port have struggled for generations to preserve its character in the face of modern times and tourism. No concessions are made to cars. Traffic winds up one-lane cobblestone streets. Few signs spoil the mood; drivers seeking the road to Deauville are on their own. Honfleur's centerpiece is the old boat basin it came within a hair of losing forever.

During World War II, the Germans planned to use Honfleur as a submarine base. No one told them about the mud.

Silt from the Seine builds so quickly that only steady use and frequent dredging can keep the harbor gates working. With most coastal traffic stopped, the gates stayed closed. Germans had no time to dredge. At the end of the war, Honfleur was hopelessly mudbound. The basin was thick with reeds and high grass.

Some people wanted to pave the basin for a parking lot. Others had a more progressive idea. They would make a shallow reflecting pool so tourists could appreciate quaiside buildings. A kernel of diehards refused. Two volunteers in underwater apparatus were lowered by ropes down the harbor gates. Bit by bit, like prisoners digging a tunnel, they cleared away the muck. A pair of shovels saved Honfleur harbor.

◈◈◈◈◈◈

Before wrapping up my look at the Seine, I took a drive from Paris back to Honfleur and to Le Havre, with stops along the way. I had some ends to tie up, and I wanted to give the river a last shot at amazing me. Most things had fallen into place. I'd taken *La Vieille* into back corners. Old books turned up, and experts were generous. My one regret was that I had not found Philippe's friend Alain Bridiers and the *Exelmans*. I had just missed it once at Conflans and then again in Paris. It was working somewhere, and I had not been in one place long enough to track it the *marinier* way—checking with the locks.

At Duclair, a pleasant portlet below Rouen, some inner voice told me to hang a left. I backtracked on a parallel lane along the river and admired the waterfront houses. Nearly at the end, I pulled onto a wide patch and shifted to reverse. Keep going, the voice said. At the main road, I started to head out again but noticed a moored barge I had already

passed. Something about it made me check it out. Closer to
it, I read the name: *Exelmans.*

It was a *chaland de Seine*, at seventy-one meters nearly
double the length of a *péniche*, with five times the capacity:
fourteen hundred tons. I could see right off that the Bridiers
were of the new wave. Alain's wife, Laurence, was wearing
shorts and not a dress. Nothing essential had changed from
her grandmother's time, however. She was sweeping the
deck.

The *Exelmans* was docked at the edge of town, powered
by its generators, and linked to shore by a sort of jungle-gym
ladder. Inside, the living room was sitcom Middle America.
It was vacation, and the kids—Grégoire, fourteen, and
Ludovic, eleven—were watching cartoons on television.
Doilies protected furniture from flower vases, and the carpet
was wall-to-wall. Phone and fax nestled on a bar counter,
which was amply stocked. Two shaggy dogs sniffed at ankles.
Framed pictures and tossed-around memorabilia gave no
hint that this happy home had no fixed address.

Up a companionway, the wheelhouse was high-tech.
The old wooden wheel was gone, replaced by a short black
joystick to direct the hydraulic steering. A fancy new apparatus allowed Alain to shift to autopilot on straights or
curves. Radar picked up anything detached from the shore.
Four handsets operated the VHF radio, the telephone and a
fax line. Buttons abounded.

Forward, however, was galley-slave country. Laurence
does not have to strap on a *bricole* and haul the barge up a
towpath, but otherwise it is the old days. There is a large
hold that is filled with dusty, smelly bulk cargo. Captain and
wife wrestle two dozen curved zinc sheets over the hold
to keep it dry. At the other end, the covers come off. The
cargo is scooped out, leaving filth to be swept from every

crevice. At every lock, there is heaving and hauling on the lines. Meantime, there are the surprises. It's always something.

Both Bridiers are of tribal stock, born and married on the river. They sniffed the wind early, raided scant savings, and traded up to the future. Independent minded but shrewd, they landed a contract to haul sand, as secure a deal as you get on the Seine. An optimist, Alain now looks back to the beginning and wonders if he screwed up bad.

"I don't know if we're going to make it or not," Alain. He is thirty-eight and hopes to ride the river another three decades. "Maybe it's just the crisis that affects all of France. If construction stops, no one can work. That will pass. But maybe it is something else."

It is a simple drama waiting to be played out. Harder-working, more affable people you will not find. The attributes of their profession are unassailable: Their *chaland* can hump the equivalent load of sixty-three trucks, emitting only one exhaust pipe of diesel fumes and not using up a square inch of roadway. If it takes a little longer to cover the distance, it also serves as a free warehouse for cargo not immediately needed. River traffic may increase, and they will stay on the water. Or it may not, and they'll go bust, with everything they own sunk into a hunk of metal no one will want to buy.

∽∽∽∽∽

Le Havre is the ugliest city in France, possibly the world. This takes some doing, given its exquisite location on a hook of hilly land between the Seine estuary and deep blue water. A friend had warned me: "It's like Russia, those drab buildings and abrupt people with sad faces who never have any fun." I don't know if she was right about the people, since I did not stick around long enough to find out. But to compare the architecture to post-war Soviet awfulness is an insult to Stalin.

It was not always ugly. In Roman times, the location of Le Havre was somewhere on the ocean floor, and the port was Harfleur. Medieval accounts tell of lively activity at Harfleur, including the annual Loonies' Festival, when respectable townsfolk did silly things. The Seine silted up the harbor, however, and Harfleur is forgotten somewhere on land. François I, about to civilize much of the world, built a new seaport.

"Le Havre is among the greatest cities in the world, second only to Constantinople in beauty," wrote Casimir Delavigne, the nineteenth-century poet who lived upriver at Les Andelys. Great ships brought passengers from America and beyond. Merchants awash in wealth built homes in the coastal suburb of Sainte-Adresse and in the heights above the city. It might still be beautiful had the Germans not holed up there for a last stand in 1944.

Piece by piece, Le Havre was taken apart by Allied guns. Except for the odd wall of old stone still emerging from the rubble, it was flattened. The city was rebuilt fast, cheap and cheesy, with little apparent thought as to what went where. From what should provide a stirring panorama in the Haute Ville, you can see the result. A gray Stalinist tower dominates a ragged skyline of boxy apartments and office blocks, factory stacks, port cranes and silos, all jumbled together with no space to breathe. When you get to the edges, however, if the wind direction is right, the air is fresh and clean.

I had come to see Michel Lemoine, the supervisor at Pilotage de la Seine, the quasi-official group of seamen like Queré and Mevel who shepherd heavy traffic upriver to Rouen. He keeps track of the river's moods and informs his men. Using electronic soundings and computers, he knows when shifting sandbars have caused the two-hundred-yard-wide channel to collapse. And he helped determine when it was time to dredge.

Until recent times, the Seine went every which way after its last meander. It climbed banks, barely covered sandbars and dodged islands. Records show that 112 ships sank from the French Revolution to the steam age, but no one counted the near misses.

"Now it is straightened, diked, almost a canal," Lemoine explained. Wavy colored lines on old charts showed what he meant. I had seen the stone banks, solid in places but collapsing along the few miles of shoreline where the odd-shaped Department of the Eure had no interest in a river that brought it no benefit.

As Lemoine spoke, I had a sudden sense. This was it. The Seine had reached its end, and I should, too. I had brought a stack of other files to explore: A new report detailed the level of pesticides and metals in the estuary, making it four times more poisonous than the mouth of the Rhône. I'd seen the culprits from the river and on my drive down. But enough already.

In fact, I realized, saying good-bye to Philippe at Honfleur was the climax. Even more than his friend Alain, he represented the past and the present. And I was not about to guess the future. Philippe's grandmother piloted a wooden *péniche* on the Seine, and his history goes vague before then. His parents taught him the river, a brave in the tribe. He bought his own *péniche* early and then exchanged it for another. Both were kept in perfect condition, with all the technology he could afford.

When Philippe saw crisis coming, he moved swiftly. By the time his kids grew up, he knew, they would need some options. He sold his boat while there was still a market, and he broadened his skills. Several of his friends struggle at the old life. A few drive *bateaux-mouches*. Some have good jobs on land, but others scrape by as night watchmen and laborers. Philippe captains a lord of the river; he has become a notable of the tribe before his forties.

"It's too early to say what my son will do," Philippe said. "He's in school, interested in what I do but also in other things. But I hope he comes to the river. It is what we have always done, and it is what I love." He used *la rivière*, in the singular, and I asked if his family had roamed more widely, like most other river people did.

"The Seine," Philippe said. "Always the Seine."

∽∽∽∽∽

At the edge of Honfleur is a impressionist holy site on a plane with La Fournaise and La Grenouillère. La Ferme Saint-Siméon was where Boudin taught Monet about portable easels. Over the years, everyone spent some time there, painting light and trying their luck with the servant girl, Rosie. It was cheap and family style, with lumpy beds and a sumptuous table. Like most of the old spots, it had fallen on hard times. Over the past fifteen years, however, a family of innkeepers had brought it to glory.

I knew I was in trouble when I saw the crowd. The more informally dressed men wore bright ties with their dark suits. A guard dog sat sipping champagne on a plush couch, one of those nonproductive, nondecorative women who let you know the world was created specifically for them. She observed my boat clothes and was not pleased. But this woman had no official status. The hostess and owner was charming.

The large dining room was polished to a glare. Every

flower had had its legs waxed. In the lounge, a burnished black piano played itself, and I had no trouble recognizing the tune: "*tum*-ta-tum, *tum*-ta-tum, *tum*-ta-ta-ta-tum, M-I-C-K-E-Y, M-O-U-S-E." Under my shoes, I felt a slight tremor. It could only be Eugène Boudin back-flipping in his grave.

My taste buds screamed for lobster, but nearly a hundred bucks seemed a bit excessive. I'm not miserly, I rationalized; I'll be in New England soon and should try something Connecticut can't offer. That turned out to be *bar*, a delicate white fish, in a crispy sesame-tinged crust. It was delicious. I found a Sancerre that would not disrupt my mortgage payments and relaxed. What the hell. If some people can afford this stuff all the time, who said life was fair? An early Monet Honfleur ain't cheap, either.

I walked outside, planning to stroll around in search of a last image to match that picture in my mind of a wonderful old man offering me the first waters of the Seine cupped in his hands. The moon mugged me. I mean, this was a moon, so huge and round it looked like an exaggerated stage prop, and it was the color of a blood orange. I watched until it was no longer startling, just an unbelievably lovely source of light that splashed gold over the estuary. Its human face seemed animated, but this was no man. I swear to God, Sequana was talking to me.

~~~~~~

By the time Sequana spills into the sea, she no longer looks like *la rivière*, let alone the tiny trickle of sacred water the ancient Gauls used as chicken soup. Until the last spits of protecting land, it is a great, wide river. Then, without the indignities of muddy deltas or marshes, it is gone. Salt kills off whatever life ran the gauntlet of pollutants. Low-slung barges can't handle the waves. And the Seine's last secrets wash away, unrevealed.

As for me, I was hooked. *La Vieille* was built for big waters. With enough time and a tender full of fuel, she could chunkachunk on to the Panama Canal. But that's not where she is going. First, she and I have to figure out what is down there, in the center of Paris, rocking her at dawn before anything goes by to throw out a wake.

Don't bet on our finding out. If Sequana's super serpent is still around, he has yet to be seen coming up for air. As for the rest, above the waterline, a hundred generations of poets and painters have tried to capture the shifting spirit of the Seine, and no one has managed yet. That is probably just as well.

Glossary

Amont, upstream; *aval,* downstream: These same terms are used for uphill-downhill. Unless the current is strong, it's a lot easier to spot the difference on a ski slope.

Babord, Tribord: Port and starboard, respectively. Bargees keep these straight with the French word for battery, pronounced "ba-tri." Dyslexic bargees are on their own.

Batellerie: Collective term for inland boats and freshwater navigation. Refers mainly to commercial barges.

Chaland de Seine: Large motorized barge, usually about 250 feet, which can haul as much as five *péniches.*

Crue: Current; river level. *Le grand crue* comes with the winter rains, usually after the first snows melt.

Duc d'Albe: A-frame pilings for mooring. Named for a Spanish duke who tied prisoners to such structures and let the rising water ruin their day.

Ecluse: Lock. Most locks on the Seine are combined with adjustable dams, or *biefs,* to help control the river flow.

Ecluser: To pass through a lock.

Freycinet: See *péniche*.

Immatriculer: In normal French, this means to matriculate, or enroll. Among bargees, it means to hit something, another boat or a fixed object. Also see *Merde!*.

La Fluviale: River cops, equipped with Miami Vice–style launches, who patrol the Seine around Paris.

Marinier: Bargee, freshwater sailor. A sea-going sailor is a *marin*.

Merde!: What boat captains yell upon striking a fixed object, throwing a rod, or missing the last lock at the day's end.

Péniche: River barge. Historically wooden-hulled and drawn by horses but now metal and diesel-powered. The most common are the Freycinets, 126 feet long by 17 feet wide, named after a 19th century transportation minister who standardized canal lengths.

Pousseur: Tugboat that pushes rather than pulls, used for hauling barge convoys as well as maneuvering in port.

Terriens, Terrienes (also *gens de terre*): Landlubbers.

Tirant d'air: Overhead clearance. On canals with low bridges, this is a crucial term. Careless bargees have been known to make convertibles of their wheelhouses. *Tirant d'eau* refers to water depth.

Yacht: (Pronounced with glottal noise and moisture) Any river craft that does not haul freight or large numbers of passengers, including eight-foot prams for canal creeping. Also, *plaisancier*.